PETER GILMAN

PAINTING EAST ANGLIA & BEYOND

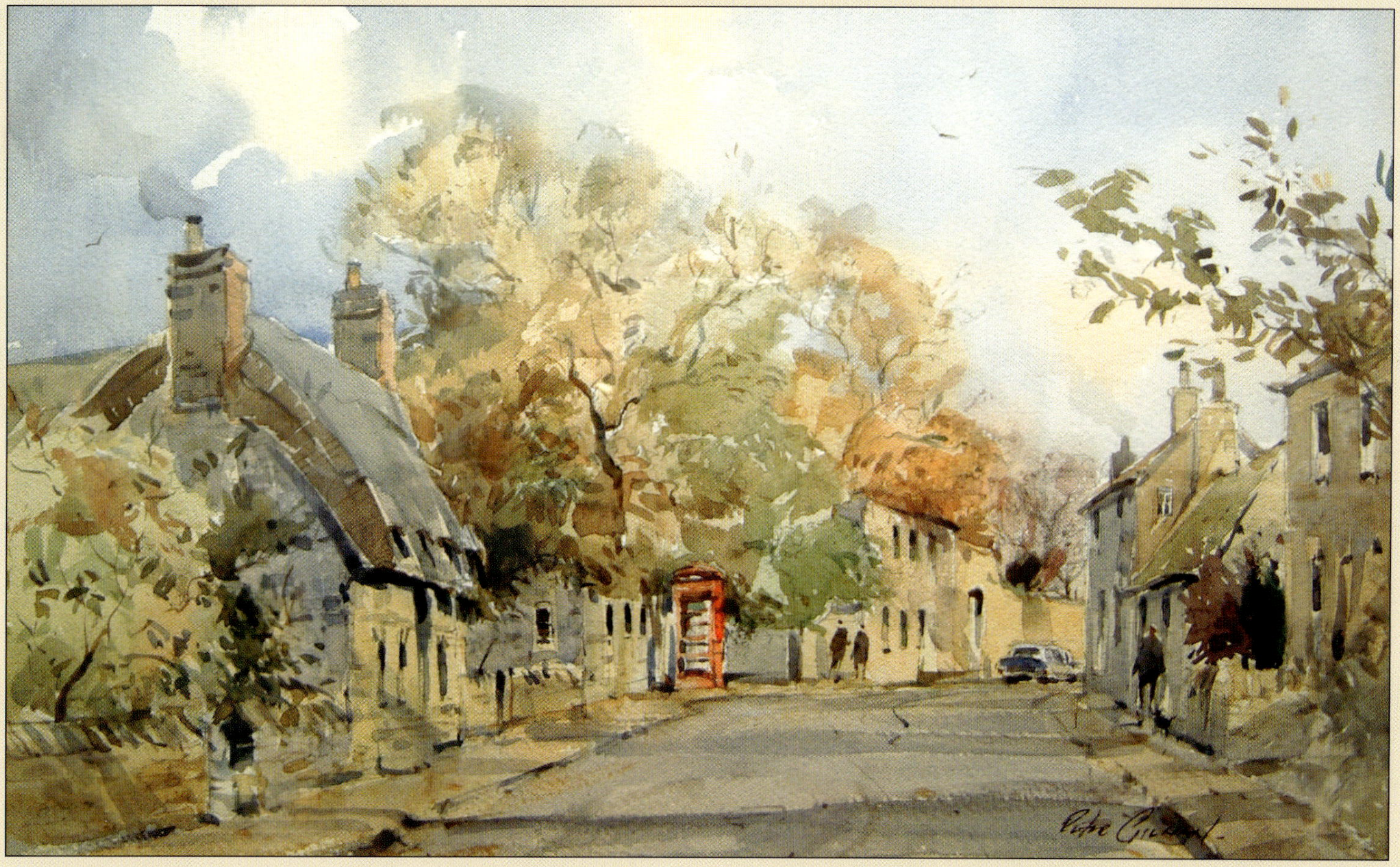

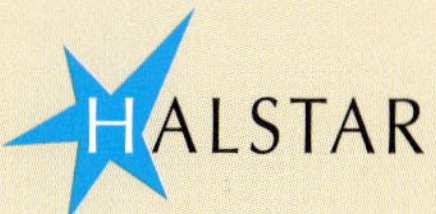

MICHAEL & ADRIAN HILL

HALSTAR

DEDICATION

To my Mum and Dad for their love, encouragement, help and support.
And to my wife Clare and my beautiful daughters Sophie and Elena.

Adrian Hill

British Library Cataloguing-in-Publication Data
A CIP record for this title is available from the British Library

ISBN 978 1 906690 20 5

HALSTAR
Halsgrove House,
Ryelands Industrial Estate,
Bagley Road, Wellington, Somerset TA21 9PZ
Tel: 01823 653777   Fax: 01823 216796
email: sales@halsgrove.com

An imprint of Halstar Ltd, part of the Halsgrove group of companies
Information on all Halsgrove titles is available at: www.halsgrove.com

Printed and bound by Grafiche Flaminia, Italy

CONTENTS

ACKNOWLEDGEMENTS

The authors would like to thank the following people for their contribution during the production of this book, without them, this would have been an impossible task!

Maxine Gilman, Jean and Barry Evans, Irene Crowhurst, Dorothy Hall, Julie and Alan Philip.

Also, Robin Mackervoy, John Stillman, Trevor Chamberlain, Sydney Cardew, The Wapping Group of Artists, June Burrows and Mary Fawcett.

Simon Butler and his excellent team at Halsgrove.

Graham and Daphne Heaton.

Keith, Graham, Carol, Michael, Brian, Ann, Hilary, Mel, Malcolm, Roger and Janice for the kind loan of their Peter Gilman paintings for this publication.

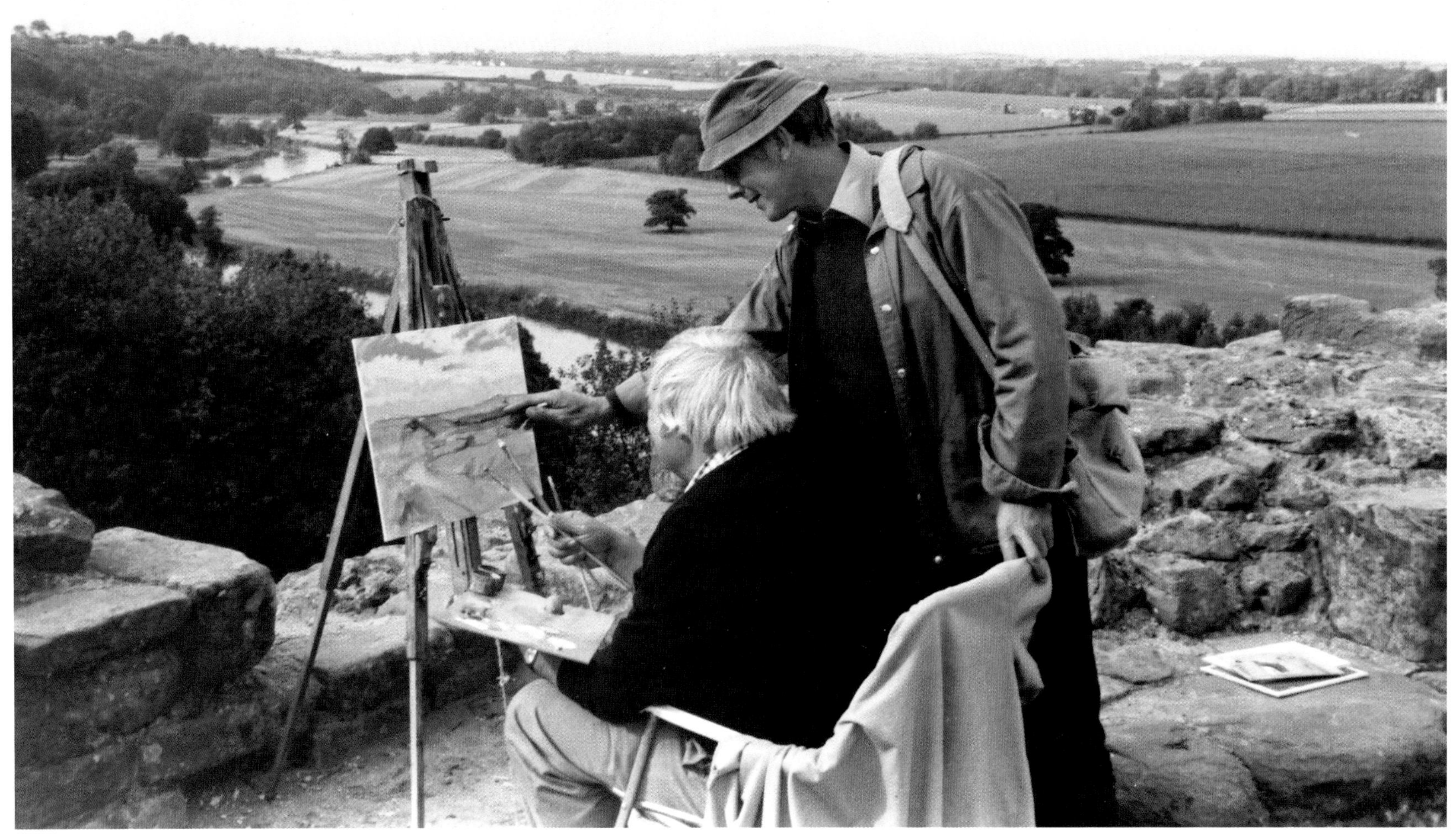

Peter Gilman as tutor offering advice to a student on a Galleon Painting Holiday.

FOREWORD

by Trevor Chamberlain

I am very pleased to write this tribute to a loyal friend and fellow painter. We painted together in all weathers for over 25 years, particularly in East Anglia and along the Thames. I always found him to be a charming companion, always ready for a joke or some humorous banter, never witnessing the hidden, melancholic trait lurking beneath his outgoing personality and which eventually manifested itself in events leading up to his death.

It was as if he left his other persona behind when he absorbed himself in his beloved artistic pursuits. I do recall he once remarked to me 'I won't make old bones'. At the time I couldn't reconcile the remark with the Peter I knew.

Peter was a very sincere painter who reacted in a most positive and spontaneous way to the many effects of nature. He worked with great speed and intensity with resulting freshness and vigour and his passionate love of the English landscape is apparent in all he did. In our earliest painting excursions to Norfolk and Suffolk we would sleep overnight in the car because we both had young families to support. We gradually progressed to a tent, and then to the luxury of a caravan as our fortunes progressed further. Later B&B became the norm and even, on rare occasions, the luxury of a hotel.

One slightly bizarre but amusing incident I recall happened in Aldeburgh in the high season. We were seeking out overnight accommodation and the only offer open to us was to share a double bed on the first floor at the White Hart Pub which we decided to accept as there was no alternative. We were not easily embarrassed having both served as National Servicemen. However at bed time I was a little unnerved to see Peter unpacking a coil of rope and a brand new pair of white gloves. Having second thoughts on the wisdom of sharing a bed I tentatively enquired what the items were for. He then explained that he always packed these in case he had to escape through the window should there be a fire!

I remember another painting trip with The Wapping Group of Artists to Leigh-on-Sea. On arrival Peter, who had never sampled the local cockles before, found that he had a taste for them. So much so that he couldn't resist two large portions, commenting to me 'better than those cheese sandwiches you have got'. Unfortunately, about an hour or so later, just when he had started on a painting, he became violently ill and had to leave for home, missing a wonderful painting day!

Peter loved animals and had two pet dogs a whippet called Ricky and a Yorkshire terrier called Taurus. The latter was not to be approached in bare feet and apparently this terrier would sometimes repel him from the marital bed. Luckily we weren't accompanied by the dogs on painting trips!

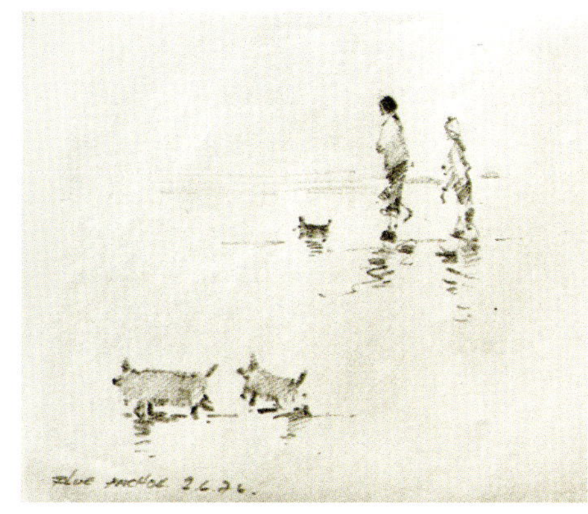

Dog walking. A spontaneous pencil study by Gilman.

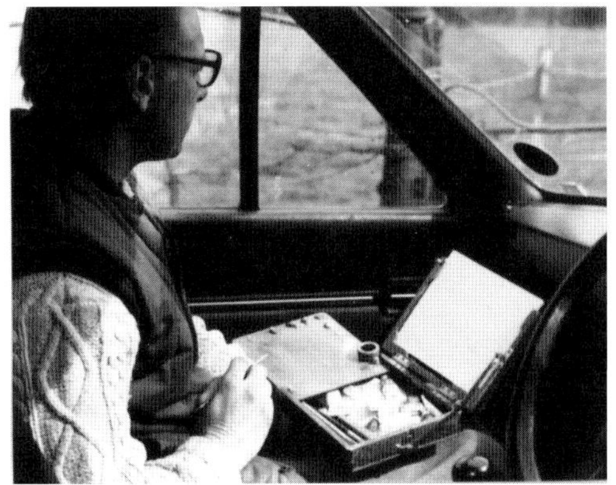

Trevor Chamberlain using the 6x8 inch pochade box designed and made by Peter Gilman.

Peter was a very gentle and generous man who took a kindly view of other people and had many friends. Although he tried to make a rule not to engage in conversation when he was working seriously on a picture he would always exchange a few words with any genuinely interested onlooker.

As fellow members of The Wapping Group we would often share travelling to and from the various venues – sometimes Peter would drive sometimes I would. On Tuesday 10 July 1984 we were both present at an evening private view in Welwyn Garden City. As the following day was a Wapping Group painting day, the subject of transport arrangements came up in conversation. I remember reminding Peter that the venue was Richmond-upon-Thames and that I would be going and was happy to drive if he wanted to come. After a few seconds thought he decided he wouldn't come on that occasion. I never saw him again; he took his own life the following day 11 July 1984, leaving his wife Jean and daughter Maxine, whom he idolised.

At the time of his death Peter was planning and working on a major exhibition to be held at Picturecraft Gallery, Holt, Norfolk. All the pictures were painted but needed sorting, framing, cataloguing etc., a task that I was happy to oversee and coordinate. The exhibition of over 100 oils, watercolours and acrylics opened on Friday 24 August 1984 and resulted in a total sell out. If only he had lived to see the result it may well have had a positive effect on that final tragic turn of events.

As a close friend I am both proud and delighted that this book, which marks the 25th anniversary of his death, will celebrate Peter's life and work. It is published concurrently with a second major retrospective exhibition of largely unseen paintings from Maxine's collection.

Trevor Chamberlain
2009

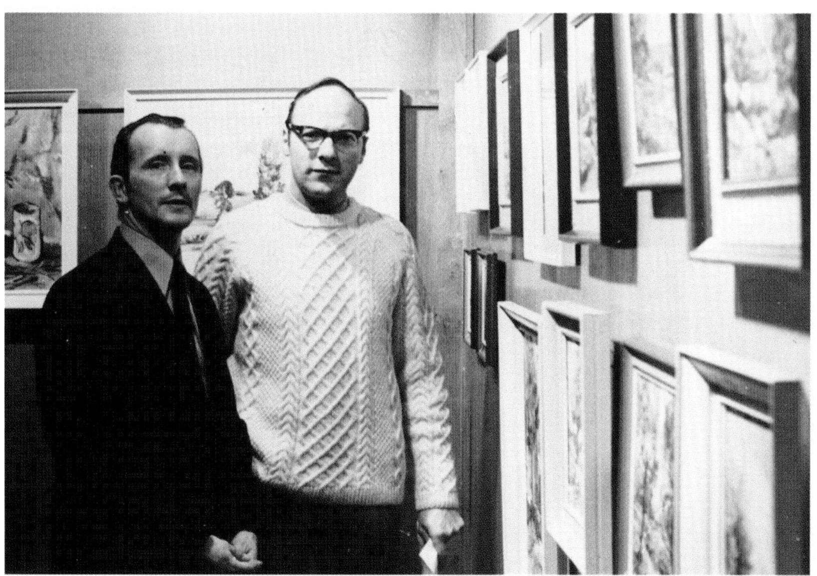

Gilman and Chamberlain regularly exhibited their work together.

INTRODUCTION
by Adrian Hill

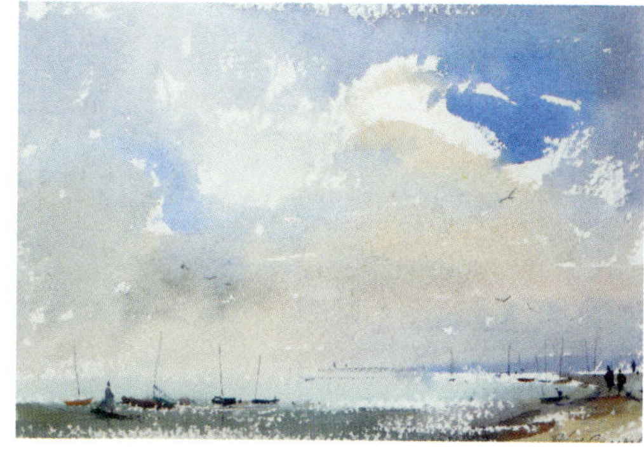

A Gilman watercolour of Blakeney, Norfolk. John Stillman Collection

The name Peter Gilman will be known by many: to artists of every calibre, to galleries, art lovers, collectors and publishers, to tutors and students, and not least to his family and many friends.

Peter Gilman was a man who touched the lives of so many people in so many different ways. I first became aware of the name and art of Peter Gilman at a very young age; I was only five years old. As children my brother and I were always encouraged to look around galleries, charged with the task of identifying a favourite painting. This enlightening situation was one of the many advantages of being surrounded by the wonderful world of art. It could be said that a love of art is in our family blood, for our grandparents and parents owned art galleries and developed art-associated businesses from a hobby of picture framing in the early 1960s.

My father always took great pleasure in showing us around exhibitions, and this passion remains still. I can recall quite vividly him returning home one day to declare that for the first time in the gallery's history every single painting had been sold during one exhibition. I found it odd that he was not excited, indeed quite the reverse. Of course, I was far too young to understand the circumstances of this exhibition and oblivious of the human cost, but I remembered the name, Peter Gilman.

I am now the owner of the award-winning Picturecraft Gallery in Holt, North Norfolk, representing the third generation of the Hill family, and it is my privilege to showcase the work of some of this country's finest painters in oil, watercolour, acrylic and pastel. I also have the pleasure to get to know, enjoy and develop special business and personal relationships with all my exhibiting artists. The thrill of selling a painting for an artist is difficult to describe. The sheer delight in knowing that the painting will be hung on a wall, admired, cherished, indeed loved, is a magical feeling which I am fortunate to share with the successful artist.

Working in such a diverse and interesting industry, there are times when a special affinity develops with an artist. It touches you and can change you as an individual, and I believe Peter Gilman was such an artist. Sadly, I never met him, spoke with him or watched him work, and yet I feel that I knew him. The legacy of paintings that he left behind speak volumes for him and maybe, as I view his work, I find the man. There can be no question that Peter Gilman was a truly exceptional painter. Perhaps also I have come closer to Peter through reading his features on painting, for these shaped and inspired a generation of amateur artists.

I have certainly been made acutely aware of Peter in his role as a father through contacting Maxine, his beloved daughter. Her recollections of a wonderful, yet rather serious father, are included in this book. I am immensely grateful to Peter's three sisters Jean, Irene and Dorothy who shared their incredible stories with me too, and I deeply appreciated the opportunity to learn more from his brother-in-law Barry; Sister-in-Law Julie and her husband Alan.

I have been enlightened by Peter's many friends, particularly those painters that he knew so well from The Wapping Group of Artists. I was to discover a story that differed with those that had been told by his immediate family. Working alongside him, exhibiting with him, and watching his journey to progress as a professional artist, they knew a very different kind of Peter Gilman – motivated, inspired and totally focused in his wonderful world of painting.

My initial thoughts to stage a small retrospective exhibition, to commemorate twenty-five years since the tragic passing of Peter Gilman, was to recognise the highly valued personal friendship that existed between Peter and my father, Michael. The launch of this book to coincide with the exhibition was furthest from my thoughts at the time, and its production has exceeded my wildest dreams.

The close business association and personal friendship between Robin Mackervoy, (current Wapping Group Chairman), the Hill family and the Picturecraft Gallery has led to the involvement of fifteen current members of The Wapping Group exhibiting alongside their, *'old painting friend, celebrating a life cut far too short and long before its time'*.

Robin kindly introduced me to Trevor Chamberlain and John Stillman, which again was to change the whole concept of the show and led to the publication of this book. They both have clearly revealed their tremendous admiration for Peter Gilman, as a man and as an artist, and the special friendship they continue to maintain with Peter's daughter, Maxine.

I am totally indebted to Maxine and her family who have now kindly allowed the release of over sixty of Peter's previously unseen paintings to feature in the tribute exhibition planned for November 2009. I was overwhelmed by the generosity of so many of my customers who have also kindly allowed their Peter Gilman paintings to be photographed to support this wonderful book.

I could not possibly complete these acknowledgments without mentioning my close and highly valued friendship with Simon Butler of Halsgrove Publications who provided the incredible opportunity and support to make this publication possible – a permanent record to celebrate the life and work of artist Peter Gilman.

Adrian Hill
Managing Director
Picturecraft Gallery, Holt

PETER GILMAN – ARTIST

Peter Gilman was born in Mitcham, Surrey, on 2 September 1928. He was the first child and only son of Charles and Winifred Gilman (née Uridge). He had three younger sisters, Jean, Irene and Dorothy. Family life was difficult for Peter. His father was quite a dominant character who found comfort through drink, making it difficult for him to tie down a regular job. Winifred struggled with the upkeep of the home and the means to scrape enough funds together to feed the family.

Peter was to experience long periods of solitude as he grew up through suffering a number of different illnesses in his early years. Bouts of diphtheria around the age of seven had him isolated from the family for months at a time, inevitably disturbing both home and academic life. The lack of physical contact through this debilitating condition, where he viewed his mother through a window, was a wretched time for him at such a young impressionable age.

Not surprisingly perhaps, Peter developed into a very serious child and, although appearing well behaved, looks deceived, for he had a very bad temper. His sister Jean recalls that he would often abandon a project if it was not working in the way he wanted, throwing it away as soon as things started to go wrong. One such project was Peter's attempt at trying to make a tent in the garden: *'While we didn't have much at that time, Peter was always so good with his hands. He could make something out of nothing. Peter spent most of the morning working on the construction of a tent in the garden when it suddenly started to fall down. Rather than trying to rescue it, Peter smashed it to the floor… if something wasn't just right, Peter would inevitably destroy it!'*

Peter would often be asked to look after his sister Jean. However, it was usual for her to be seen trailing behind him having been given strict instructions, *'Walk behind me and do not speak to me!'*. Peter always wanted to walk in front, and certainly wished to disassociate himself from his sister, not conveying to anyone that she was associated with his family. A degree of forgiving acceptance was shown at his odd behaviour, after all, *'this was just Peter being Peter'*.

Jean recalls, *'Things were not always that bad. I remember Peter and I visited the cinema to watch Robin Hood. Once the film had finished we hid beneath the cinema seats as Peter had enjoyed it so much he wanted to wait for the next showing in order to see it again.'*

Like so many children of their age, Peter and his two sisters were to be evacuated during the Second World War amidst fears of bombing during the blitz. They were all sent to

Chichester, but Peter was unfortunately separated from his two sisters and moved in with a family who, at best, proved incredibly difficult to deal with. Peter was desperately unhappy, to such an extent that his mother called for him to return to the family home leaving his two sisters behind.

A significant change in Peter's life awaited as he was more fortunate on being evacuated for a second time; this time he was sent to High Wickham in Buckinghamshire. He moved in with the Johnson family which proved to be a very happy time. Peter found himself surrounded by a lovely home and was treated with great affection and welcomed as if one of the family. The Johnson's had two boys of a similar age and Peter settled quickly and fitted perfectly into this happy, loving family. Peter thoroughly enjoyed this very different life to the one he had left behind and his wish was granted, mainly for educational reasons, to stay with the Johnson's after the war. It was during this time that he finished his schooling and served an apprenticeship in carpentry and cabinet making.

During his stay in Buckinghamshire, Peter developed a love for drawing and it was here where his artistic talent started to shine, greatly encouraged and nurtured by his wartime family. Looking back, Peter's sister, Irene, was not surprised: *'Whenever Peter put his mind to anything he would always succeed in it. He excelled in everything that he did.'* Irene remembers him being incredibly intense as a child, *'Peter was very fussy that things had to be done in a certain way… and, of course,* his way *was always the right way!'*

Having deferred his National Service to complete his carpentry and cabinet-making apprenticeship, Peter finally returned to Mitcham, and was faced with a very different family unit. Peter's father was out of work and drinking very heavily, something that Peter particularly struggled to deal with. During his lengthy absence, Peter's mother had given birth to Dorothy, who he was to discover had also been evacuated with Jean and Irene during the latter part of the war. All three sisters had returned home from Chichester having experienced a very different evacuation to that of Peter's, albeit a happy one with a loving older family.

The Gilman's family home at Mitcham had been bombed, so all six of them now found themselves crowded into a small flat above a three-bedroom house. This proved to be a major shock to Peter's system, almost torture. He had experienced the joy of living happily and had been greatly encouraged and influenced by the Johnson family, but now he was forced to share extremely cramped conditions and the trauma of watching his mother endlessly struggling to put food on the table and trying her best to make ends meet. Needless to say, Peter was desperately unhappy… but was still passionate about his art.

Irene remembers that Peter was always drawing, *'He would often sit in silence for hours sketching almost anything he could find. He once drew for me some Disney characters and I took them to school and proudly showed them to all of my friends. They couldn't believe how good they were.'*

The feeling that Peter needed a change of scenery, and maybe a new direction, came in the form of National Service where he served in the Royal Air Force between 1946 and 1948. He was drafted in as an Airframe Fitter, a role utilising the skills he had acquired as a carpenter. Later Peter became involved in the Berlin Airlift, a vital operation to bring much-needed supplies from Western Allies to those who had become isolated in Berlin, starved by the occupation of the Soviet Army. Peter was responsible for aeroplane maintenance and

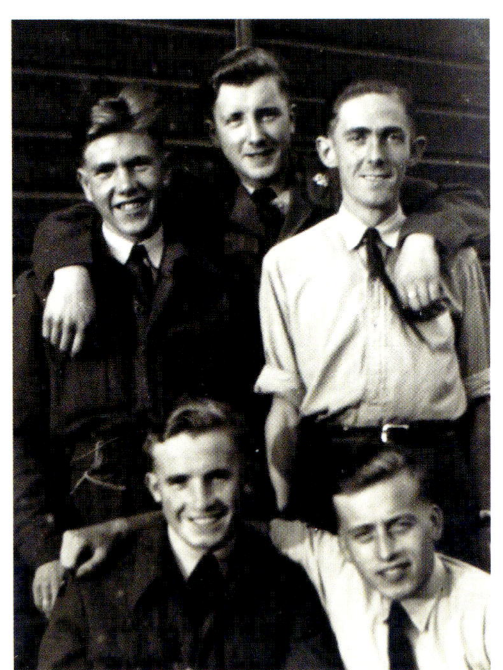

Peter Gilman (top centre) with fellow National Servicemen at Weston-Super-Mare c.1947.

was stationed in Germany. Peter chose not to talk too much about his National Service but it was obvious that his experiences played a significant part in shaping his character. The disciplines which he had gained during his wartime childhood years were reaffirmed by National Service and would feature in just about everything that he would do in the future.

On completion of his National Service in 1949 Peter, once again, returned to his family in Mitcham. Some aspects of home life had become easier as his parents had now secured a house which gave room for them all to live much more comfortably together. Peter began working at London Carriers, owned by Phillips, an electrical company situated in Pearly Way, Croydon, fitting interiors of wooden framework in commercial vans.

During this time, Peter became interested in cycling and joined the British League of Racing Cyclists based in Streatham. Peter had a bicycle made, but soon found it to be too small as his interest was leaning towards racing as opposed to leisure riding. Peter's sister Jean purchased the smaller bike and joined the club too, often cycling with her partner Barry.

In 1951, during one of the cycling meetings, Peter was to meet Jean Parkes. Their friendship blossomed and Jean became Peter's girlfriend. They enjoyed the company of Jean's sister Julie Parkes and her fiancée Alan, who was also very involved in cycling.

Alan recalls those early cycling days, *'I found Peter to be quite an awkward kind of character, although he was a very genuine, loyal man with an extremely caring nature. He was quite reserved and certainly had very strong opinions and personal ideas. He was a little bit like his bicycle… always immaculate, nothing was ever out of place! Although Peter attended the majority of social events at the club he always kept himself to himself.'*

Alan vividly recalls the first time he met Peter at a cycling meeting which he had arranged in Bournemouth, *'Things weren't like they are today and we used to organise cycling events in quite a homemade kind of way where everyone interacted socially and had a bit of fun. Peter had made the trip down to Bournemouth and had competed alongside the other cyclists. I remember him being a dapper man, very neat and tidy. He was quite abrupt and a little aggressive to start with, but he joined in with the rest of us and seemed to enjoy the weekend. There was no doubting that he was obviously a man with an incredible amount of ability but he seemed to lack the true passion needed to really make it competitively. I can't ever recall him winning a race… although it was evident he would have been more than capable of doing so.'*

Irene recalls Peter putting every ounce of energy into his cycling too. *'My brother was passionate about his cycling… I think he would have given anything to have had that little bit of extra stamina needed to really break into the racing scene properly. Peter and a friend used to do a race called the "Bath and Back", this was an evening event, cycling throughout the night. These races really took their toll on Peter and he would often suffer for days after a race. I remember sneaking home one evening, later than I should have been, having been out courting with my boyfriend Frank. I almost got to the top of the stairs when Peter shouted out in the dark having had a nightmare about a certain race… I was so scared that I almost fell down the stairs backwards!'*

Peter and Jean were married at St Leonard's Church, Streatham on Saturday 27 March 1954 and spent their honeymoon in Bournemouth.

Peter enjoyed his friendship with his brother-in-law Alan, who remembers what may have been a particularly poignant moment in Peter's artistic career, *'Peter was always sketching and often had a pencil and pad with him wherever he went. I was heavily into photography at*

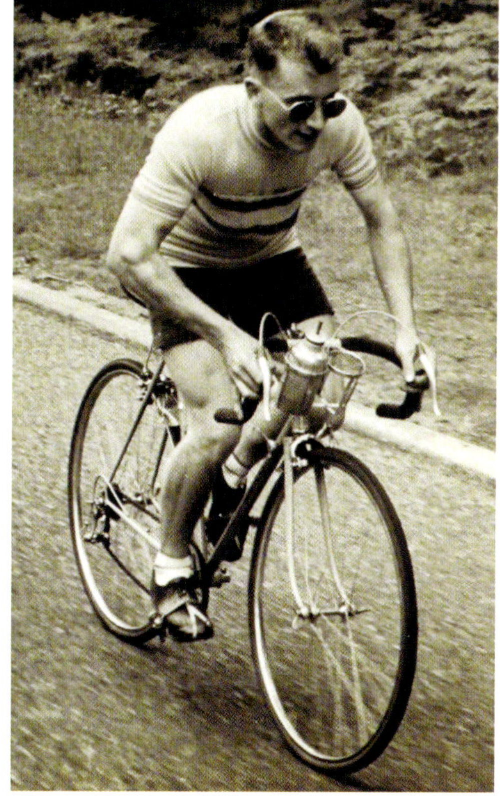

Peter competing in a road race in 1954.

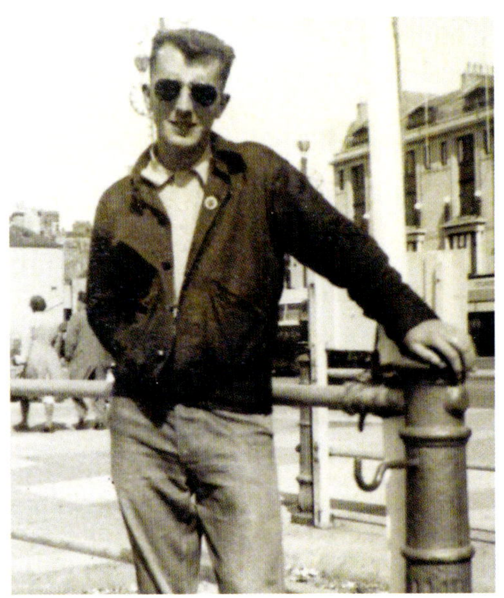

Peter in Hastings, 1952.

that time and we often found ourselves discussing compositions where we shared notes and had varying opinions. I repeatedly mentioned to Peter about using oil paints in his work, but my comments had very little success for my suggestions generally were ignored!'

It was by chance that the two of us came up with a scheme for a gift for our mother-in-law. It was quite fashionable to hand-tint black and white photography in the '50s, colour photography still being relatively in its infancy. I had been photographing some swans at the local park and had the images developed on to an emulsion-based white Whatman paper. The paper surface had a bit of a tooth and could easily take a good coating of colour. I suggested to Peter that if we used my photograph he could undertake to colour it in and this would make an ideal present for our mother-in-law. Peter reluctantly accepted the task and, of course, made a wonderful job of bringing my photograph to life with colour. Once finished, Peter made a beautiful fire-screen frame, and that hand tinted photograph was used for as long as I can remember. This probably was Peter's first real use of oil.'

A year later Peter and Jean seized the opportunity to move into their first married home situated in New Town Stevenage in Hertfordshire. The local authority were making available affordable rental housing to anyone who held a job, so Peter started employment with English Electric, a British manufacturer specialising in industrial electric motors and transformers. He worked as a designer and model- and pattern-maker using plastics and wood. This new role meant that he could work creatively for the first time and provided independ-

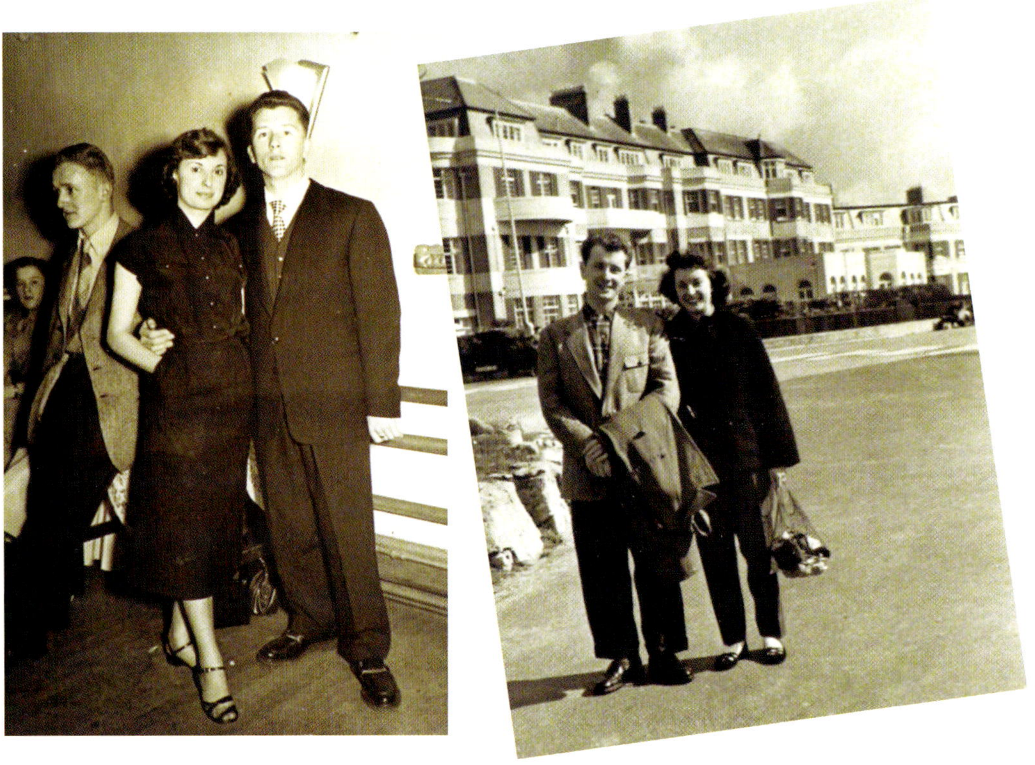

Peter and Jean Gilman in 1952 (left), and on their honeymoon in Bournemouth in 1954.

ence for the newly married couple. In 1963, Peter and Jean were blessed with the birth of their first and only child, Maxine, who quickly became the centre of Peter's world.

Throughout his time living in Hertfordshire, Peter continued to develop his keen love for drawing and painting. As he progressed and nurtured his skills, he began to expand a portfolio of art work and, through networking with other local artists, he eventually joined the local art group in Stevenage.

It was during art group meetings that Peter met fellow artists John Haskins, Trevor Chamberlain and David Green. Regularly painting together formed lasting friendships. Peter's ability to tackle any subject was astounding. He showed confidence at all levels whether the subject was still life, figurative, marine, town or landscape, in any medium. A highlight was his love for line and wash work, particularly accentuating his skills of fine draughtsmanship which developed from his wartime childhood days of drawing and sketching.

A change of jobs led to a new role at ICI in Welwyn. His position as a draftsman brought benefits in wages and reduced the pressures in paying bills. His hard work ultimately provided the opportunity to get on to the property ladder, and he bought his first house in Stotfold. Whilst working for ICI, Peter was tasked to an assignment to work on the Blue Streak Missile project. This involved being flown to Scotland on a regular basis to make full-scale models in wood.

Peter was perfectly suited to ICI projects and the company were deeply impressed by the quality of his work. During a spell of redundancies a decision was made to retain Peter, but this caused a great deal of unrest and dissatisfaction amongst fellow workers and ex-

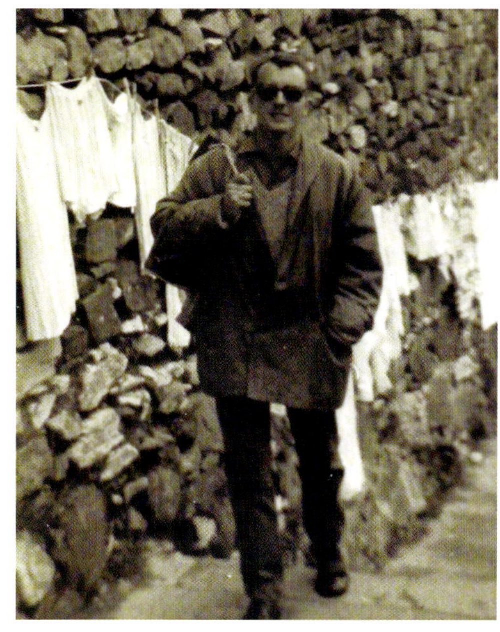

Peter on holiday in St Ives, Cornwall, 1963.

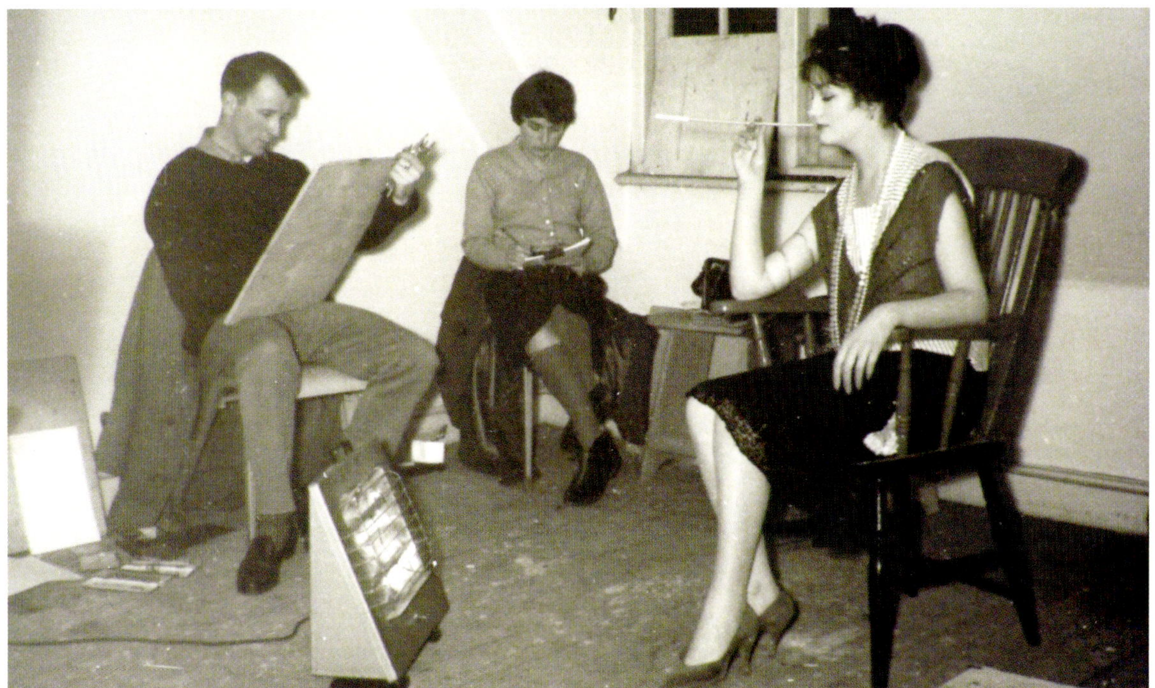

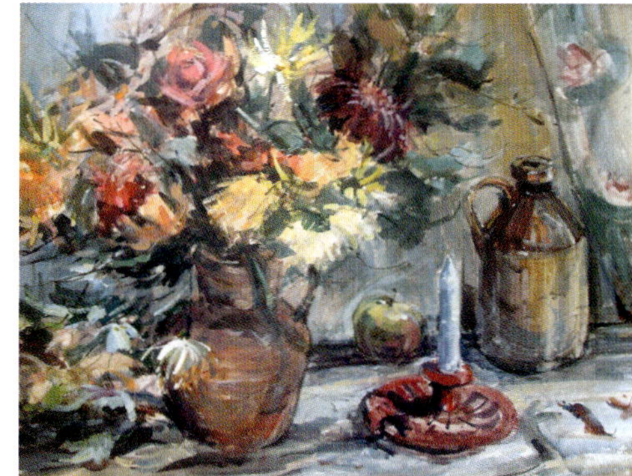

Still Life with Candle. Oil.

Peter sketching in a life class.

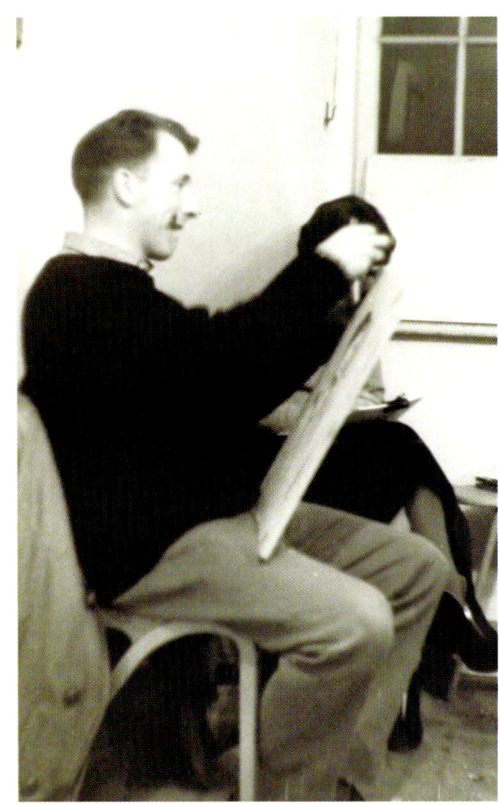

The life class.

employees. Peter, and his wife Jean, suffered a number of unpleasant situations from the families of redundant workers and this significantly disturbed Peter, becoming a very low time in his working life. In hindsight, this was to be a blessing, for this period of unsettlement was to be the catalyst to launch a new career as a professional artist, achieving that long-burning ambition to make a career in the art world that had obviously always been his aim.

Peter had developed a real flair for his painting, using oil for a strong base of colour and then overlaying with lines of black ink. He had submitted works to local society exhibitions with a good degree of success, but he longed to take the next step and have art works exhibited in a gallery.

Brother-in-law Alan was delighted to tell Peter of an opportunity which had arisen via a client. He was advised to make himself known to the Dorric Galleries, a new gallery in Bromley that had opened in 1965, for they were in the stages of planning an exhibition. Peter visited the gallery and showed them some of his paintings, a daunting task for any artist. The gallery enthused, likening them to 'Walt Disney creations'! Trevor Chamberlain was to share this exhibition, and Peter's first entry into the world of galleries was secured. The exhibition was very successful, with both artists returning a good number of sales, and the experience provided Peter with the confidence to show and exhibit his work in the future.

A move in 1969 to the picturesque village of Ashwell, near Baldock, was a move spurred by lovely romantic views in and around the village. Peter often quipped, 'great painting material!'. The new family home was built on the site of the disused Old Bull public house, but Peter's attention was drawn to the old garage at the bottom of the garden, which would satisfy a craving for his own studio. This was to be an artists' studio like no other. Every paint tube had its own place, every brush was in its right series and size, even the pencils were in an order… all lined up like soldiers. Everything was kept in immaculate condition and nothing was ever out of place.

There can be no question that the move to Ashwell greatly inspired Peter. He had finally achieved his ambition to become a professional artist, had a family and a beautiful home. He was totally content, possibly for the first time since his evacuation with the Johnson family during the war.

As Peter's confidence in his own ability grew, he found himself being invited to exhibit in more society shows. He was a long-standing member of numerous local art groups including Letchworth, Hertford and Welwyn Garden City, exhibiting regularly at their annual Exhibitions. Between 1971 and 1977, Peter also exhibited continually at the Royal Society of Marine Artists and Chelsea Art Society. However, one of his greatest achievements was to be elected as a candidate for membership for The Wapping Group of Artists. This culminated in his holding full membership in 1977, whereupon he contributed to each of their Annual Exhibitions. A proud 'Wapper', Peter would often include in his biographies and write in his painting articles about the pleasure and privilege he experienced when painting in situ beside the Thames alongside other Wapping Group members.

This love of life led to some of Peter's happiest years and this was clear to see in his paintings. His increased time to paint allowed his style to develop, gaining him extensive recognition and the confidence to diversify into teaching. In 1975 he took a major step forward and joined the Galleon Painting Holidays tutor panel, where his genteel manner and infinite patience proved particularly appealing to beginners. As with everything that he undertook, Peter's professionalism, sensitivity and sense of humour gained him many friends and he found himself in tremendous demand as a tutor. News reached artists' material company Daler-Rowney and Peter was recruited as a demonstrator, and he became an ambassador in promoting their products.

In 1979 Peter proudly wrote three articles for *Leisure Painter* magazine, focusing on watercolour, oil and marine painting. It was during these articles Peter's great love for painting was revealed, and the pressures he placed upon himself, '*…we are better at our work if we are not tired mentally and physically. Painting is not easy; it is an intense and unique time in our lives when we are producing a work and feel prepared to cope with it. Feeling has a great deal to do with our painting; how wonderful the excitement prior to beginning a work we have been looking forward to doing.*'

As with his way of life, Peter's writing was precise and extremely well structured. He would go into great detail to express everything to an amateur painter that would enable them to get the best from their painting, informative and yet simple to understand, the mark of a true teacher.

The Leisure Arts Book entitled *Painting in Oils* includes particularly fine examples of Peter's detail and sense of humour: '*How you dress to deal with the different seasons is very important for comfort. In warm weather we must keep cool. Wear a shady hat – never paint in sunglasses. Insect repellent is a useful item to carry in hot weather. In winter keep your feet warm with wool socks and good boots. Thermal underwear is very helpful. A coat with a pure wool lining is a good investment. A pair of gloves with thumb and forefinger removed from the brush hand is a must. Remember, always keep your feet and hands warm; you cannot concentrate if you are cold.*'

Sidney Cardew, a current member of The Wapping Group of Artists and the Royal Society of Marine Artists, recalls with great affection his first meeting with Peter Gilman. *'I first met Peter when I did a Galleon Painting Course at Ross-on-Wye in 1980. I found him to be a very friendly and committed artist and it was an honour to know him. I had many pleasurable hours of painting with Peter but I will always remember his demonstration, a painting in oil on hardboard near Flanesford Priory, Goodrich.*

There were about twelve or more of us watching, but it was obvious that Peter was not very happy with his progress. When lunchtime arrived most of the class left but a few, including me, remained while Peter struggled on. He suddenly called a halt to his painting and, whilst wiping his brushes and cleaning his palette, declared, 'I have had enough of this!' Other words were uttered as he seized his painting and threw it into the field of corn in front of the Priory. He picked up his easel and away we went to lunch.

During lunch I asked Peter if he would mind if I could search for his throwaway painting, as I had considered that it really wasn't the right thing to do. He was not at all bothered and after a considerable search I managed to find the painting intact and undamaged. On taking the painting back to Peter I asked if I could keep it and he said, 'leave it with me and I will finish it for you'.

The next morning he presented me with the completed painting, duly signed 'Peter Gilman'. It remains hanging in my lounge, nicely framed and greatly admired!'

In 1982 Peter had his first book published entitled, *Oil Painting Outdoors*, and this title featured significantly in the highly popular instructional Leisure Arts series. This book was

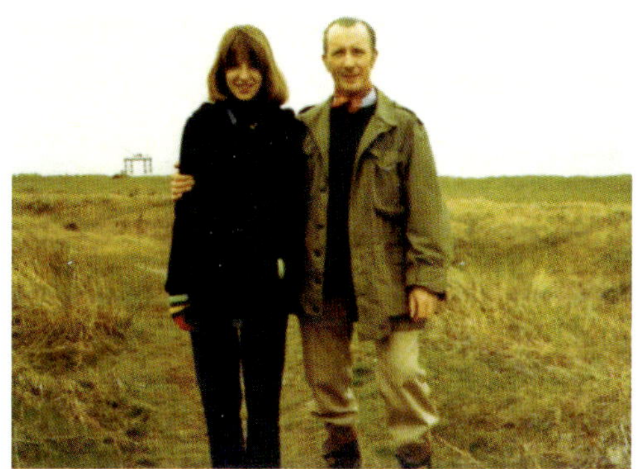

Peter and Maxine, May 1977.

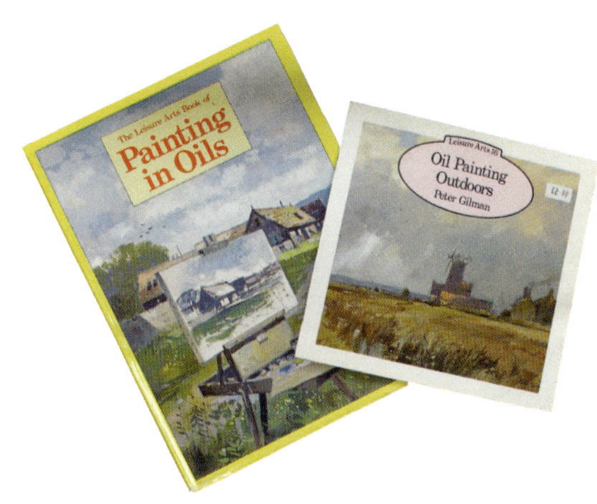

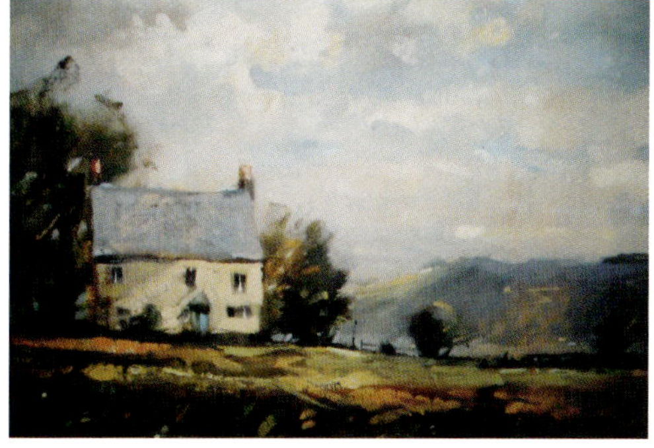

The Gilman painting 'rescued' by Sidney Cardew..

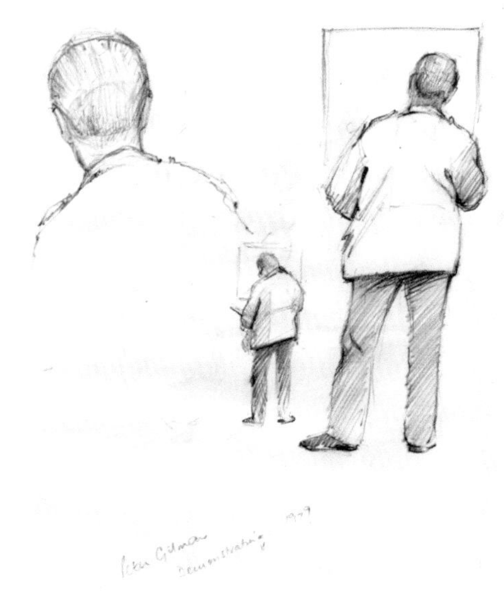

A sketch of Peter Gilman demonstrating to an art group, by Robin Mackervoy.

an informative step-by-step guide to painting in oils and was considered worthy to be incorporated, virtually in its entirety, to feature in a combined book of oil tuition entitled, *The Leisure Book of Painting in Oils.* Peter was delighted to feature alongside tutorials and artworks by some of the most prestigious artists at that time, Norman Battershill, Clifford Bailey and Dennis Frost. His original paintings were now featured in many mixed exhibitions, including that of the prestigious Claridges Gallery in London's West End, and he staged numerous joint exhibitions alongside his good friend Trevor Chamberlain. He was working with the best, writing with the best and exhibiting with the best!

At a point which could have been considered the pinnacle of Peter Gilman's artistic career, and notably at the happiest point of his life, personal circumstances were to change. As a man who strived perfection, living by a personal code of conduct where the very highest standards were attained, he chose to leave his family home, a decision that would emotionally affect him and all those closely around him. He set himself up in a mobile home in Lower Stondon, at Henlow, where he lived and worked alone.

It was around this time that Peter was to hear of a gallery in North Norfolk that had developed a new display system where paintings were sold without deducting commission. His initial journey to discover this gallery and the subsequent friendship he made with the owners is told by Michael Hill in the following chapter.

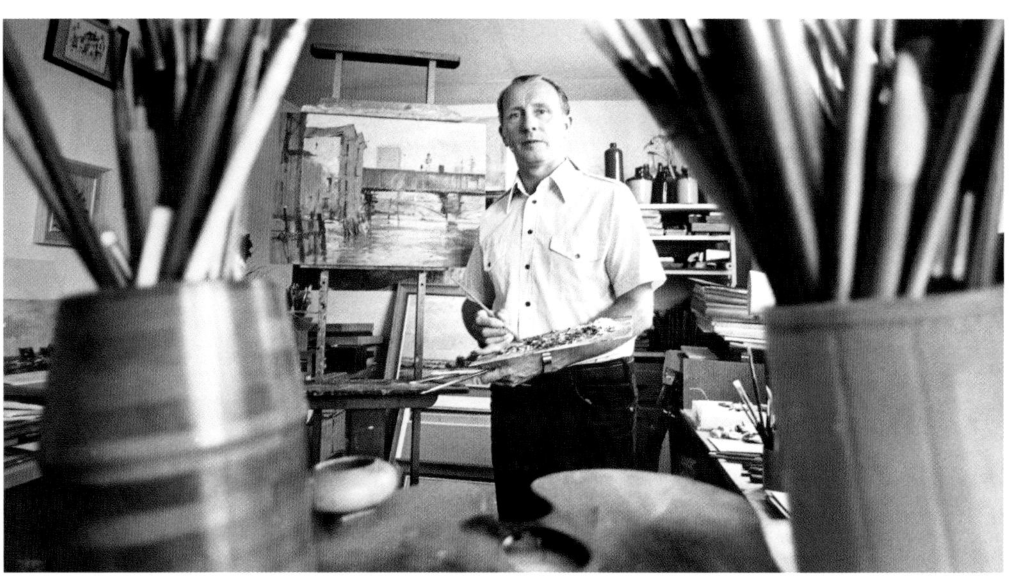

Peter in his studio. Photo © Alan Philip.

A PERSONAL TRIBUTE

by Michael Hill

I feel greatly privileged to have this unique opportunity to record my personal recollections of Peter Gilman, a truly exceptionally gifted artist who I had the pleasure to promote and represent at Picturecraft until his most unexpected and untimely death in 1984.

In order to fully appreciate the circumstances of our initial meeting I need to explain why Peter Gilman decided to journey to North Norfolk in order to find our gallery.

An incredible amount of hard work saw our family business grow at an alarming rate from the humble beginnings of a hobby of picture framing in 1963. On leaving school, at just 16 years of age, I formed a partnership with my parents in 1968. Our diversification into selling paintings and artists' materials was encouraged by customer demand and our ongoing desire to provide a first-class service at every possible level.

My father's erratic and impulsive decision to purchase Lees Yard in 1971 at a cost of £9,750, may not appear reckless in this day and age, but the pressures that it brought to bear could justify a book being written on this subject alone. However, this purchase secured us with substantial warehouse premises which, for financial reasons, we were forced to quickly develop into an art gallery. The majority of the work was undertaken by ourselves, and the Picturecraft Gallery opened to the public on 1 April 1972. The reaction from artists and the public was immediate, for the gallery at that time was recognised as one of the largest privately-owned galleries in the county.

After some time it occurred to me that, whilst happily supplying artists with frames and paints and generating two areas of profit for our business, it seemed grossly unfair to deduct commission from the full selling price of a painting when an artist exhibited at our gallery. I challenged myself to provide an alternative by adopting the role as an artist and setting out a list of requirements which I would deem to be the absolutely perfect scenario for exhibiting in 'the ideal gallery'.

A particular failing with our gallery display system was the quantity of work being exhibited and the inability for an artists work to be viewed as a collection. It was obvious that the random display of over 1000 paintings around the gallery proved confusing for the public, and also created difficulties in book-keeping. What a joy if an artists' work could be displayed together and contained within one space! Other thoughts revolved around allowing an artist the freedom of choice to decide where and when they would like to exhibit in the gallery. The majority of artists had already expressed their preference that the gallery should be responsible for planning an effective layout design and to undertake the hanging of their paintings, so these simple observations formed the foundations of my deliberations.

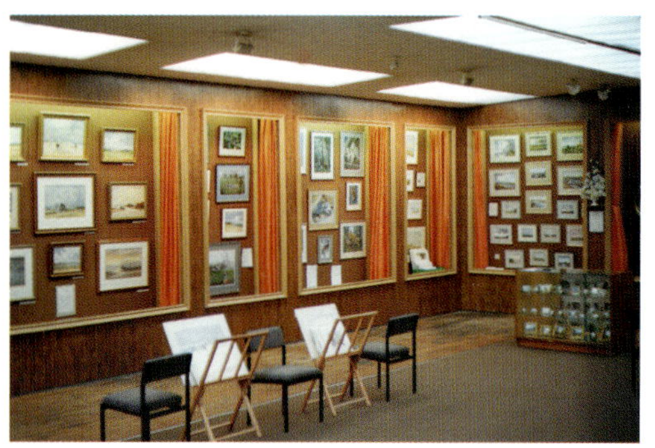

Picturecraft Gallery in 1980.

There were two further ultimate aims. One was to totally eliminate gallery commission charges, but the other was to try and assist any artist who felt that they had reached a point in their career where they wished to show their paintings to the public, perhaps for the first time. Artists had already made me acutely aware of appalling selective procedures, restrictive contracts and the humiliation experienced when their work had been severely criticised and rejected by gallery owners. It was time for change.

In very simple terms, I eventually designed and implemented a completely new display system where nineteen individual display spaces of varying sizes were built around the gallery walls. The year was then divided into three-weekly exhibition sessions. The concept was very straightforward, an artist was offered the opportunity to select a display space and date session. Once display space had been secured, detailed instructions were provided when the paintings needed to be delivered to the gallery. The layout design, hanging of paintings and management of sales would be the full responsibility of the gallery and no commission would be deducted from sales. The public, in effect, could purchase directly from the artist.

Of course, in order to provide all these services, some form of income had to be generated for the gallery. My solution was to introduce a rental charge totally dependent on the amount of space required and, thankfully, this new structured way of exhibiting was very warmly welcomed. It was an extremely proud moment when our display system eventually won the National Westminster Bank's Streamline Gold Business Award in 1991. Today the display system still operates, albeit following a total refurbishment programme in 2003 when the gallery was enlarged and redesigned to incorporate 32 display spaces.

News of our gallery spread far and wide and attracted attention from artists from this country and also overseas. It was a very busy time and the enhanced manner in which paintings were being displayed, combined with the regular three-weekly changes, increased sales dramatically.

Before long, professional artists fascinated by the size, space and layout of our gallery started to enquire if it was possible to rent every display space in the building in order to stage a one-man show. It was obvious that the cost of renting the entire gallery for a three-week period would be too prohibitive for one artist, but I was tremendously attracted by the idea of establishing an exhibition centre. In order to address the problem, I introduced a secondary display system which enabled us to quickly transform the normal layout of the gallery into a stunning new setting for exhibitions to take place over a period of just one week. This unique system proved to be the turning point for our gallery and is also used to this day, albeit significantly modified during the 2003 refurbishment.

And so to Peter… One day a seemingly shy gentleman arrived at the gallery. I acknowledged his presence and ensured him a warm welcome, but it was clear his mission was to view the paintings rather than to become involved in conversation. Our policy was to always allow freedom of space and he was left to quietly spend time perusing the paintings without interference.

After a period of considerable time he eventually worked his way around the gallery and nervously approached the desk. In a quietly spoken, gentle manner he enquired, 'Is this the gallery in Norfolk that doesn't charge any commission on sales?' He appeared so relieved to know he had found the place and was quick to respond, 'I'll bring my paintings in then!'

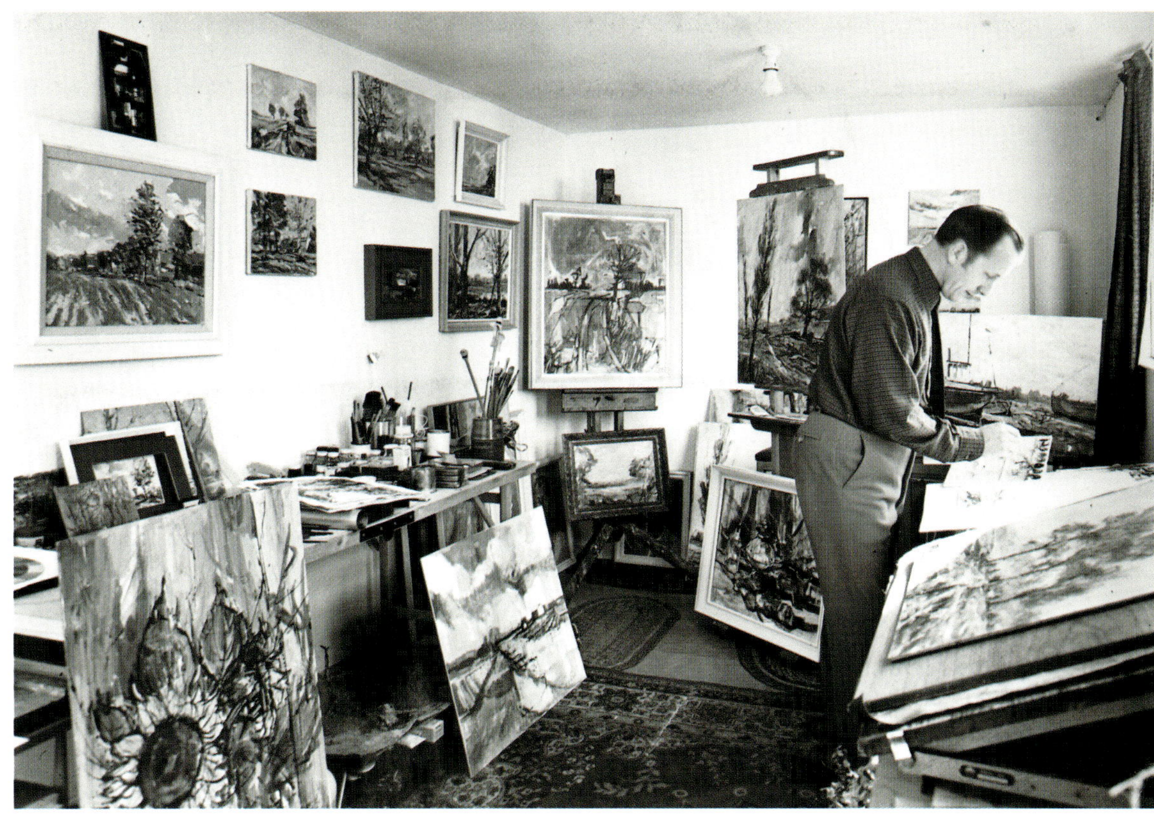

Peter at work in his studio.
Photo © Alan Philip.

His face turned to despair on learning that the gallery was full, it was necessary to book in advance and that rent was charged to secure space. 'I've come such a long way', he explained, 'and my car is filled with paintings'. Fully expecting my father, forever tactless at every occasion, to question how a gallery is expected to live on fresh air, and still oblivious to who this modest man was, I suggested that we should view his work and escorted him to the green Morris Traveller standing outside. It was true. Clusters of paintings, framed and unframed, were randomly scattered around the vehicle. Flustered at the dreadfully untidy state of his car he introduced himself, 'My name's Peter Gilman and I would so much like to exhibit here'.

It was a bright, sunny day and my first viewing of Peter's work was to see them hastily piled up and propped against the rear wheel arch of his car. Each painting glowed in the dramatic, strong sunlight, and each received a brief verbal anecdote from Peter, 'Gosh! I remember it was very cold when I did that one'.

My enthusiasm and admiration melted Peter's shyness away, for I was absolutely enchanted by his paintings. Comparable to nothing I had ever seen before, perhaps bearing a likeness only to Marcus Ford in their freedom of execution. A breath of fresh air.

Peter continued to rummage around in his car, eager to please and to show more, but my awareness of the heat from the sun bearing down on this scattered collection concerned

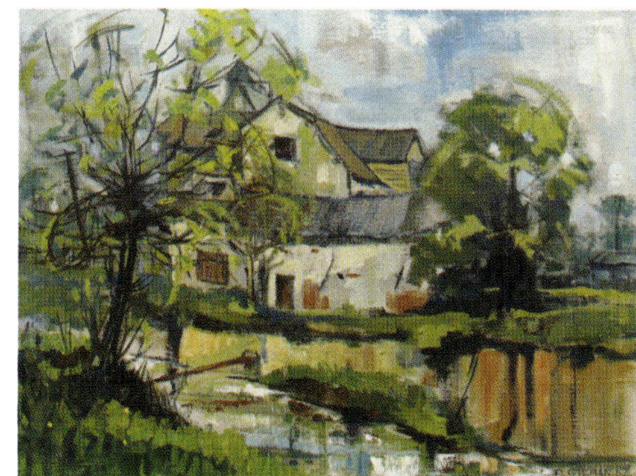

An early Gilman painting from 1962.

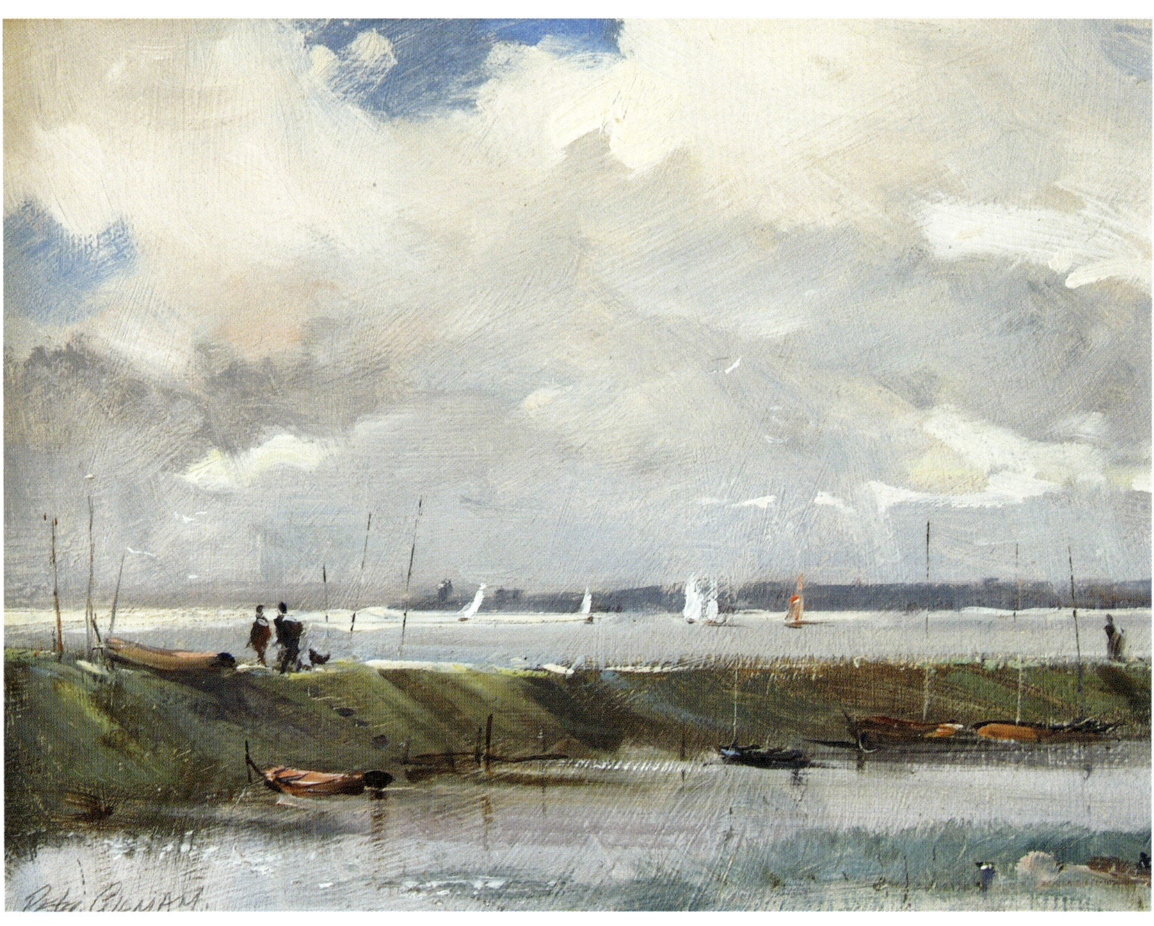

A Gilman painting showing the freshness and freedom of execution in style.

me. I hastily suggested he should stop and invited him to bring some of the framed work into the gallery for my father to view. The suddenness of my decision halted him in his tracks and seemingly brought him crashing back down to earth. He nervously looked directly at me, dispirited in tone he confessed, 'The truth is, I've got no money'.

There could be no question that I was in the company of a tremendously humble man, acutely embarrassed at his naïvety in failing to recognise how we made a living from running a gallery. Clearly he was struggling, and it was at this moment when I first detected the genuine extent of his utter desperation. I reiterated my suggestion that we should take some of the paintings into the gallery and this immediately raised his spirits and his relief was clear to see. Unsurprisingly, given sight of Peter's paintings, my father endorsed my enthusiasm. But how could we help?

The stringent controls in renting display space simply had to be overturned. There was no question that we could allow Peter to return home with all his pictures. Our offer was to show his work on the understanding that we would only charge him the cost of renting space should sufficient sales take place. Peter appeared deeply moved by our confidence in his ability and there was a genuine sincerity in his gratitude. The strength in the grip of his handshake left no doubts to his feelings as he left to go home.

It was fortuitous that one of our exhibiting artists was unable to exhibit for the next three-weekly session and this provided the space to exhibit all the paintings that Peter had left behind. It is difficult to imagine today just how successful sales in the gallery were at that time. Saturdays proved particularly busy and there were many occasions when the number of visitors far exceeded our capabilities to manage the gallery appropriately. It was not uncommon for customers to remove the paintings from the walls themselves in order to make a purchase.

It was during one of these busy Saturday afternoons when the telephone rang, and when I responded I had difficulty in hearing a faint voice say, 'It's Peter'.

'Peter who?', I enquired.

'It's Peter Gilman, and I'm wondering, has anything sold yet?'

'Of course', I enthused, 'there's hardly any left'.

Peter told me many months later that it had taken a glass of whisky in order to pluck up the courage to telephone that day. I totally failed to recognise the significance when he freely confessed, 'I don't know what I would have done if you'd said, nothing's sold'.

The early success with sales of Peter's paintings was certainly not short lived. He made an enormous impact in the gallery and eventually rented 'his special space' on an annual basis. Peter was highly motivated by this positive feedback and he spent considerable time painting in North Norfolk to enable local landscapes to significantly feature in his display.

Strangely, Peter never spoke of other galleries or places where he had held exhibitions. I was unaware of his background, other than his involvement in teaching art with the Galleon Painting Holiday Group. He was clearly proud of his Leisure Art Series publication entitled, *Oil Painting Outdoors*, and was delighted that it had sold very successfully in our artists' material shop. Peter was happy to sign a copy should this be requested.

Peter was extremely complimentary of our business and expressed great joy when visiting Holt, 'I love coming here', he once told me, 'for I'm surrounded by all the things that I love the most… paints, frames and paintings!' Because of this, I never saw a sad side to Peter and we enjoyed happy times, and a very special friendship developed based on respect and total trust for each other. As our business relationship blossomed, Peter entrusted me to supply all his picture framing requirements. Frames were ordered over the telephone in preparation for his regular visits to bring new paintings for the gallery. To make ordering simpler, some picture frame mouldings were actually named after Peter and he would take great delight in ordering, 'six 10 inch x 12 inch frames in Gilman's Gold'.

Following incredibly successful sales, in May 1983, I approached Peter to see if he would consider staging a one-man exhibition in our gallery in August 1984. He appeared apprehensive at the prospect of filling such a large gallery but indicated that he was extremely flattered to have been asked and requested time in order to give it further consideration. Over the following weeks, Peter was anxious to glean as much information about staging a major show as possible. He request a plan of the gallery in order to gauge the number of paintings required, recognising that this would possibly represent his biggest ever exhibition. His attention to detail and fastidious approach conveyed his wish that this was to be a very special show. He continually questioned his ability to fulfill such an enormous

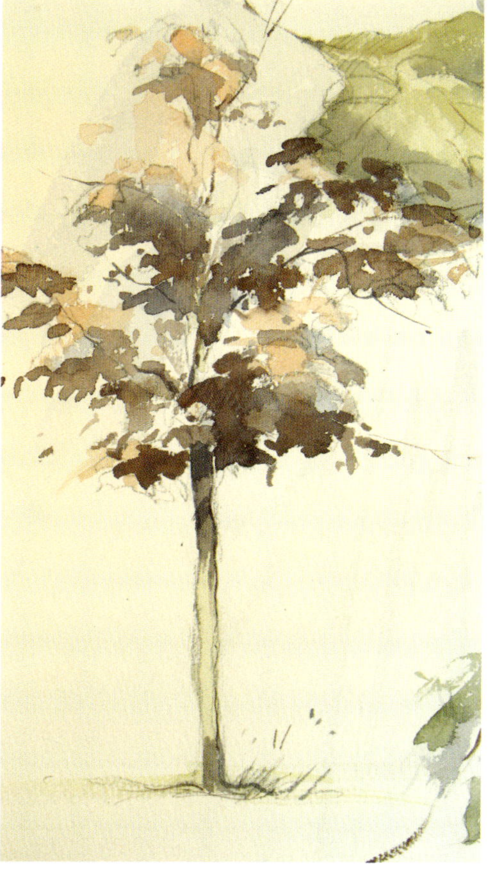

The lightness of Gilman's style is exhibited in this watercolour sketch.

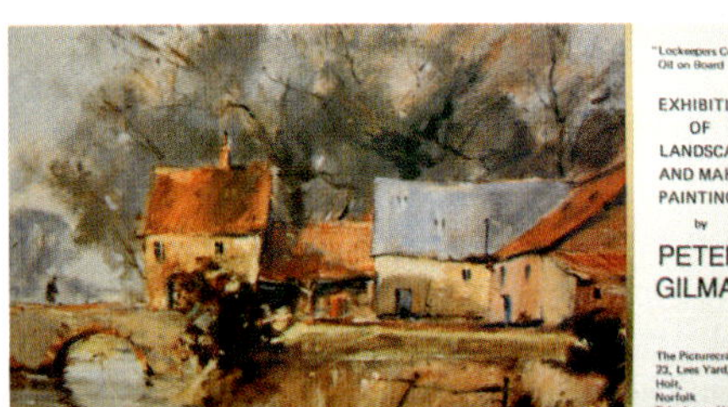

*The invitation card to Peter's one-man
exhibition at the Picturecraft Gallery.*

undertaking and was grateful and encouraged by the strength of our reassurance. I was absolutely delighted to receive Peter's telephone call confirming the exhibition, and his target was to try and accomplish 100 paintings in 15 months.

The promotion of Peter's forthcoming exhibition drew significant interest for he had amassed a great following through exhibiting in our gallery on an annual basis. He regularly kept me updated with his progress and was excited by my feedback. A local collector and tremendous admirer of Peter's paintings offered his holiday cottage overlooking the windmill and marshes at Cley-next-the-Sea for Peter to use for the duration of the exhibition. This was very warmly received and prompted Peter with the idea that he should paint every day in the gallery while the show was running. Excitement was in the air!

Closer to the exhibition Peter advised me that there were to be 107 paintings, a mix of oils and watercolours, mostly featuring East Anglian landscapes with an emphasis on the coastline. He carefully detailed the sizes for all the framing requirements. He asked me to select a good example of his work from his current display to feature on the private view card, so I chose, 'Lock-keepers Cottage, River Ouse', a beautiful landscape in oils. The mailing list labels were printed and envelopes prepared. Once all the frames were made I telephoned Peter to update him of our progress. He was deeply appreciative and complimentary of the organisation and seemed excited at the prospect of staying in North Norfolk. We had ordered copies of his *Oil Painting Outdoors* book and he was agreeable to signing copies for customers throughout the exhibition and offered to sign some in advance when he delivered all the paintings. All was well.

Peter delivered his paintings to the gallery, delighted that he had surpassed his expectations to paint such an enormous quantity and enthused at the sight of all the frames. He furnished me with a detailed hand-written list showing the title and price for each painting. Surprisingly, he was keen to pay. It is customary when an artist reaches this stage to defer payment until the exhibition has finished, but Peter insisted and paid in full. 'And now it's up to you', he said. We shook hands, he thanked me for everything and he left.

The telephone rang in the gallery on 11 July 1984. It was Trevor Chamberlain, a fellow artist and very close friend of Peter's for over twenty-five years. 'Michael, it's bad news', and the conversation that followed was one of the most unexpected shocks I have ever experienced in my professional career. To be told that Peter had taken his own life was impossible to believe and I listened in stunned silence to be advised of my mission, 'It was Peter's wish that the show must go ahead as planned'.

Despite twenty-five years passing, I still feel totally numbed by Peter's death. I had been so deeply privileged to show his work and to share in the great joy his paintings brought to so many people. Never at any time did Peter ever convey a troubled mind, and I thought that I knew him so well. Now I was charged with the difficult and extremely sad task to present a fitting tribute, a situation that I had never encountered before.

I turned to Sidney Reeves, a very dear friend for help, for it was hard to find direction. With great sensitivity we talked through appropriate ways to prepare a suitable tribute and decided to quickly publish a card to accompany the preview cards already waiting to be posted in their addressed envelopes. The card read:

'In sending you the accompanying invitation, the Directors of Picturecraft have to announce with deep regret the unexpected and untimely passing of Peter Gilman. The artist had set his heart on

this Exhibition and had worked indefatigably for many months producing a fine collection of paintings; some of which are the best examples of his work. It was his last wish that the Exhibition should be held, and that no effort should be spared to make it a fine one. Picturecraft asks its patrons to regard this Exhibition as commemorating Peter Gilman and his art'.

With help from Trevor Chamberlain, John Seabrook and artists' material company, Daler-Rowney, we prepared a folded card bearing a poignant photograph of Peter on the front cover entitled 'Peter Gilman, Artist and Man, A Tribute'; the photograph revealed to me great sadness in his eyes.

My foreword was brief, *'It is with much sadness, yet pride, that Picturecraft presents this small tribute to the late Peter Gilman. It was our great privilege and pleasure to have known him, personally, and to have worked with him for many years. During that time, our relationship was both harmonious and compatible, and we never failed to admire this kindly, gentle man, his professionalism and his great talent'.*

My friend Sidney, my mentor and master of gentle words, concluded, *'Truly, the tragic passing of Peter Gilman has sadly eclipsed the happiness of many'.*

Peter's wishes were honoured and the exhibition opened on Friday 24 August 1984. The attendance was unbelievable; at the end of the exhibition every painting was sold. The press release in the *Eastern Daily Press* contained a photograph of Peter's daughter, Maxine, viewing the paintings in the gallery with Peter's sister, Jean Evans, bearing the headline: 'Artist's last exhibition has an East Anglian flavour'.

The editorial was extensive:

'Art lovers flocked from all over Britain and from abroad to Holt at the weekend to pay homage to one of Britain's most highly regarded contemporary artists, Peter Gilman, who committed suicide two months ago.

What turned out to be his final exhibition, of 107 oils and watercolours, mainly depicting East Anglian landscapes and coastal scenes, had been planned for 15 months and the last works were delivered to the Picturecraft Gallery, at Lees Yard, Holt, only shortly before Mr Gilman ended his life.

A partner in the family-run Picturecraft Gallery, Mr Michael Hill, spoke on Saturday of his first encounter with the Surrey-born artist, whose work has found a treasured place in many private collections, including that of the Royal Family.

"He walked in here about three years ago because he had heard that there was a gallery in North Norfolk which sold pictures without charging the artists a commission," said Mr Hill.

The new system introduced by Picturecraft involves hiring out bays in the gallery for a weekly rental. "He had about 36 paintings in the car with him and when I saw them I knew just what a good artist he was. Within a week we had sold 18 of them and he never looked back after that," said Mr Hill.

At Friday's private viewing of the last Peter Gilman exhibition the trend continued, with 36 paintings being sold in two and a-half hours. By Saturday afternoon almost two-thirds of the collection had been snapped up, at prices ranging from £42 to £250.

Although some buyers took their works home with them, the majority remain on view at the gallery until Thursday.

Born in 1928, Peter Gilman was a professional marine and landscape artist, painting in the traditional style in oils, acrylics and watercolours. He exhibited regularly at the Royal Society of

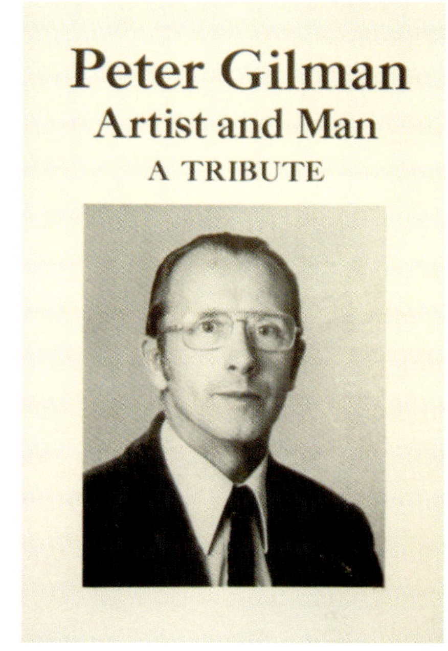

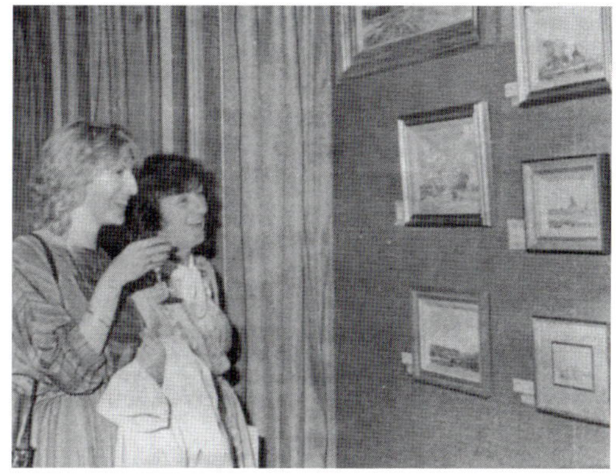

Peter's daughter Maxine and his sister Jean Evans at the opening of the 1984 exhibition.

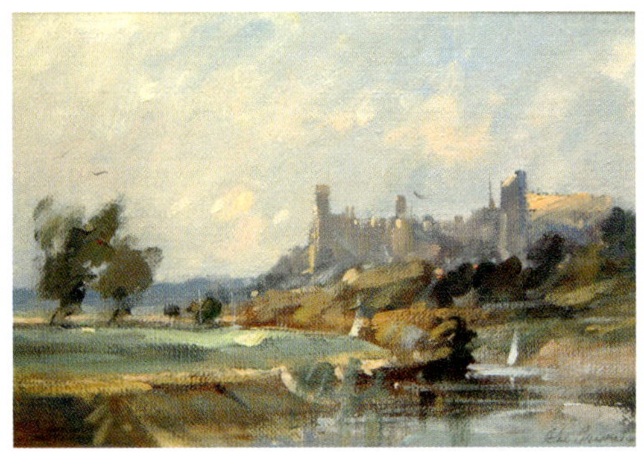

Arundel Castle. Oil. As featured in Oil Painting Outdoors. (Michael Hill Collection)

Marine Artists' annual exhibitions, the Chelsea Art Society's exhibitions and widely elsewhere in this country and abroad.

He won the John Goss Prize at the 1984 Hertford Art Society's annual exhibition. He was a popular lecturer on painting and wrote the Leisure Arts volume on Oil Painting Outdoors. *He became very popular as an art demonstrator for Daler-Rowney and as a member of Galleon Painting Holidays tutor panel.*

Among the guests at the exhibition preview at Holt were his friend of 25 years, fellow artist Trevor Chamberlain, Miss Maxine Gilman, the artist's daughter, and Mrs. Jean Evans, his sister.

"I always say he was an artist's artist. Anyone who is an artist who saw him work appreciated how good he was. He loved painting outside and was often interrupted by people wanting to talk to him about his work. But he never brushed them off, he always had time to talk to those who were genuinely interested," said Mr Hill.'

As with any artist who has passed away, their paintings remain behind to serve as a visual reminder. Amongst my personal collection of cherished paintings, I hold some wonderful examples of Peter's oils and watercolours. One was featured as a step-by-step illustrated guide in the *Oil Painting Outdoors* book and it is fascinating to see how this particular painting, of Arundel Castle, was constructed and to read Peter's accompanying notes, 'I feel I was successful in capturing a scene bathed in the light of a summer morning when the highlights and shadows dramatized the subject to particular effect'. He had every reason to be pleased.

I find myself continually drawn to Peter Gilman's paintings, charged with sparkling light and a freedom of expression where his brush appears to have danced across the canvas. Of course, Peter's style was underpinned with unquestionable precision, and each painting clearly held a happy moment for him.

For me, the wonderful memories of a gentle, charming man remain. However, the sadness and suddenness of his departure was a tremendous loss to the world of art and for all those who were privileged to know and love him.

Michael Hill
Picturecraft Gallery
Holt

Opposite: Mill near Cromer. Watercolour, 27x19cm.

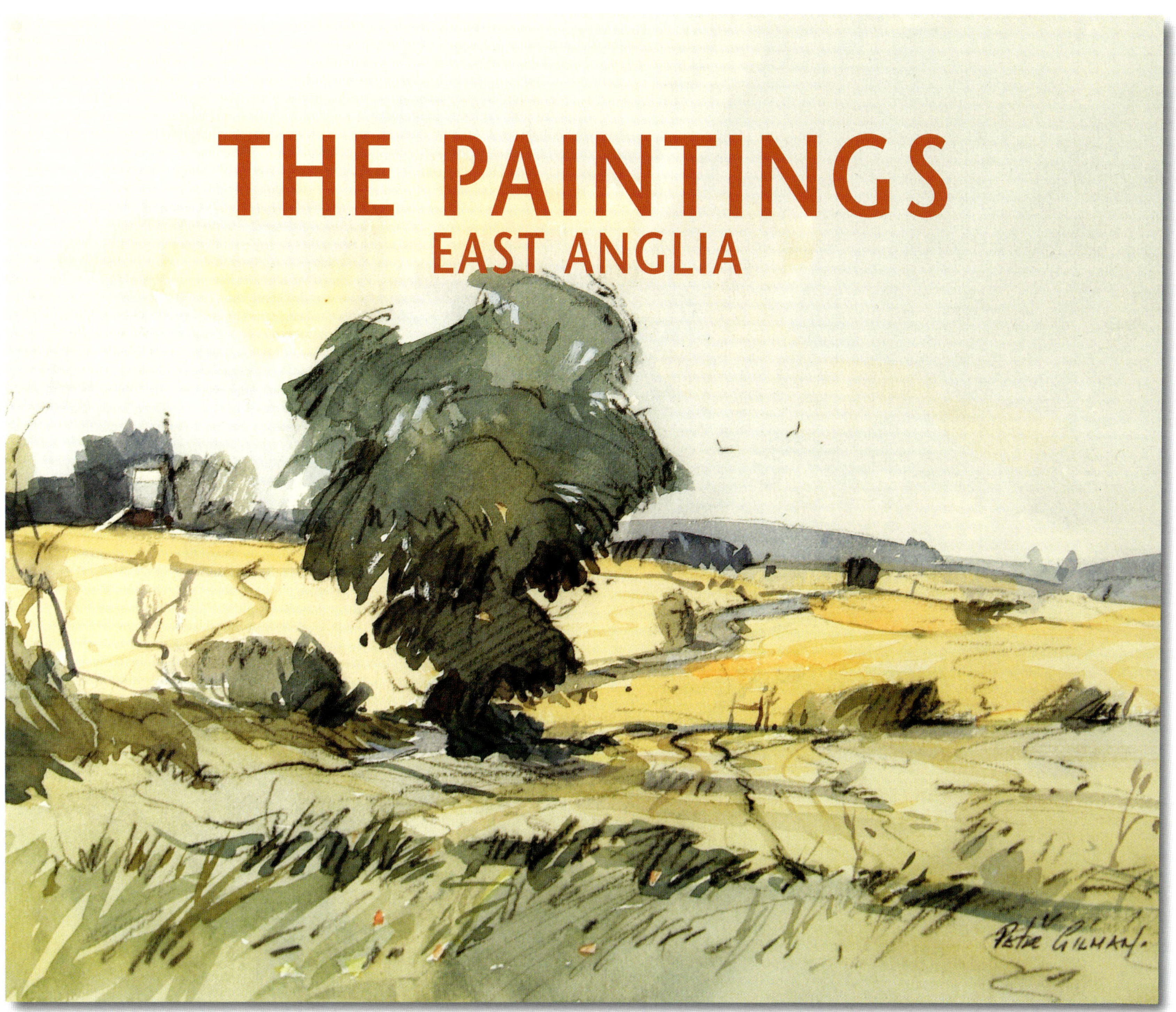

THE PAINTINGS
EAST ANGLIA

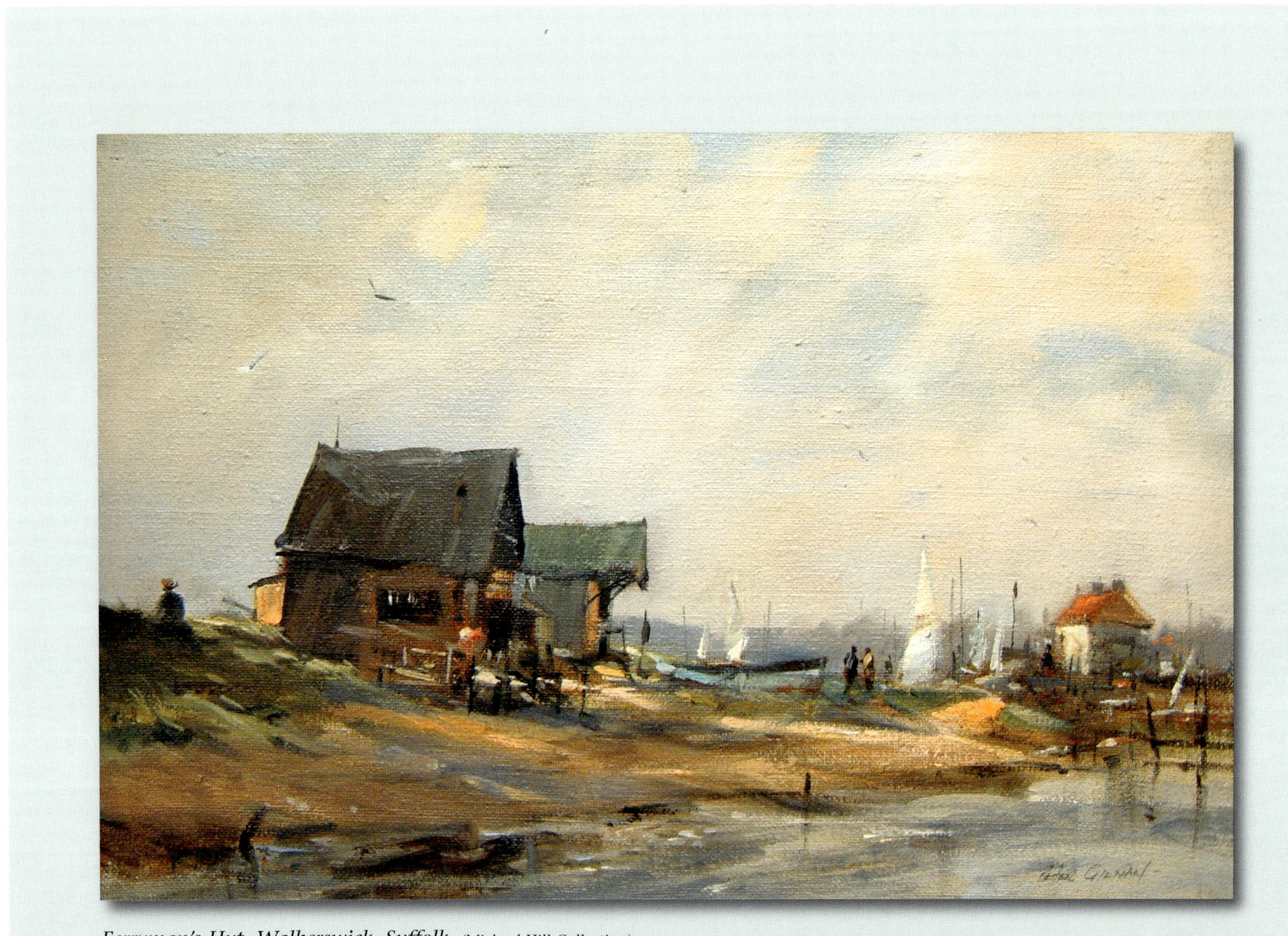

Ferryman's Hut, Walberswick, Suffolk. (Michael Hill Collection)

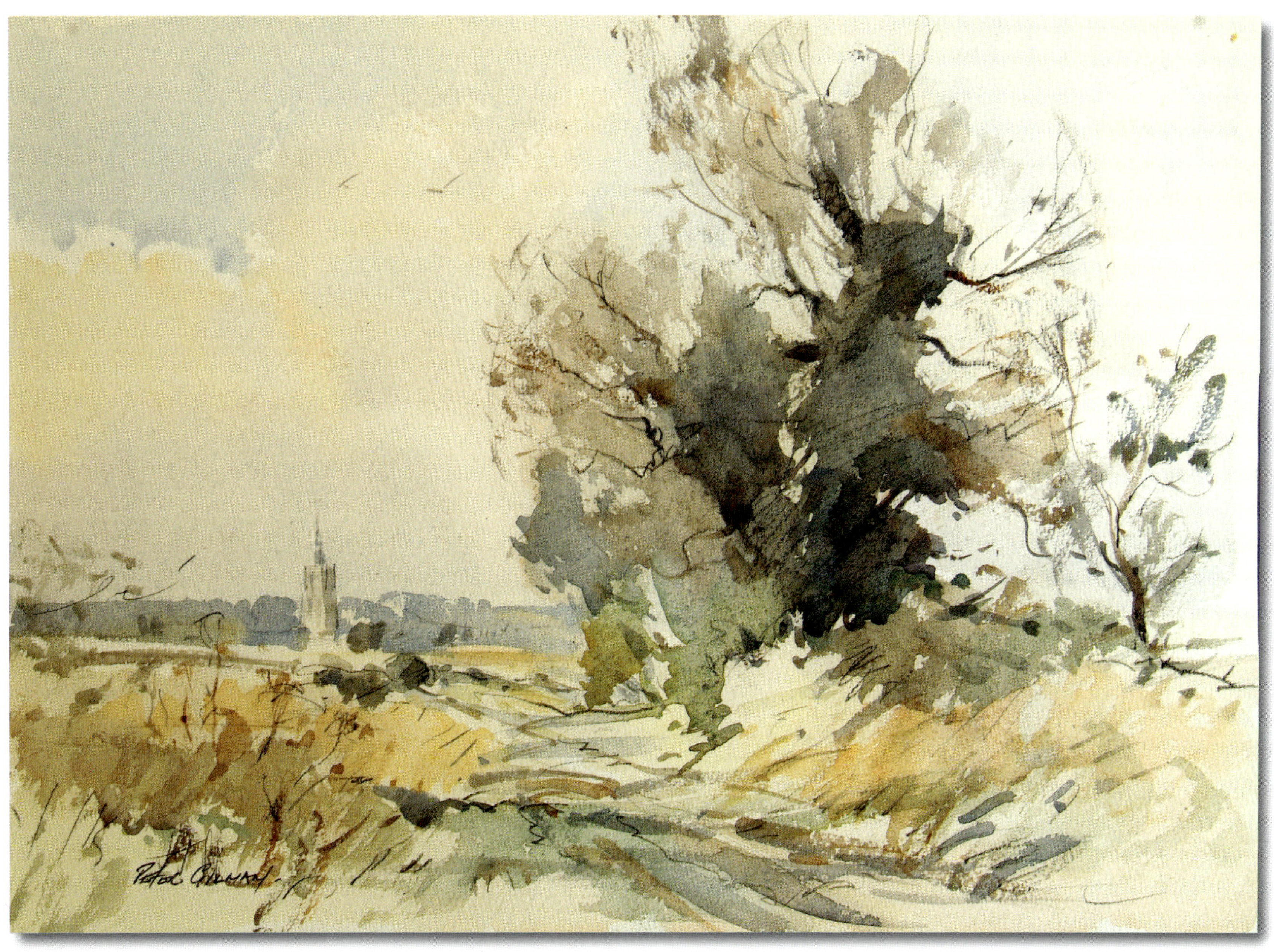

Quietly Waiting for Sunday: Suffolk Pastoral. Watercolour.

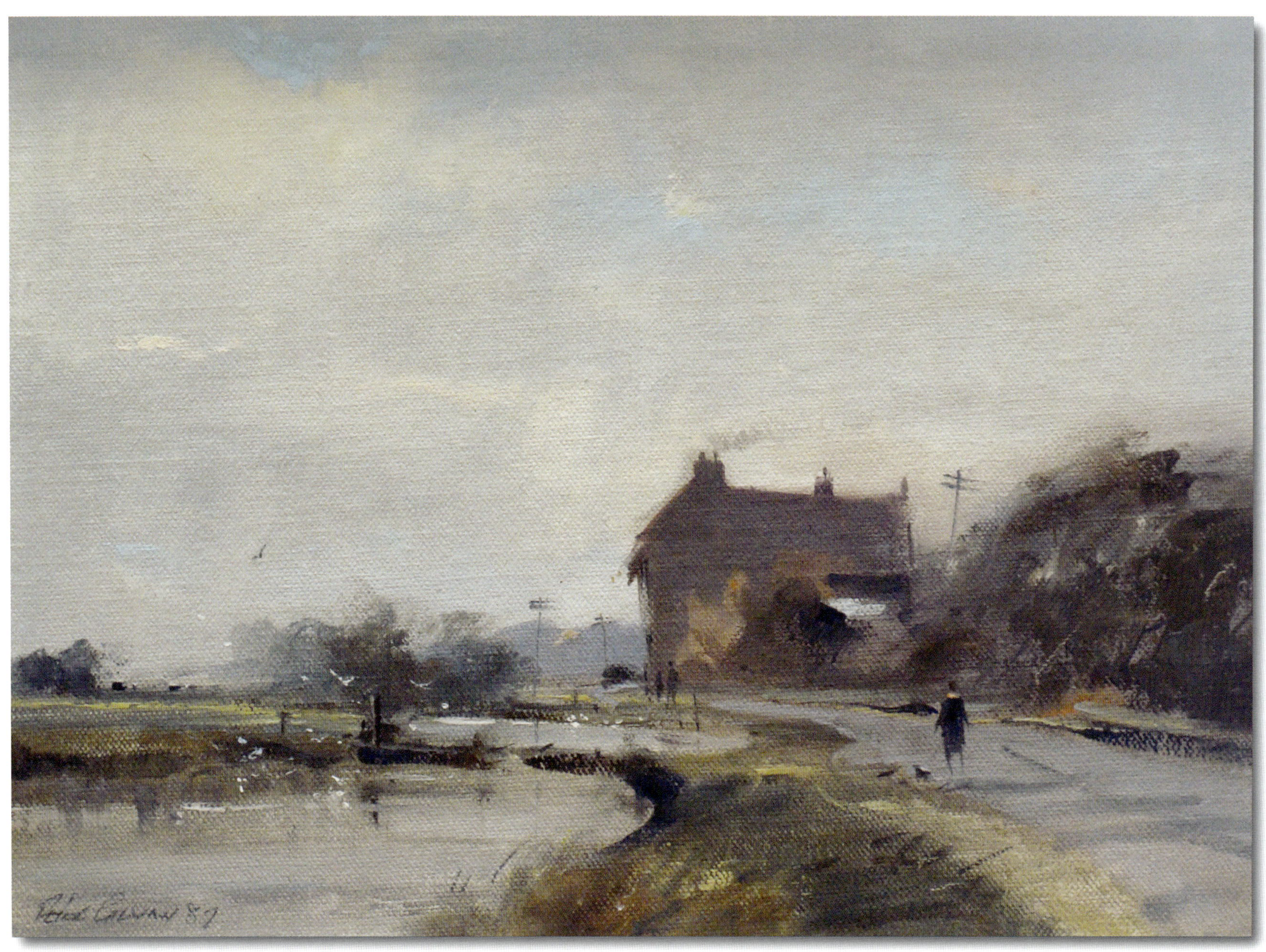

A Norfolk Lane. Oil on board.

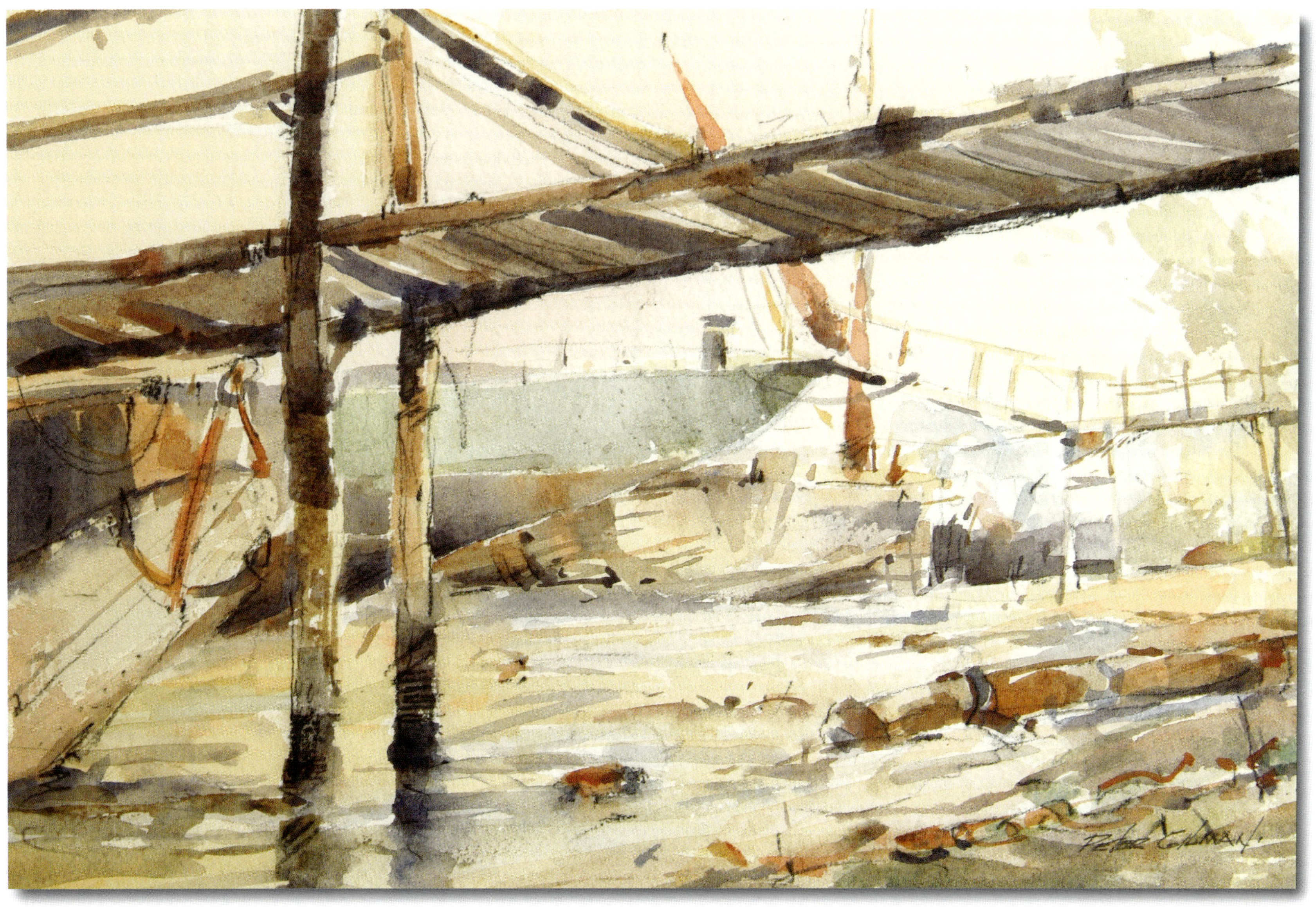

Pin Mill Foreshore, Suffolk, 1980. Watercolour.

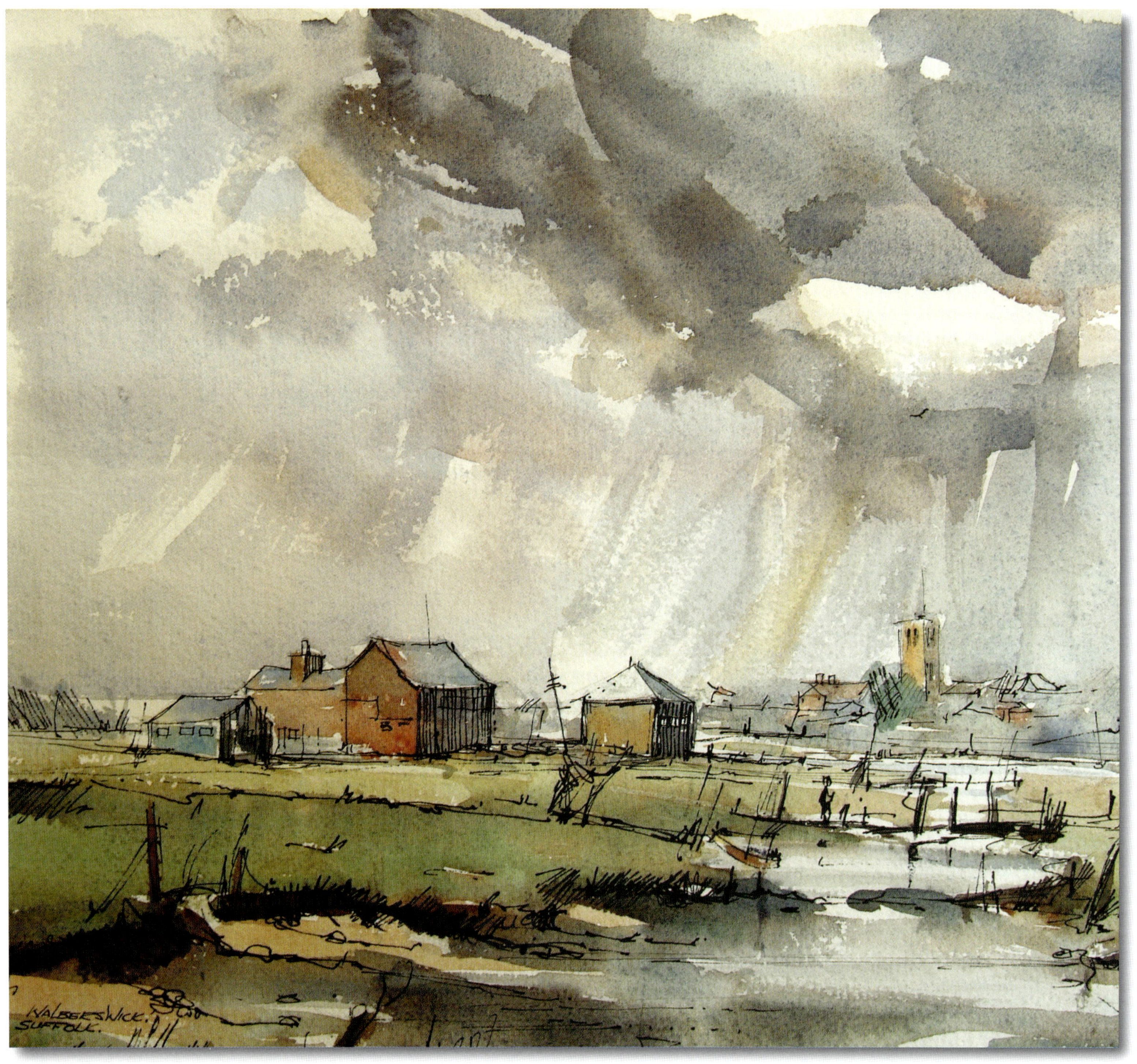
WALBERSWICK.
SUFFOLK.

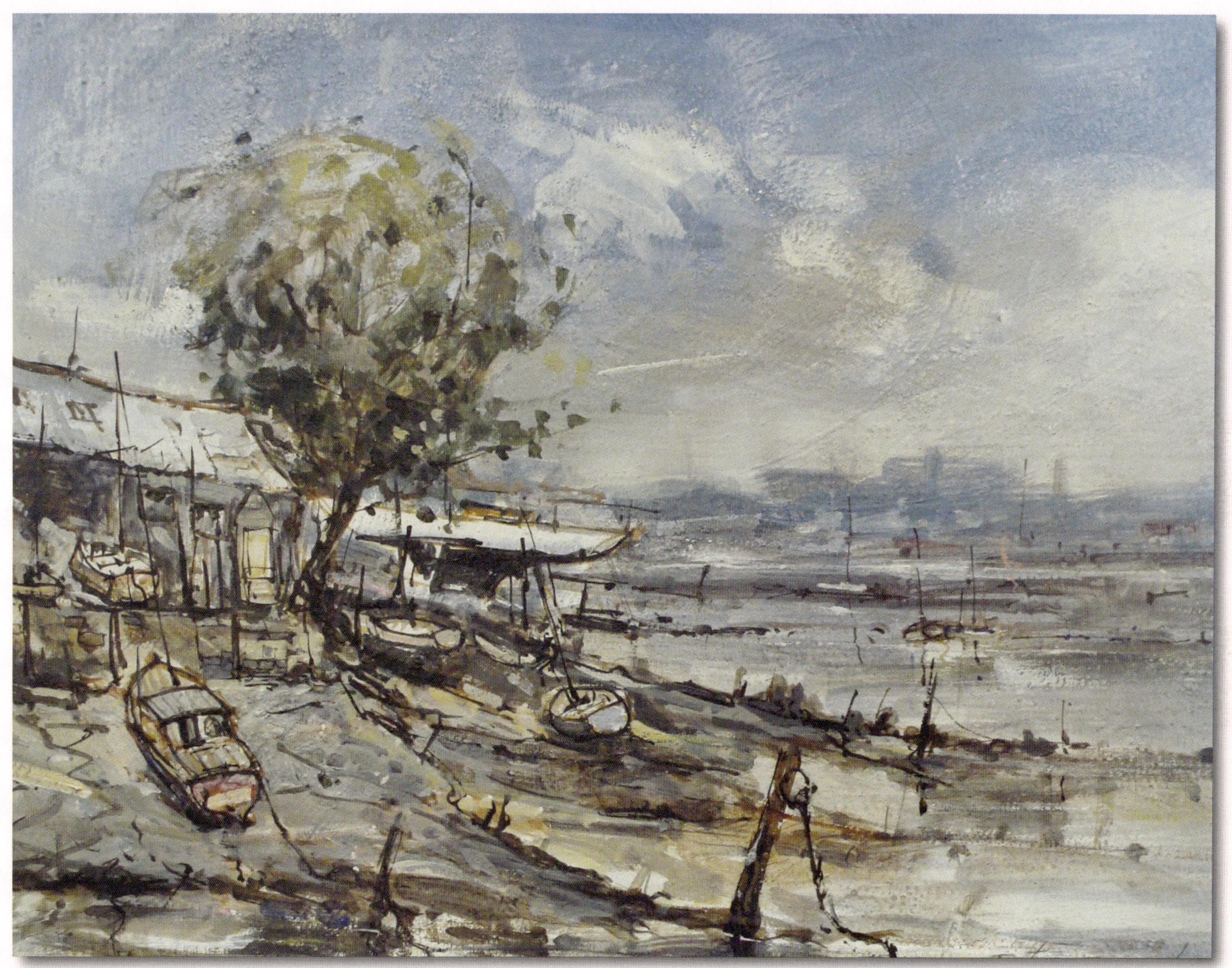

The River Orwell, Ipswich. Oil.

Opposite: Walberswick, Suffolk. Pen and wash.

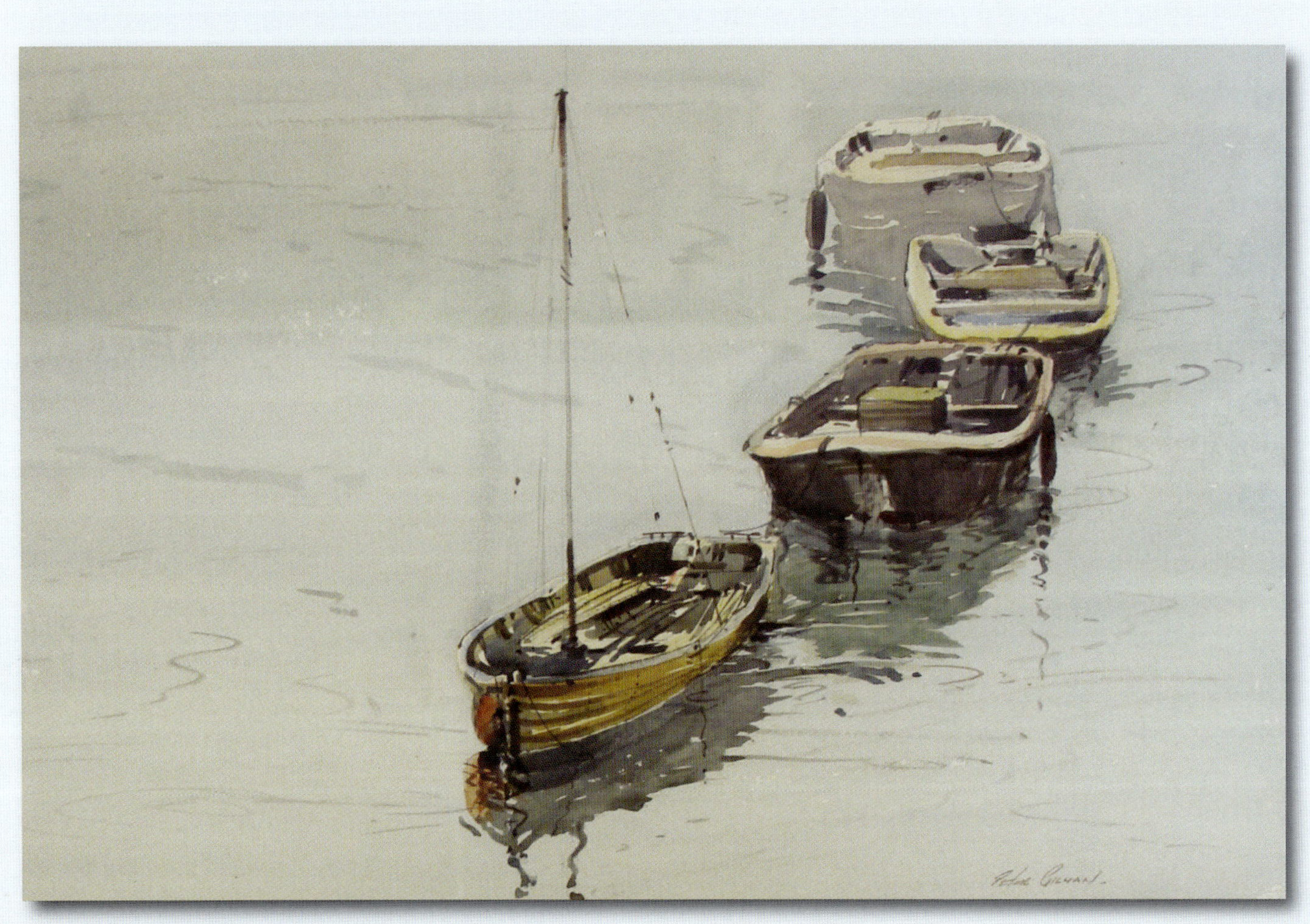

Tranquility, Blakeney. Watercolour 14x20.5 inches

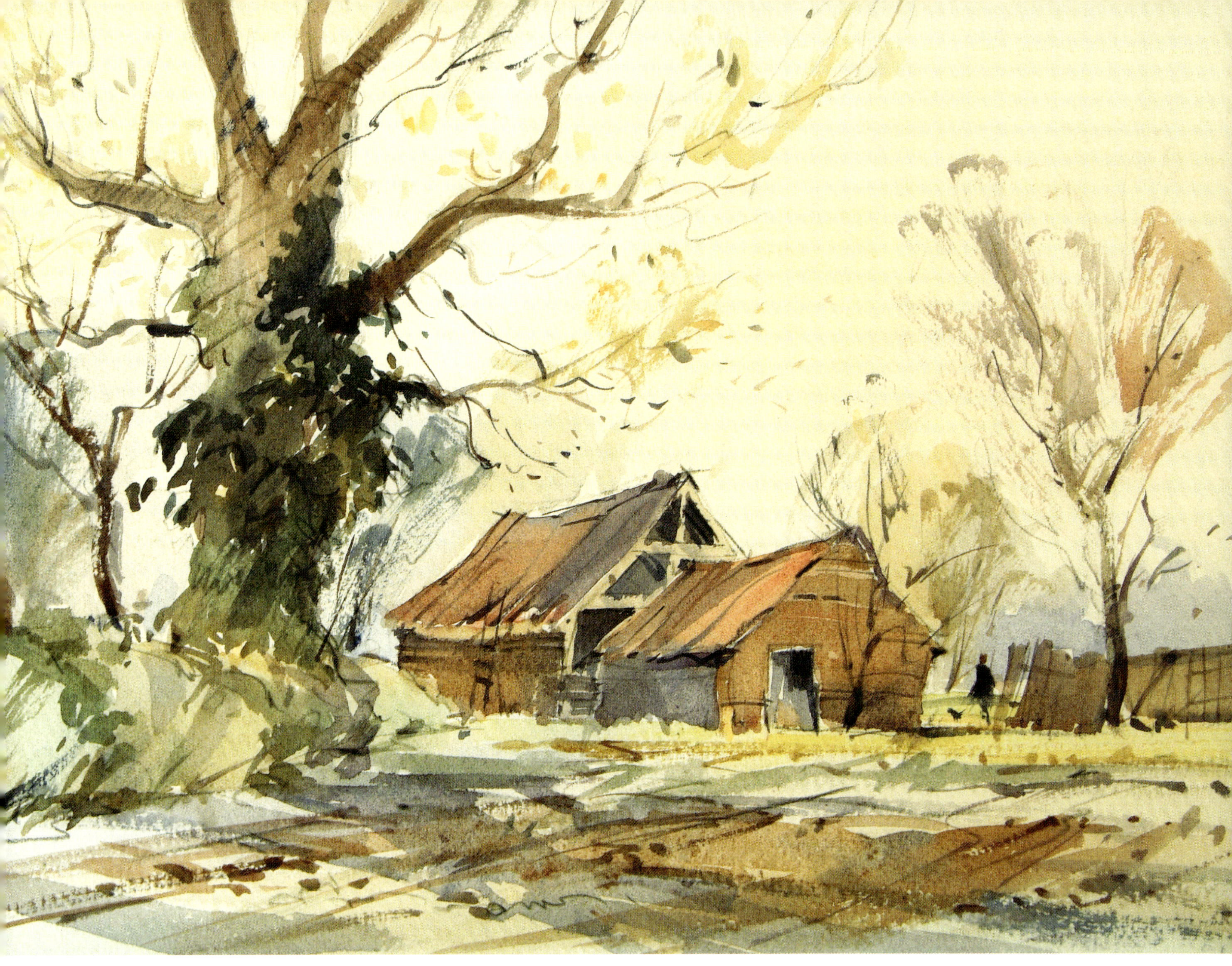

The Old Barn. Watercolour 27.5x19 inches.

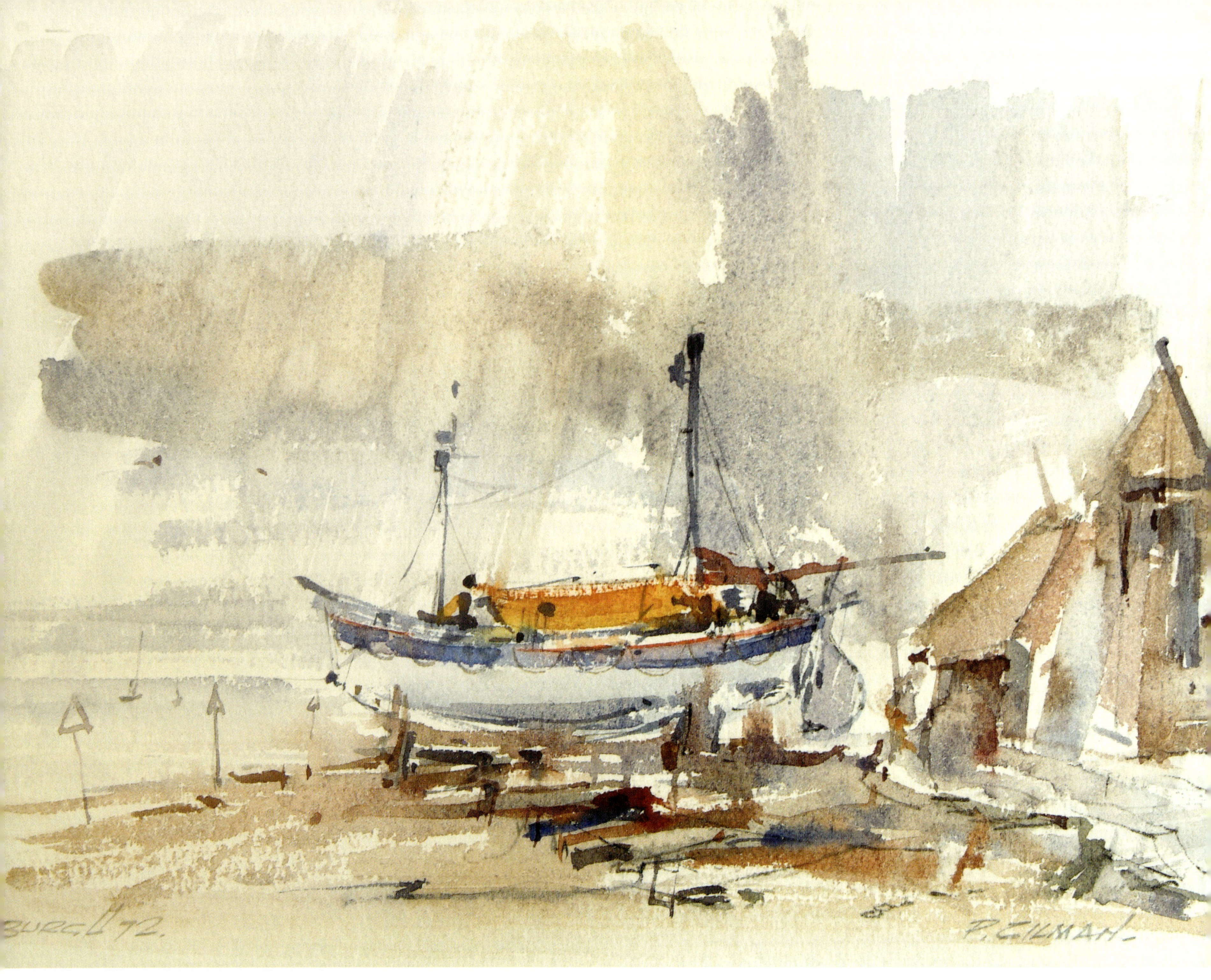

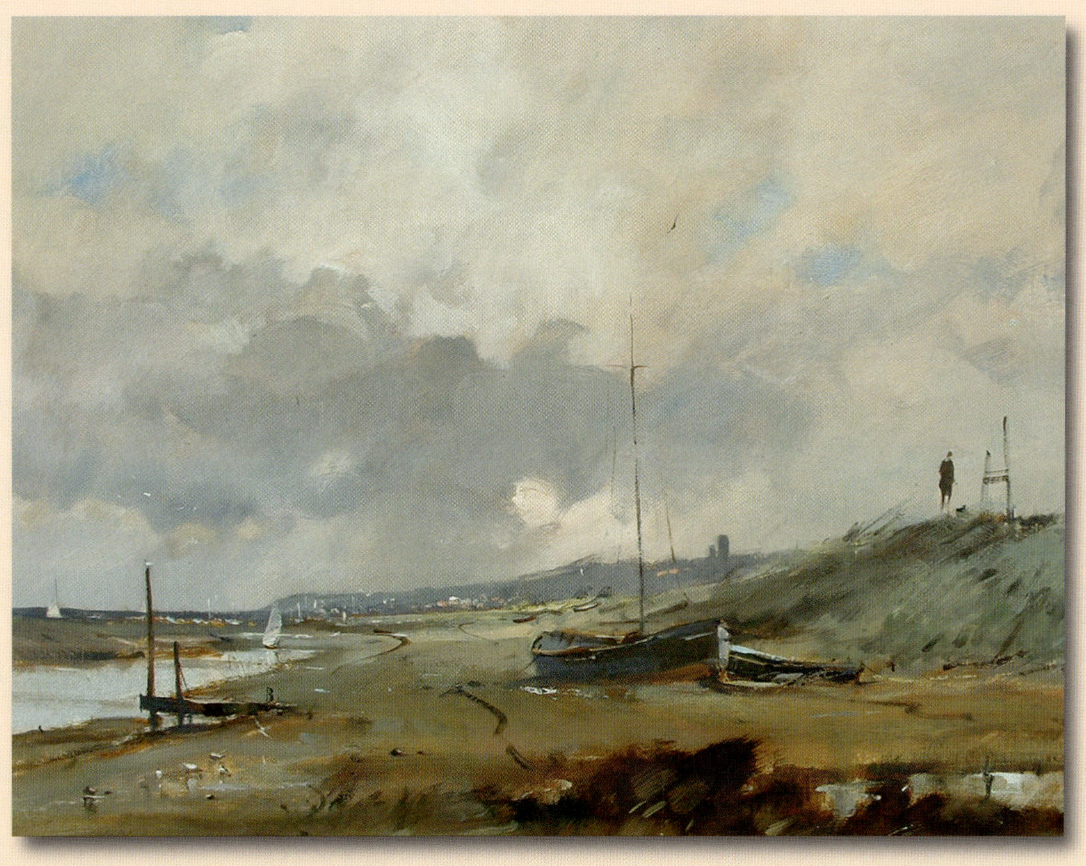

From Morston towards Blakeney. Oil 20x30 inches.

Opposite: Aldeburgh, Suffolk 1972. Watercolour 24x18 inches.

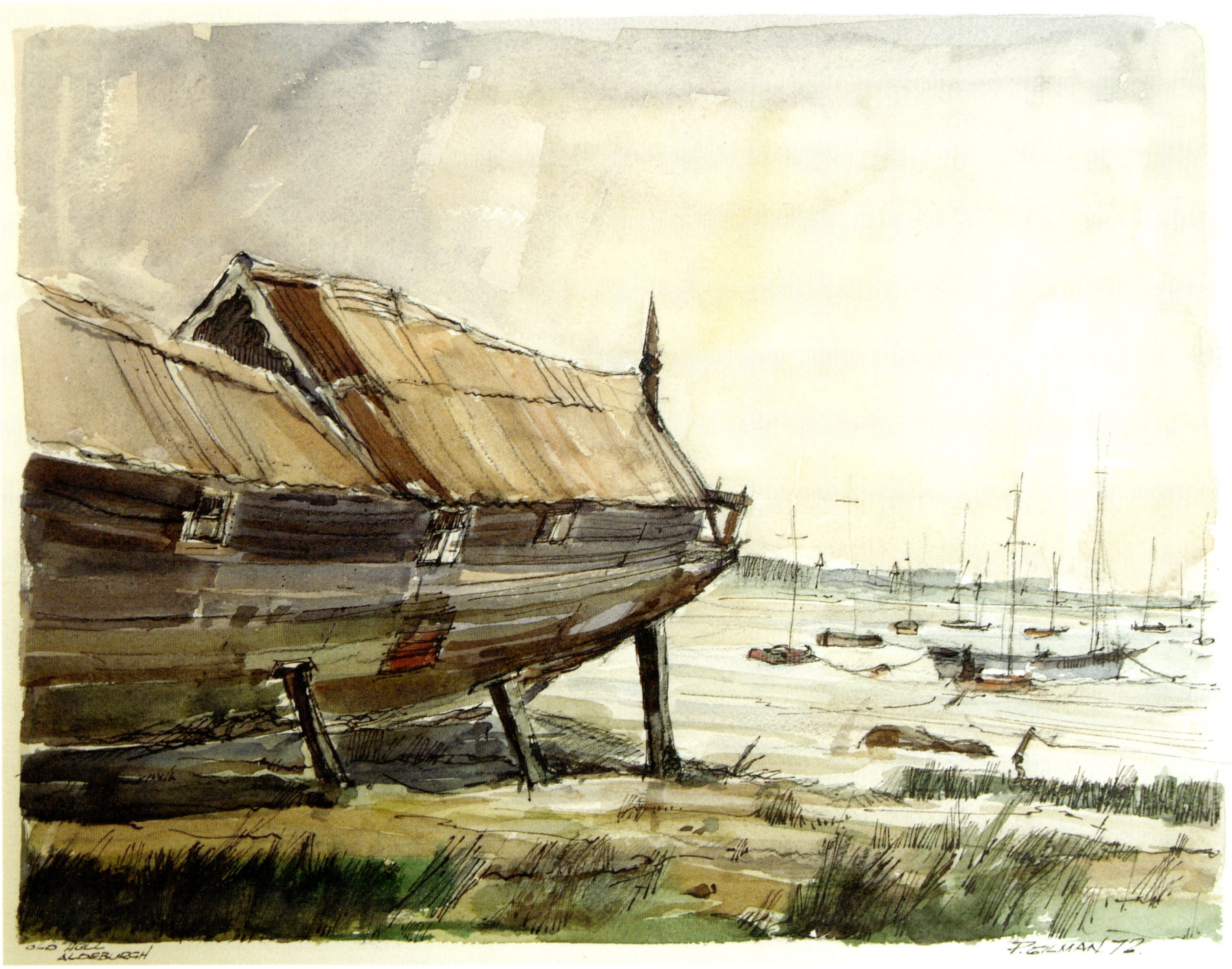

The Old Hulk Aldeburgh, Suffolk 1972. Watercolour and ink 33x26 inches.

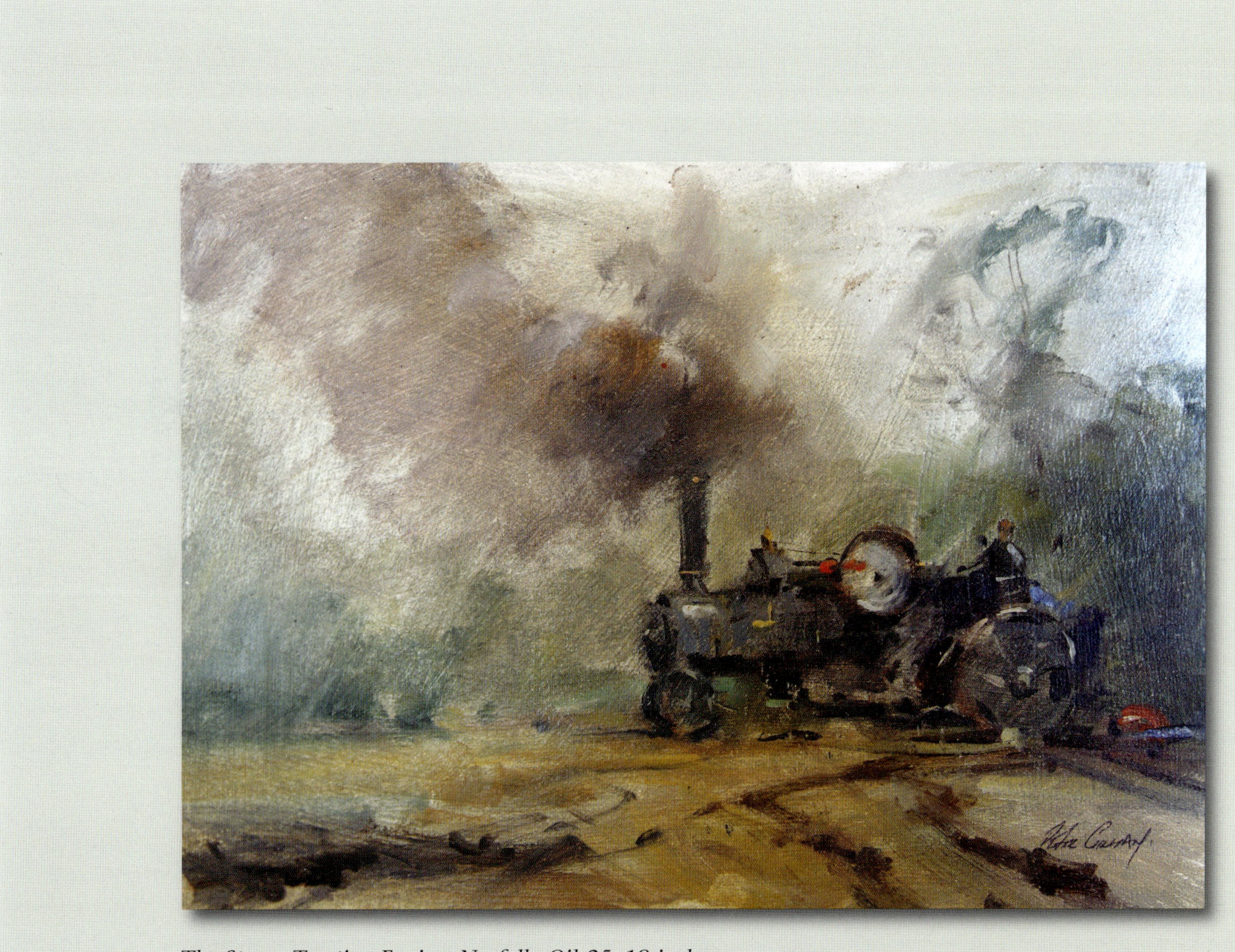

The Steam Traction Engine, Norfolk. Oil 25x18 inches.

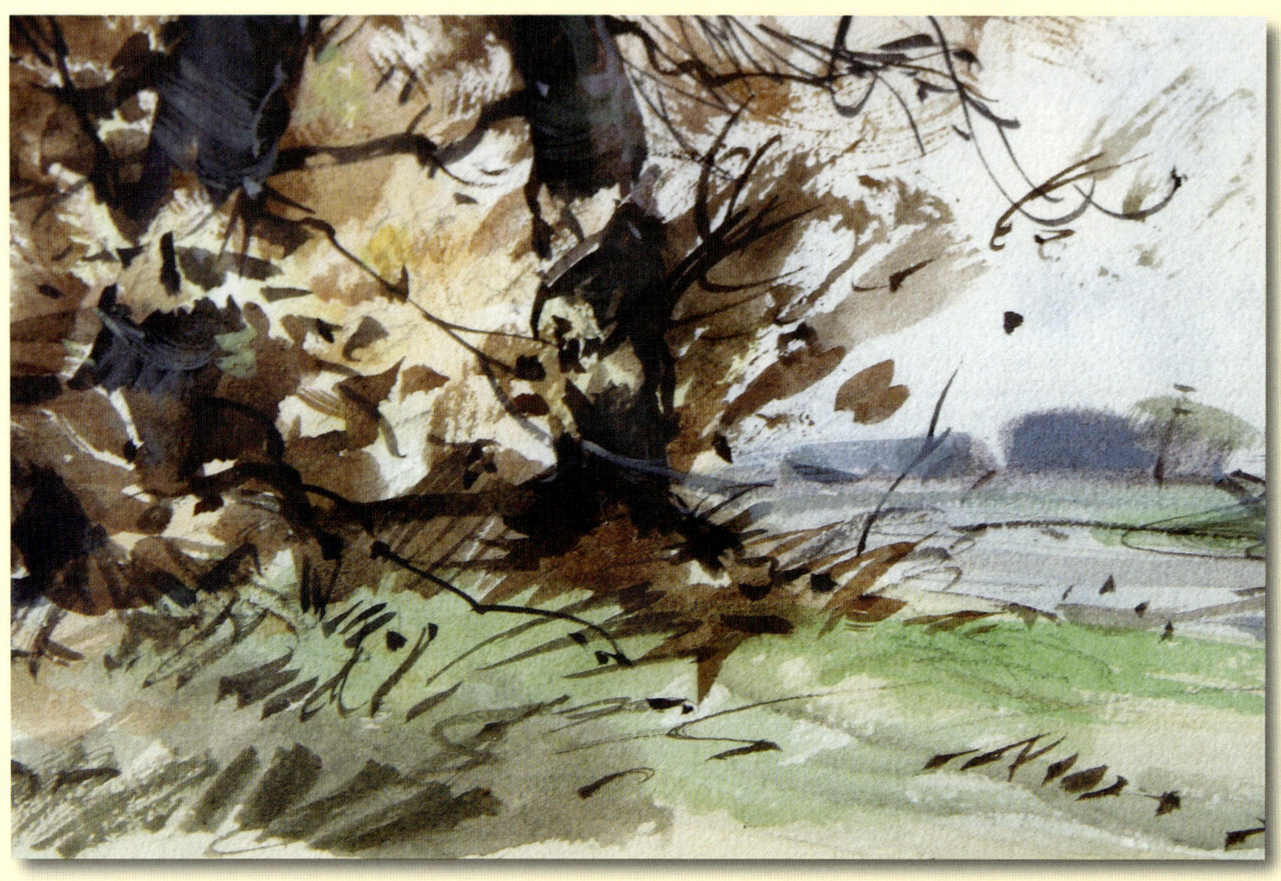

Norfolk Spring Morning, 1983. Watercolour and ink 33x26 inches.

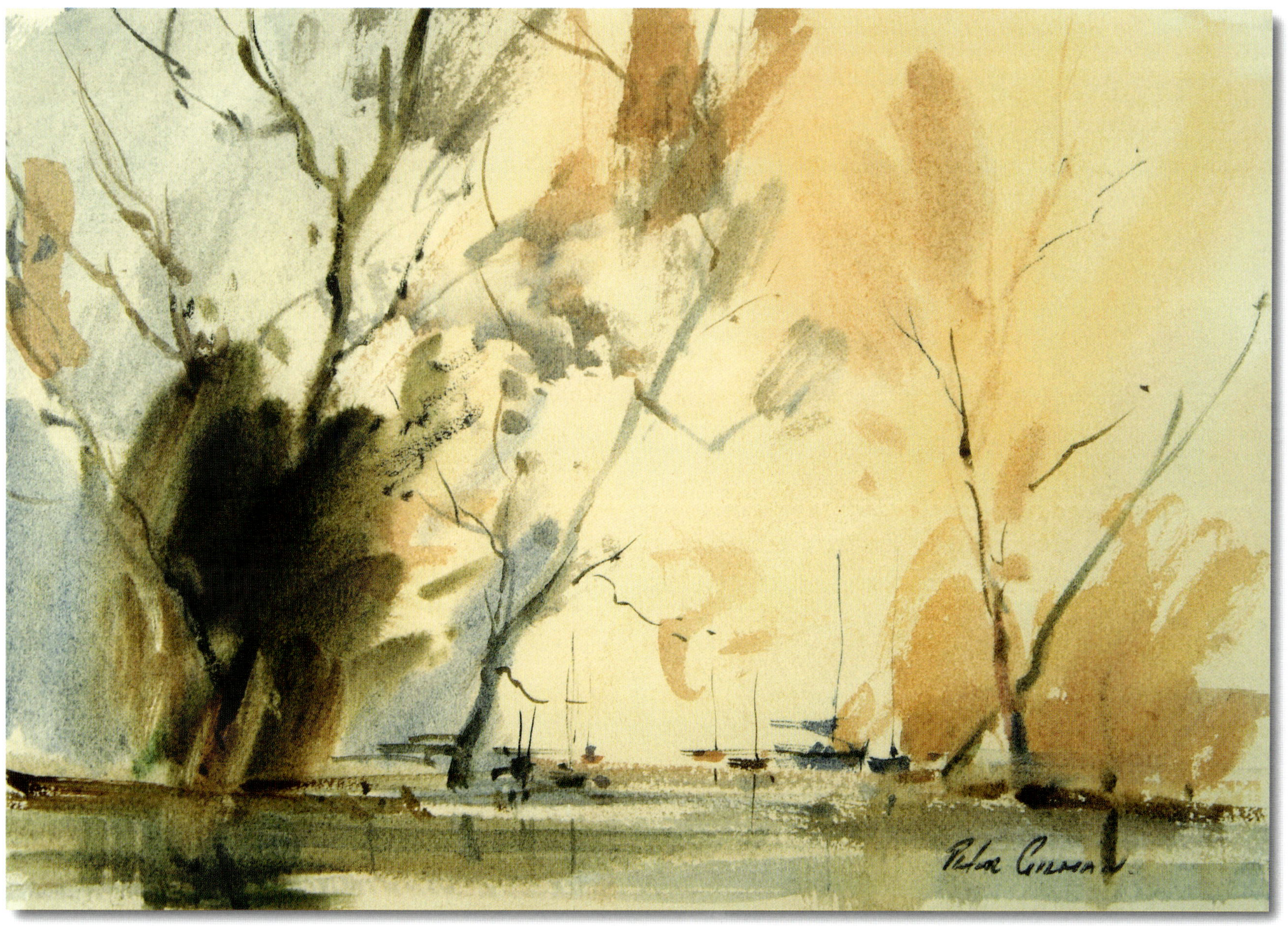

Broadland Evening. Watercolour 17x13 inches.

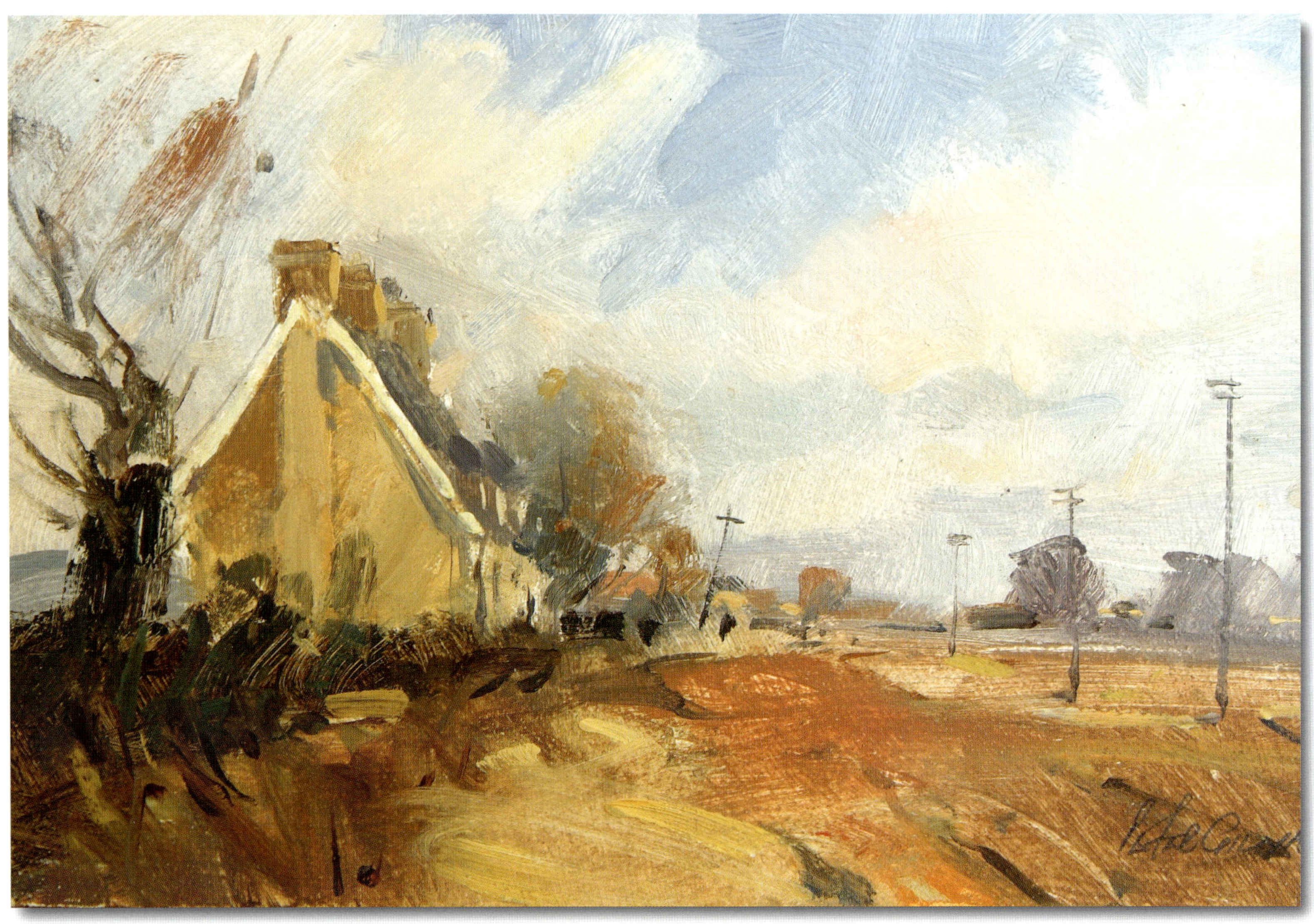

Life on the Flatlands. Oil 18x12 inches.

Opposite: Country Lane, Autumn. Watercolour and ink 14x18 inches.

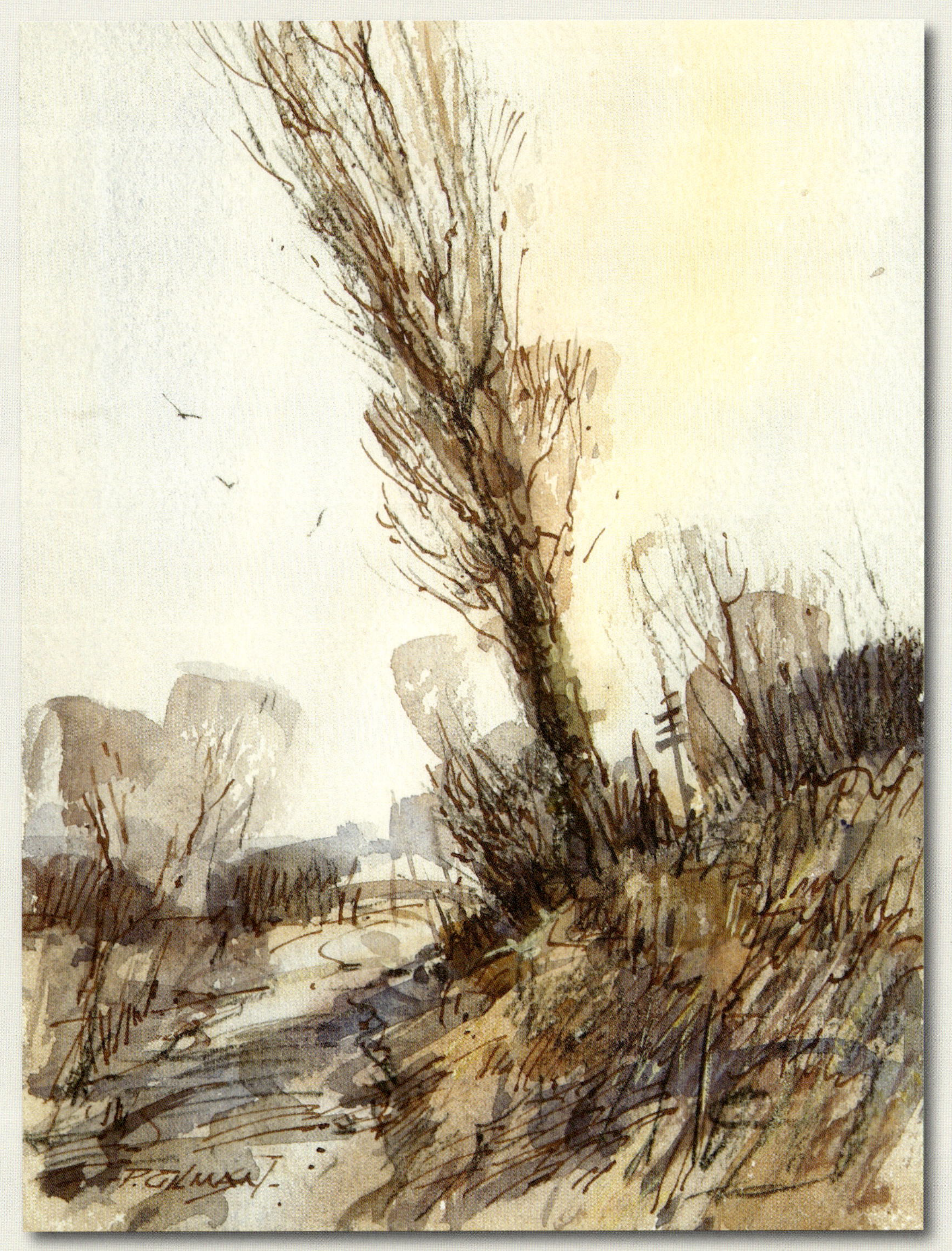

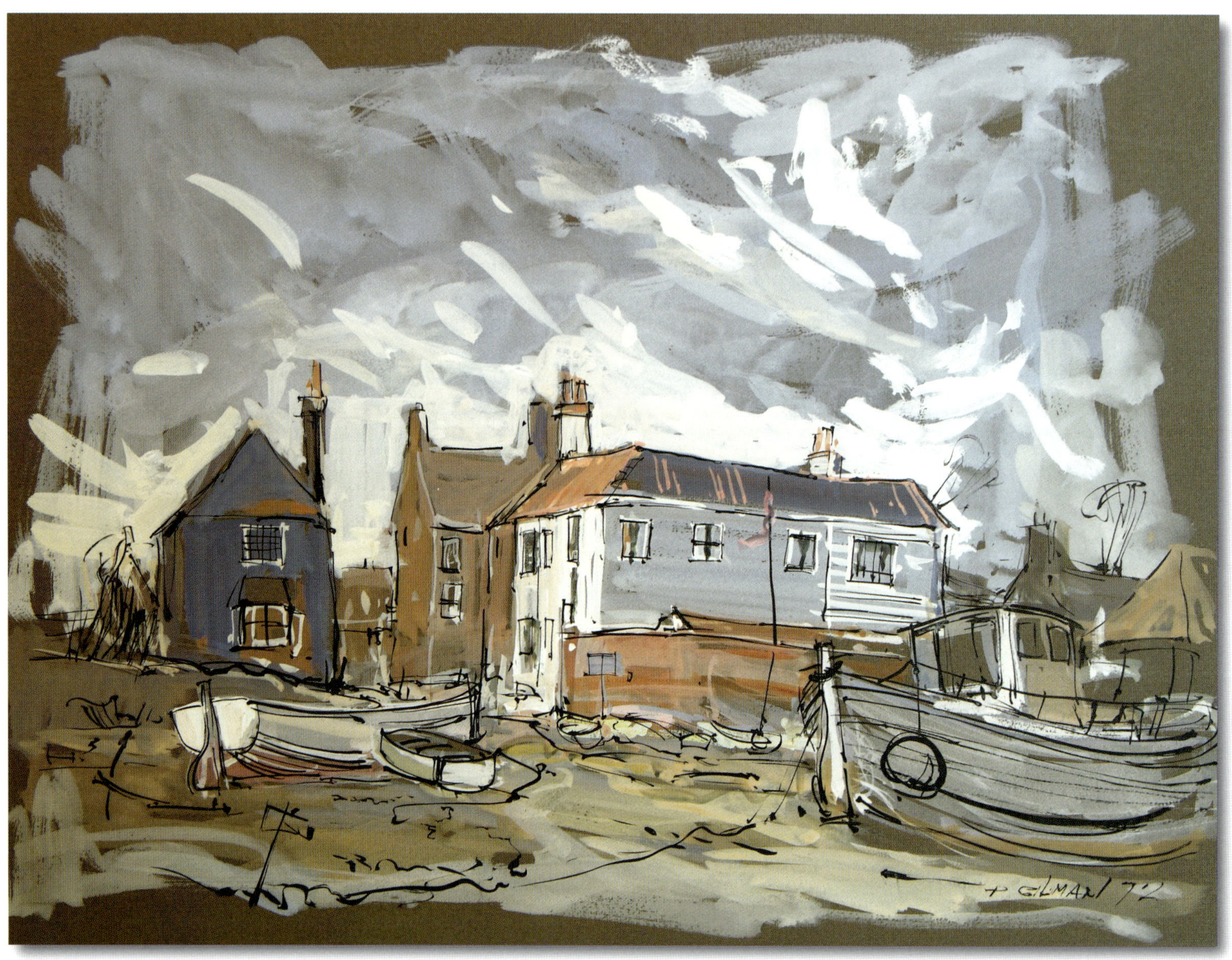

Boats Ashore. Mixed media 34x26 inches.

Opposite: Autumn Trees, 1978. Watercolour 38x30 inches.

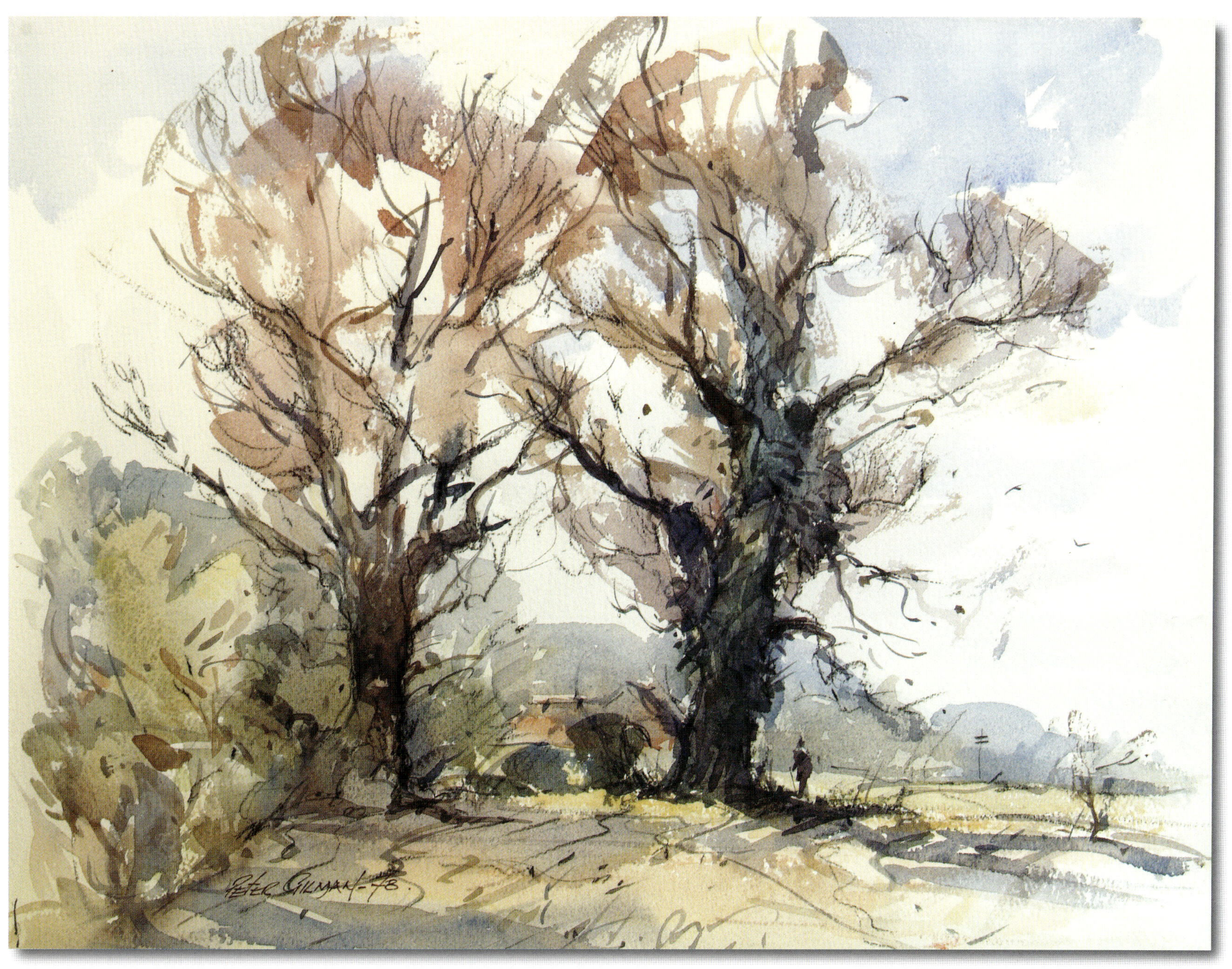

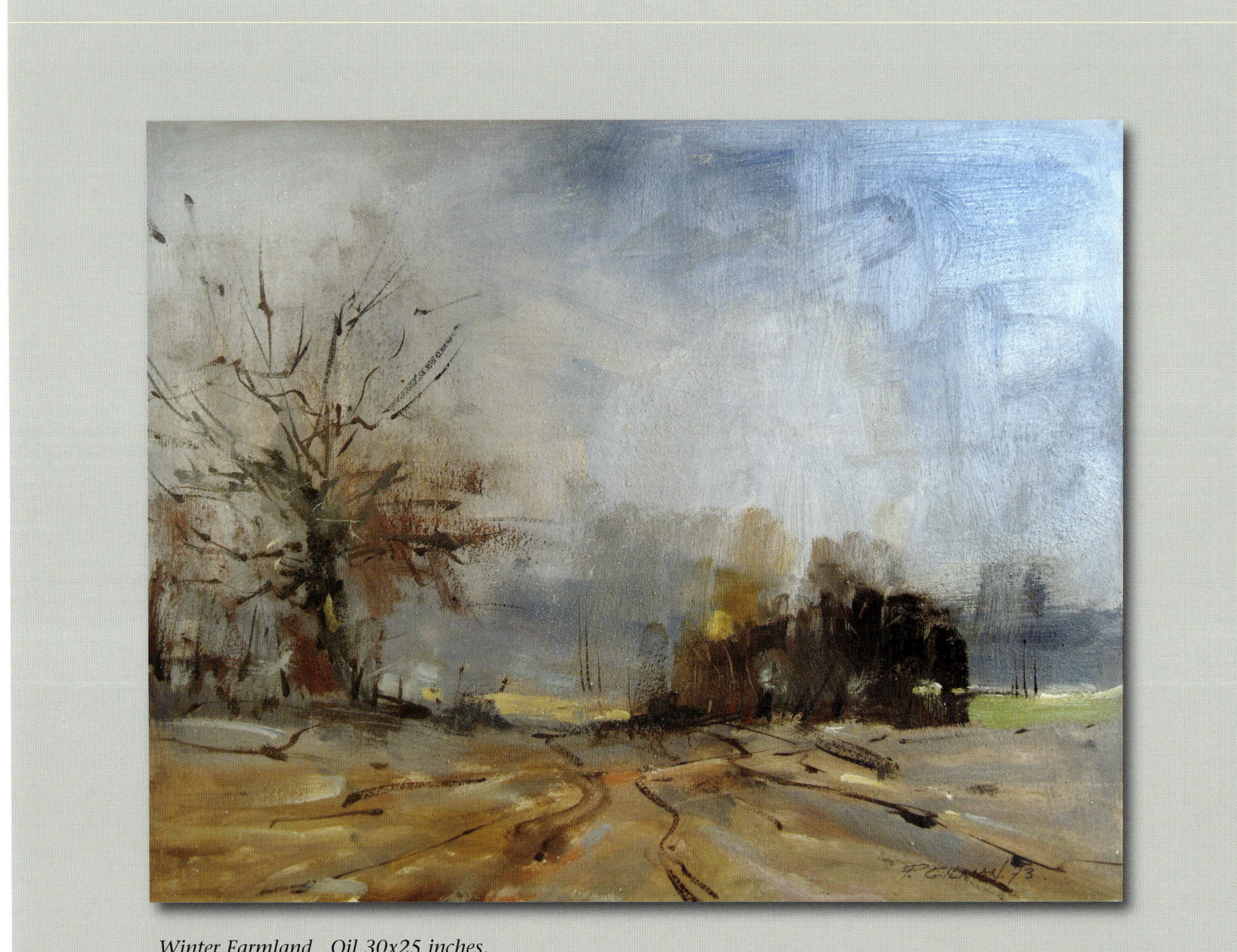

Winter Farmland. Oil 30x25 inches.

Opposite: Snow Scene. Oil 51x40 inches.

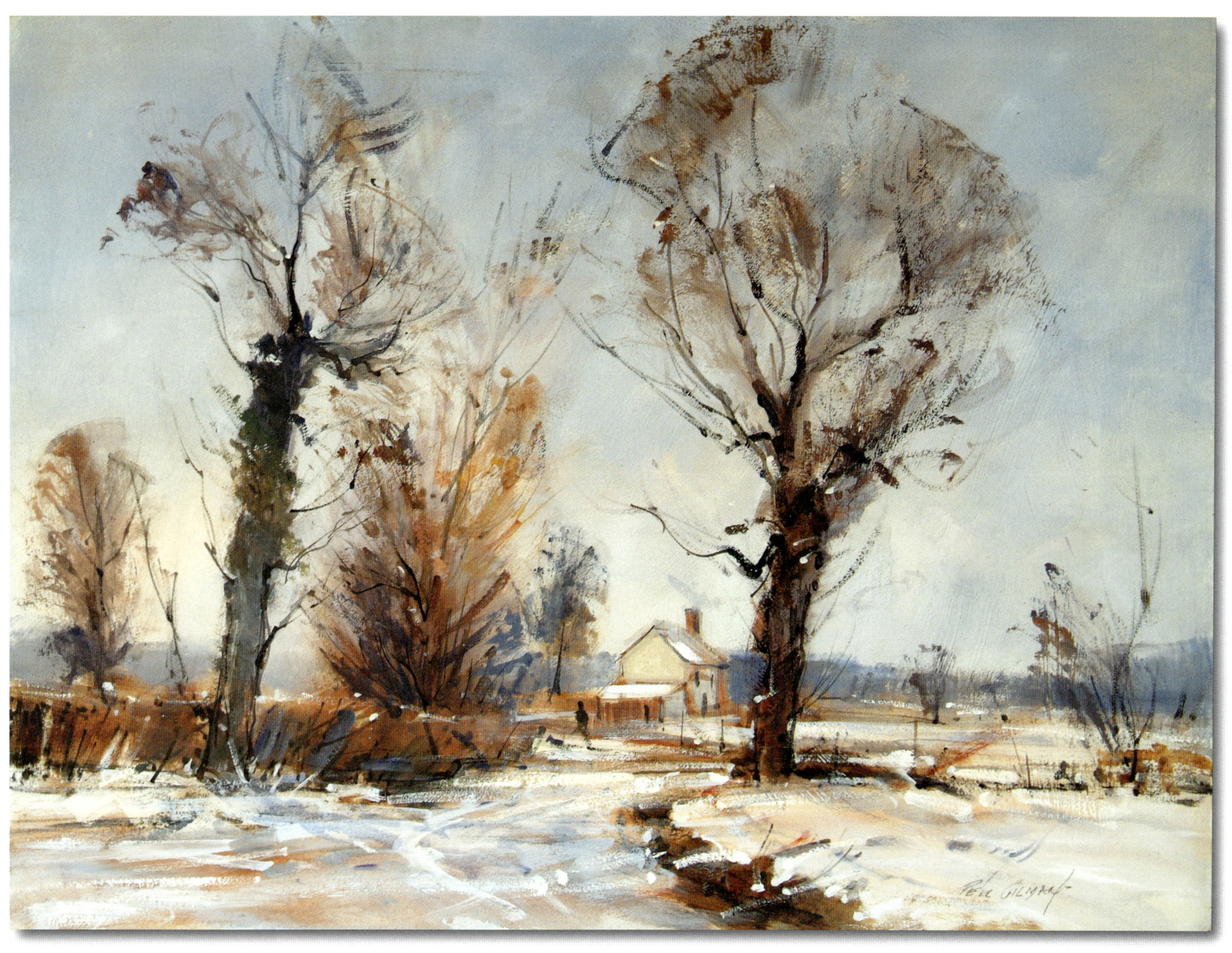

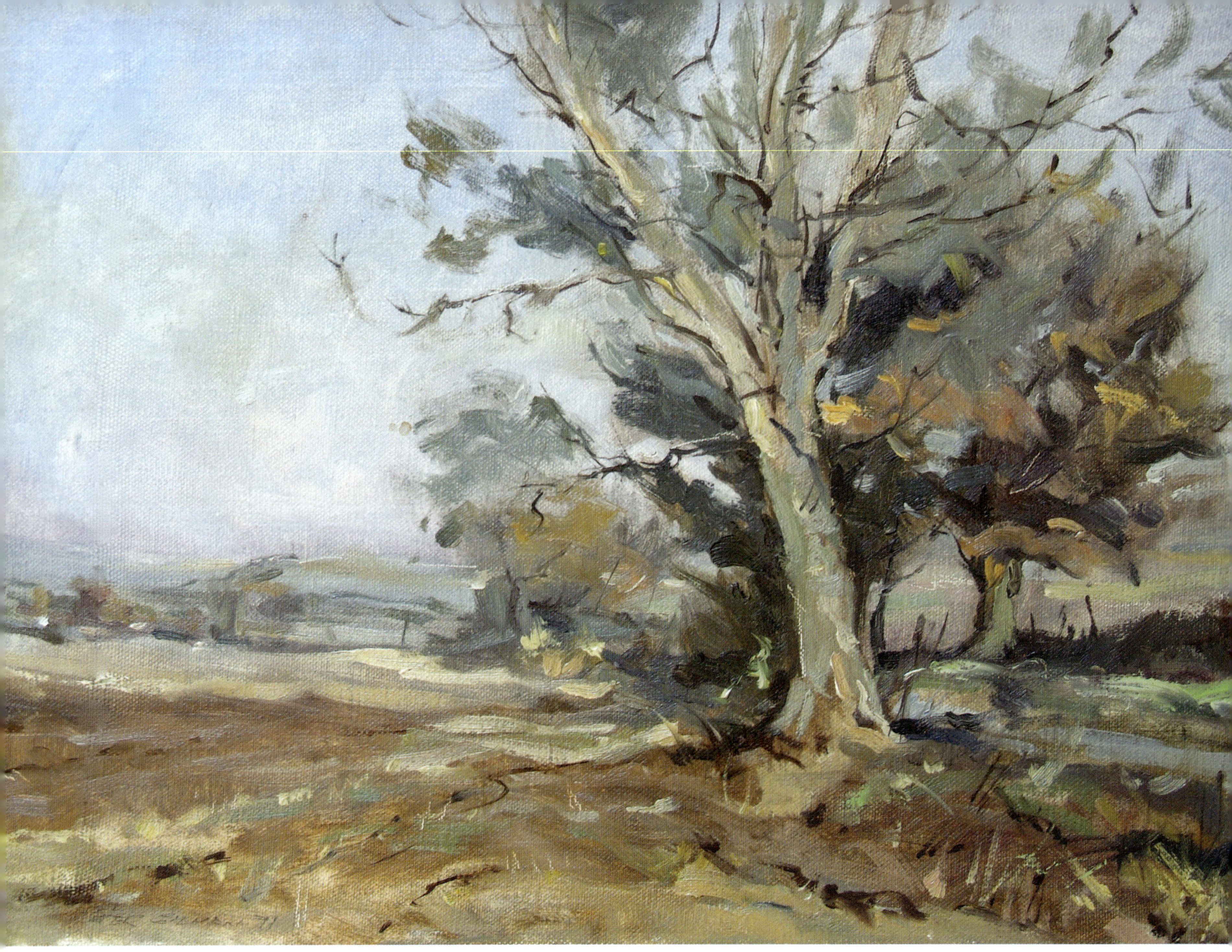

The Approach of Spring, Norfolk. Mixed media 34x26 inches.

Opposite: Billingford Mill, Norfolk. Oil 12x9 inches.

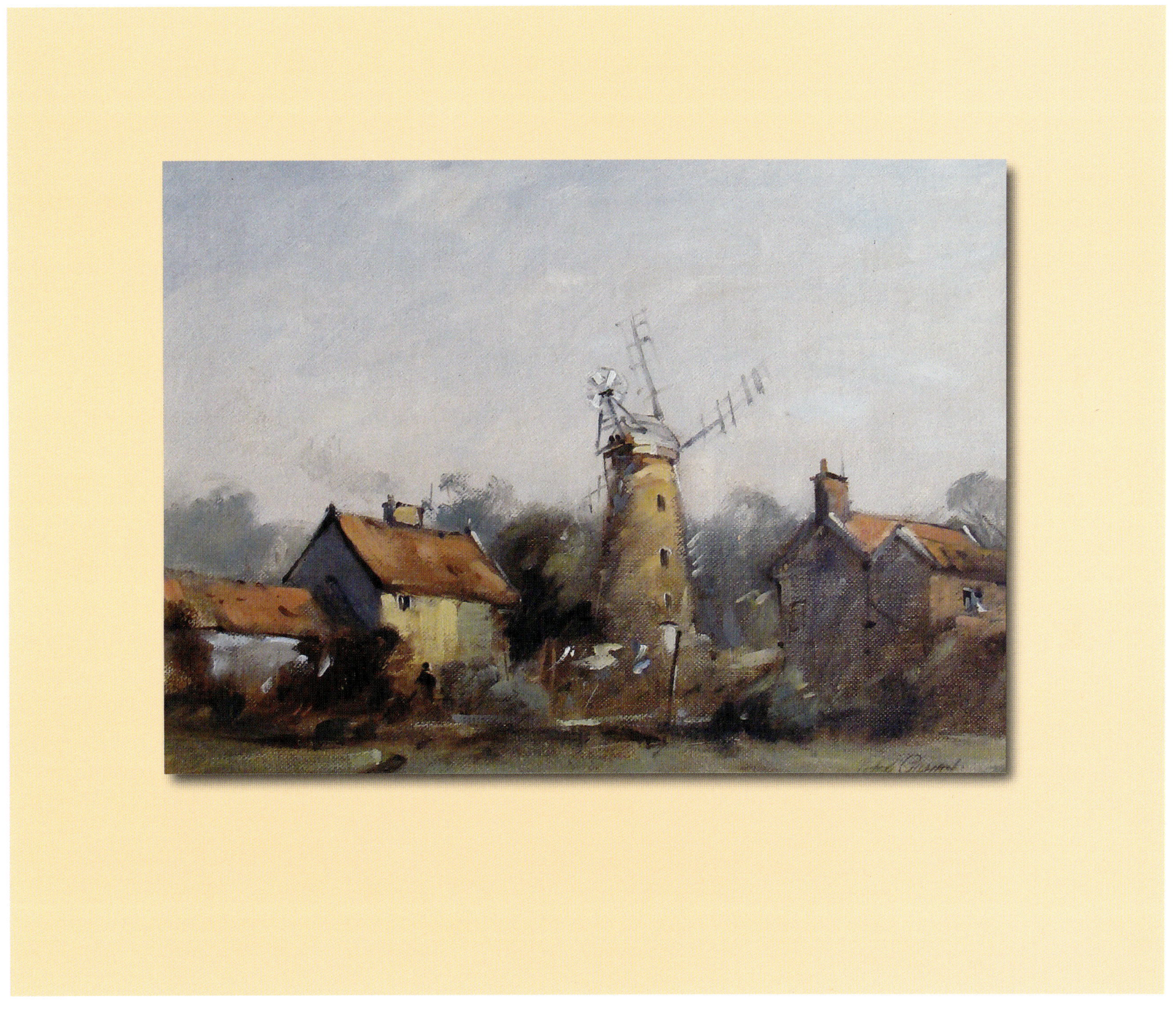

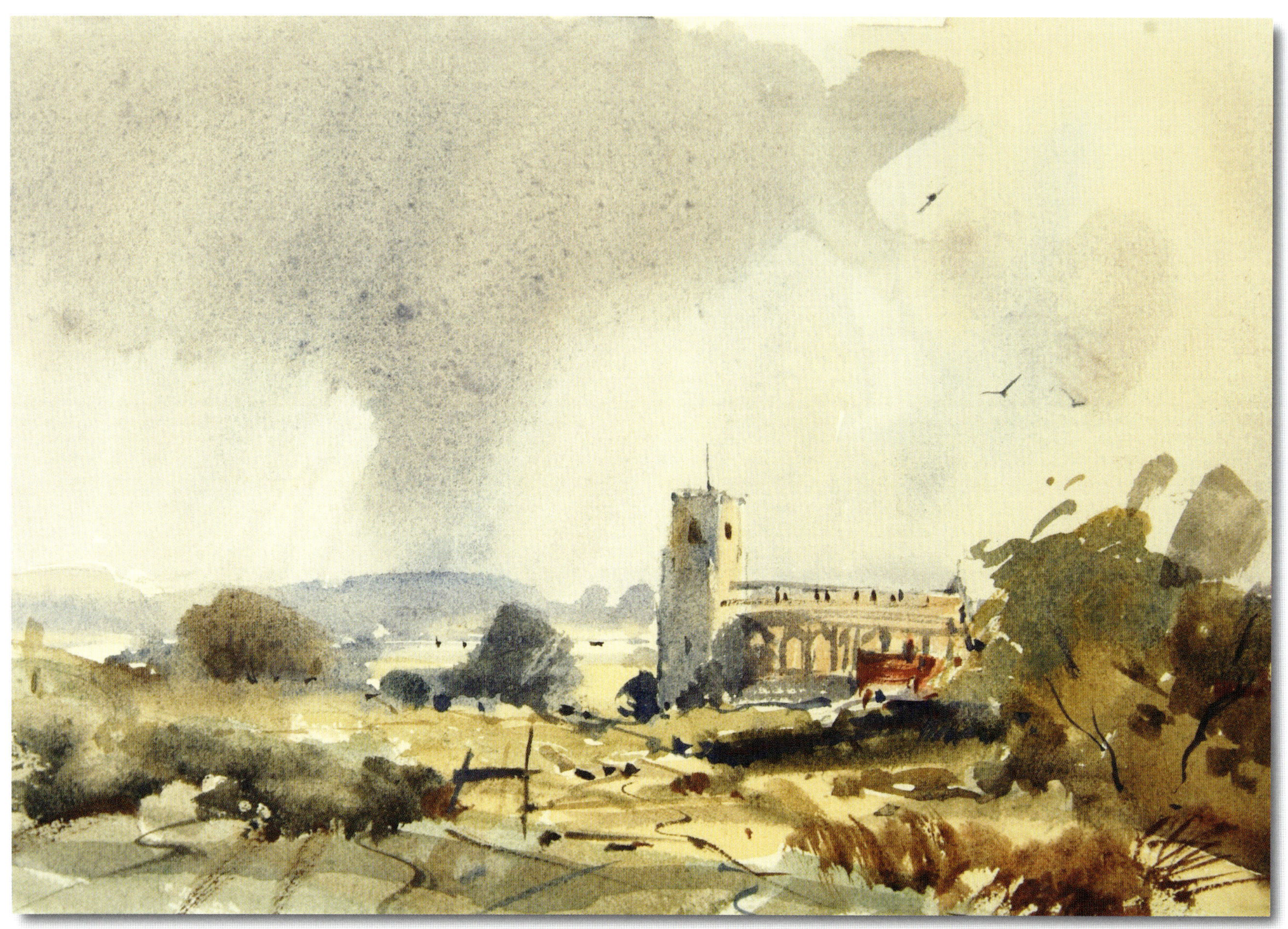

Blythburgh Church, Suffolk. Watercolour. (John Stillman Collection)

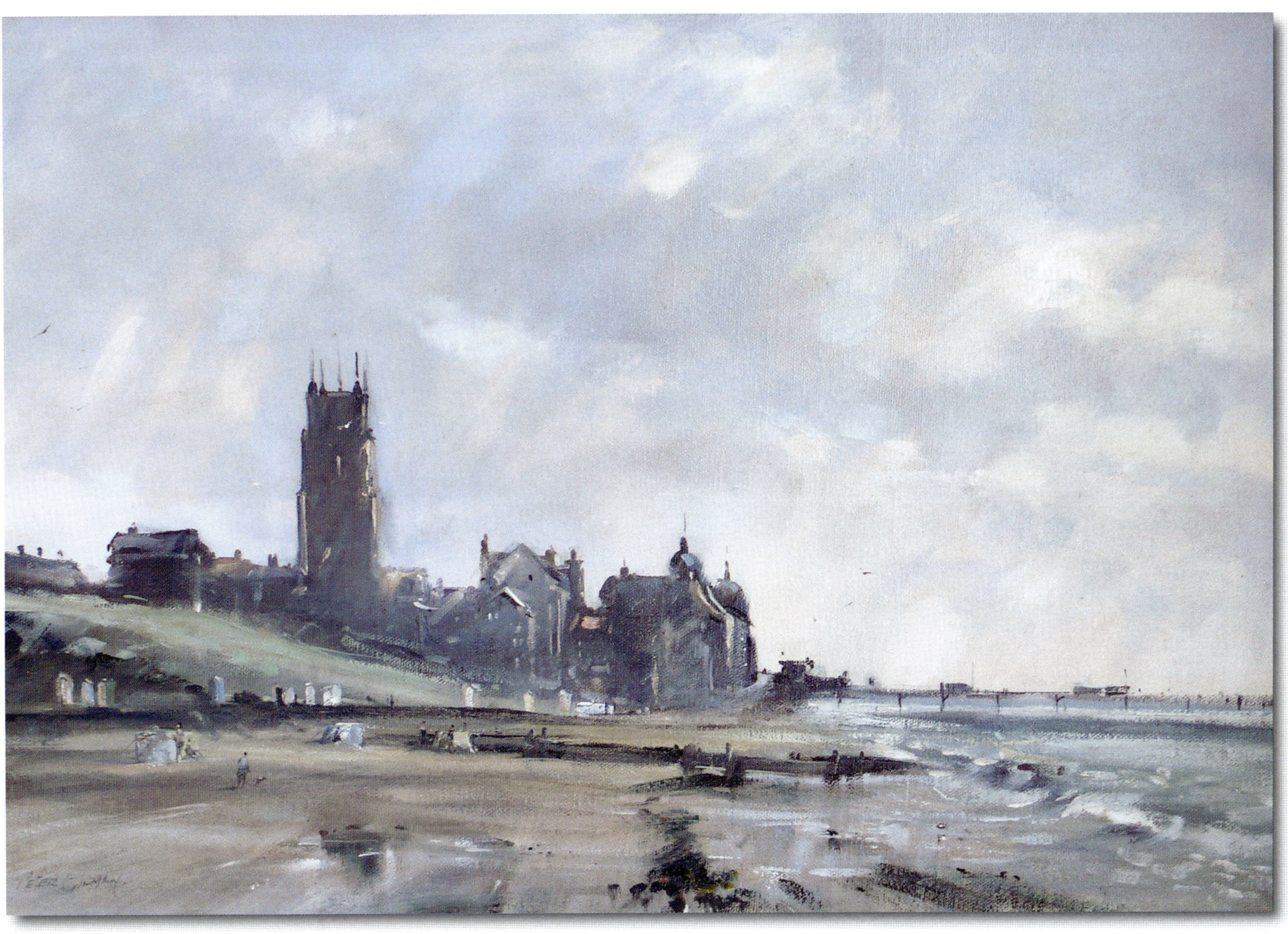

Cromer, Norfolk. Oil. (John Stillman Collection)

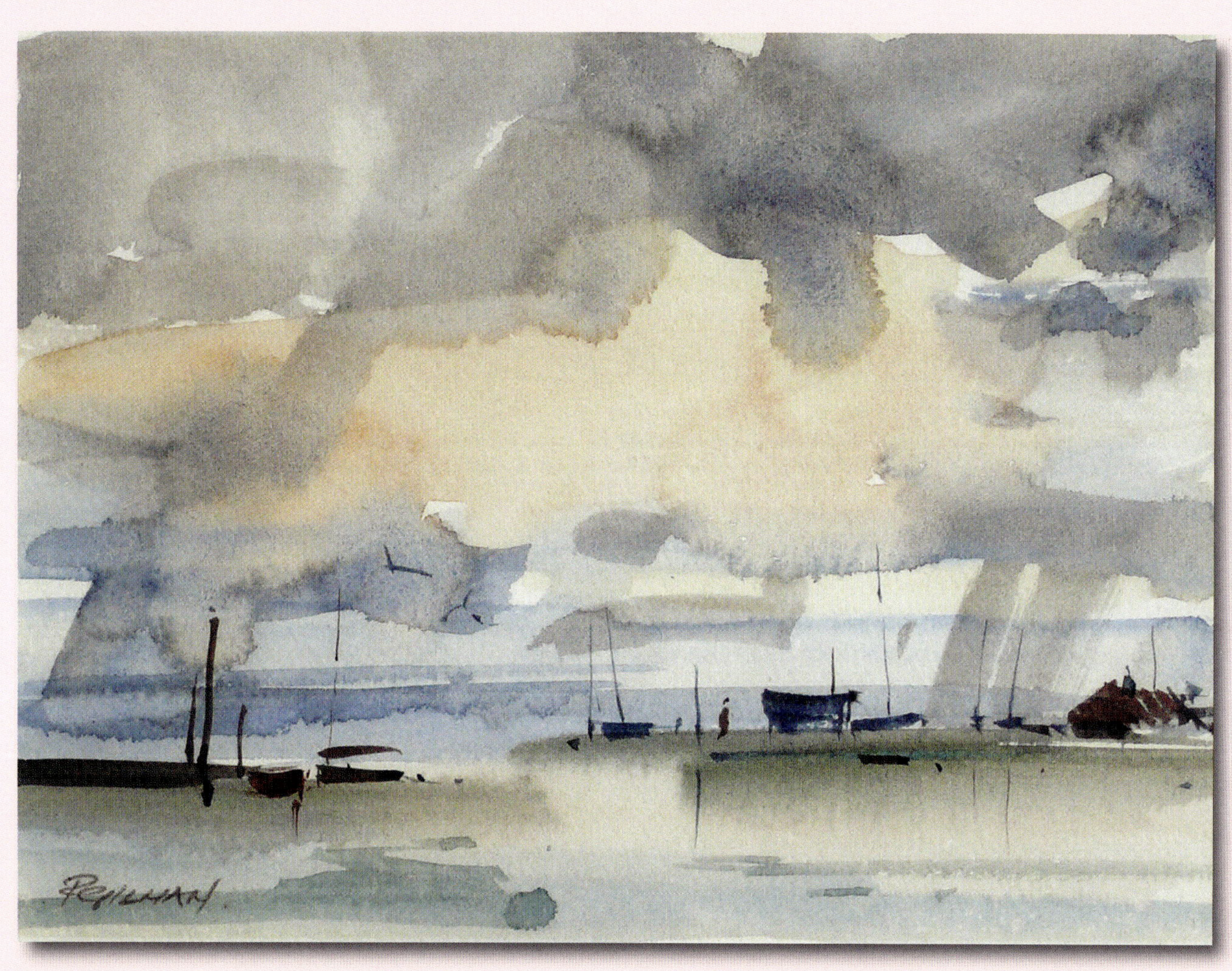

Blakeney, Norfolk. Watercolour sketch.   (John Stillman Collection)

Opposite: The Village Kiosk. Watercolour

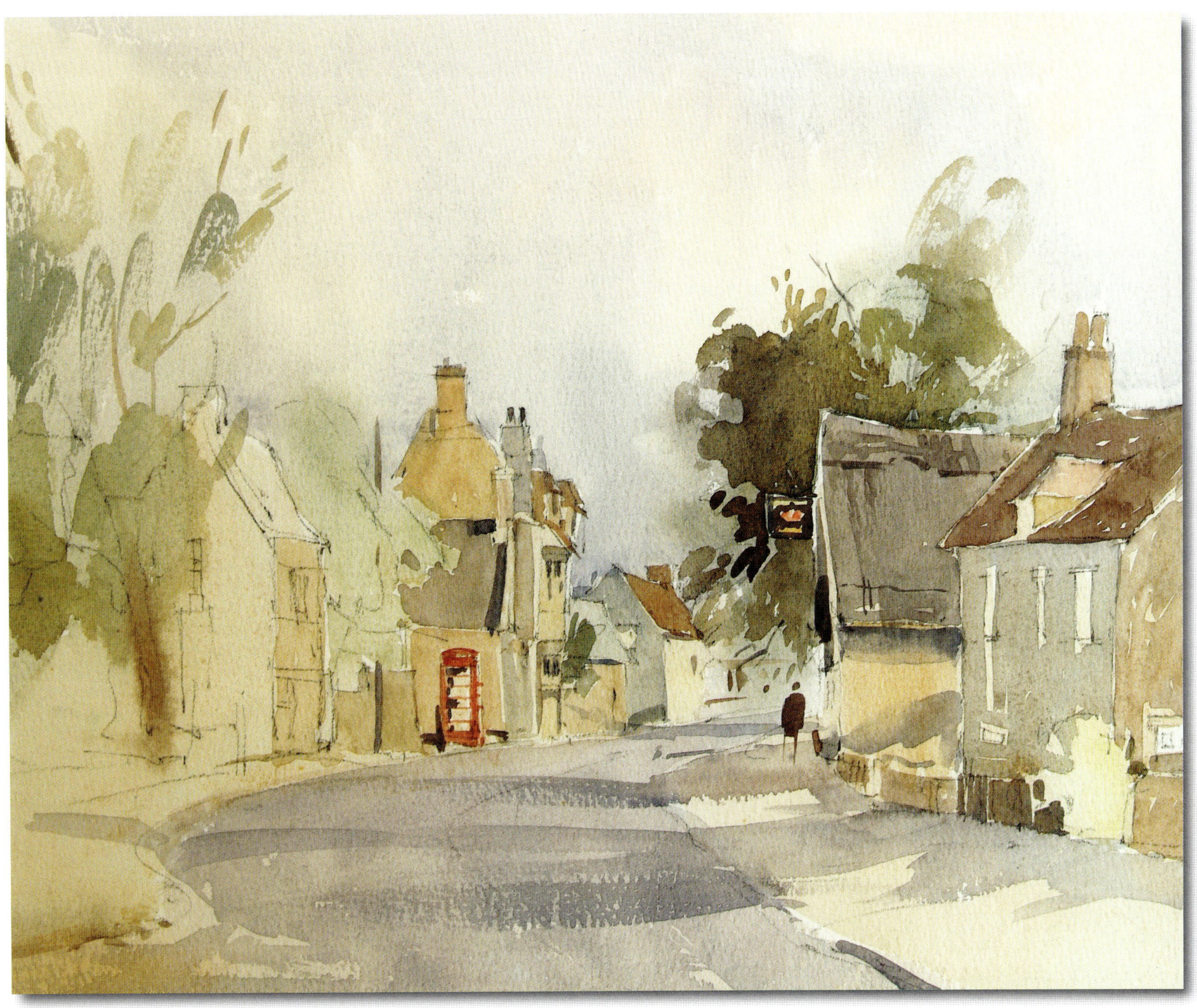

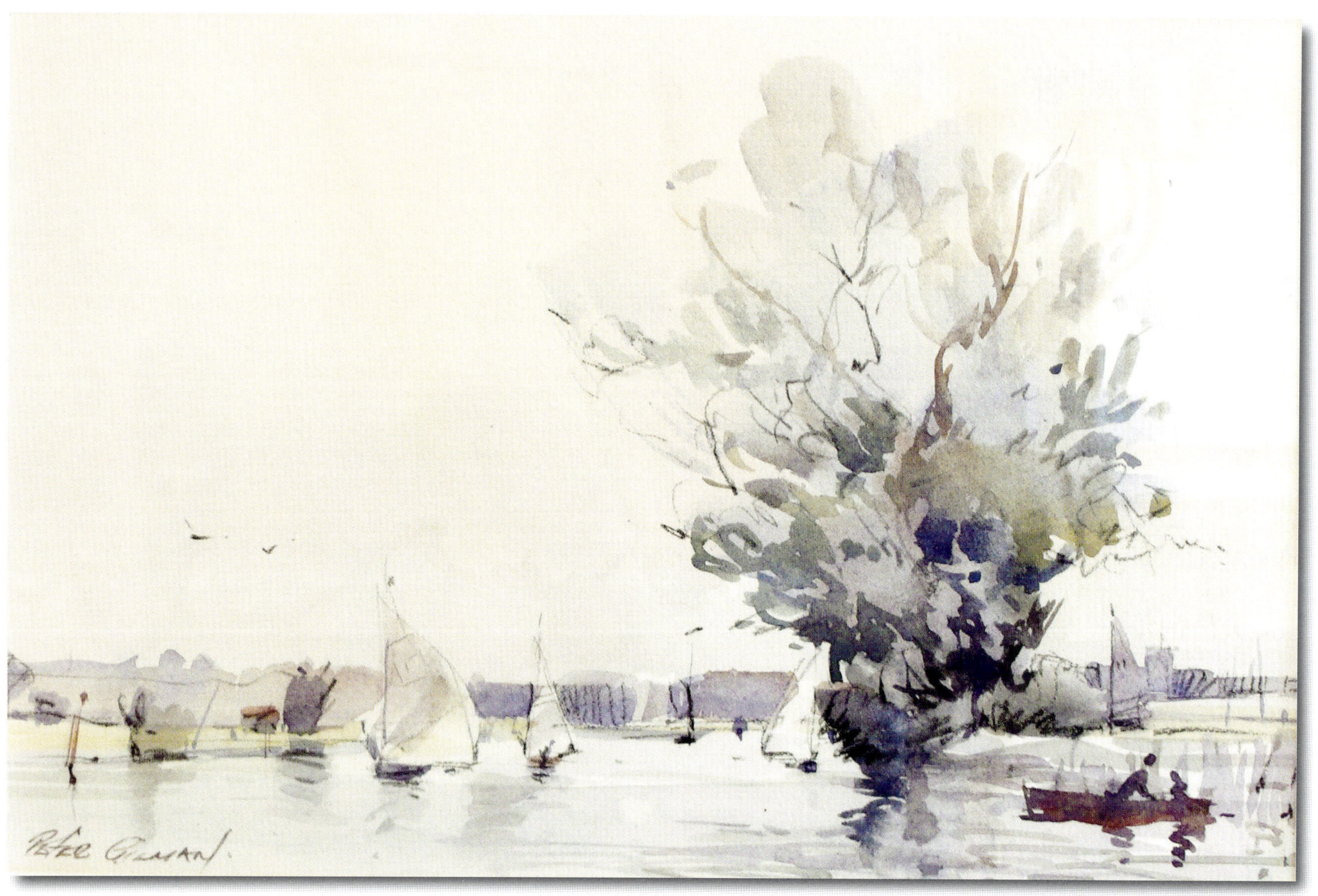

Sailing on the Thurne, Norfolk. Watercolour. (John Stillman Collection)

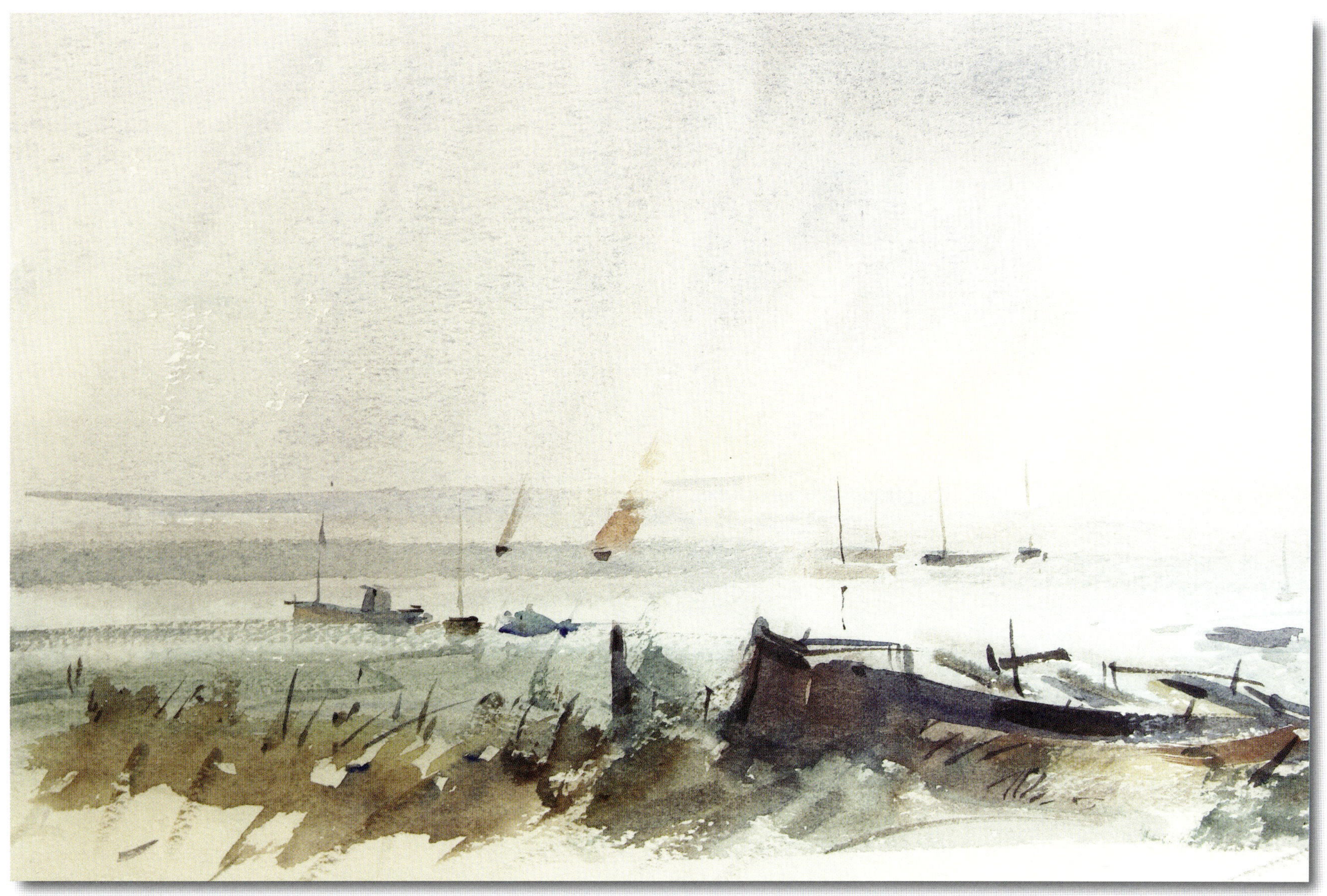

A Windy Day, Norfolk. Watercolour sketch.

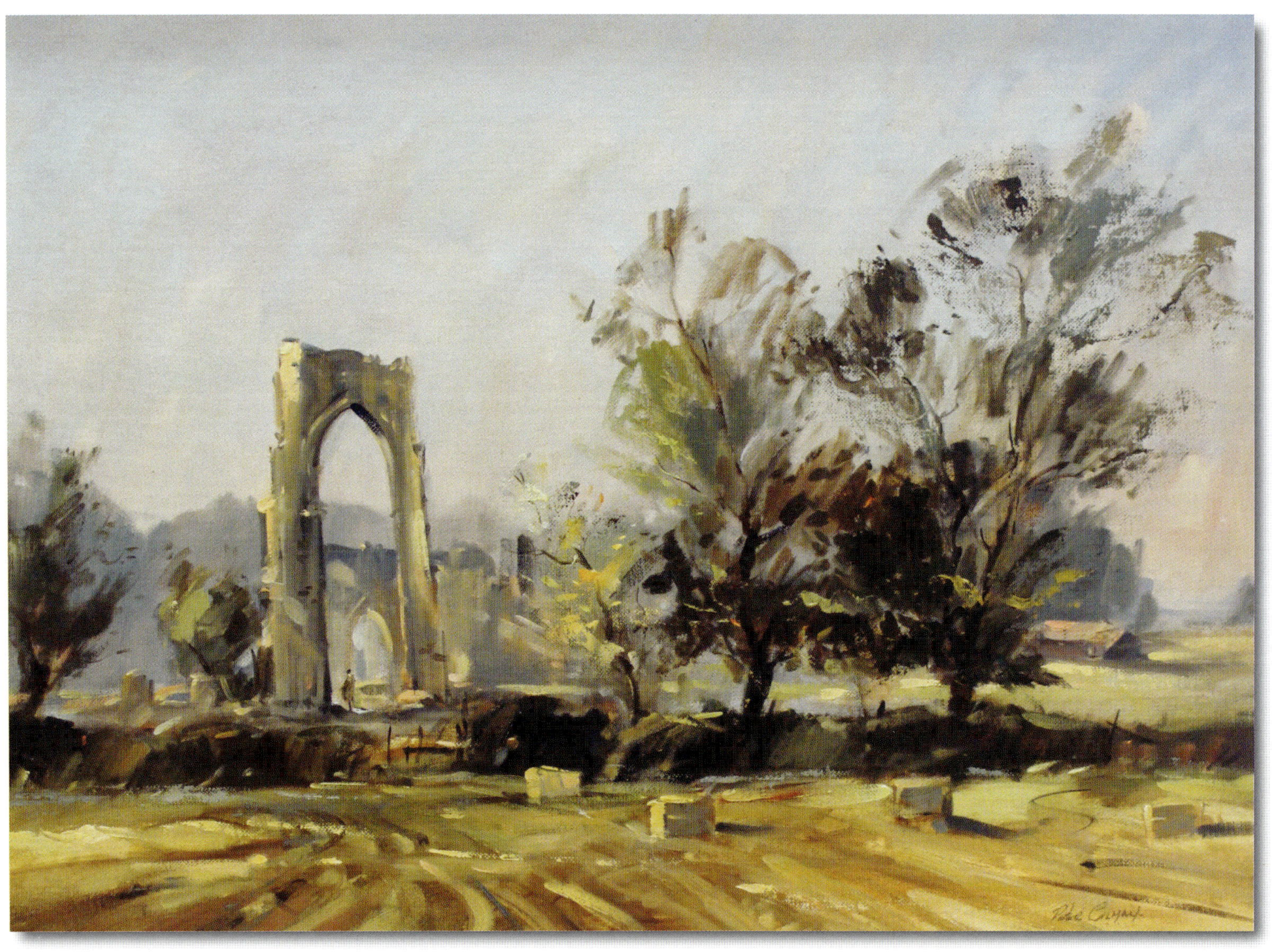

The Abbey Ruins, Leiston, Suffolk. Oil 18x24 inches.

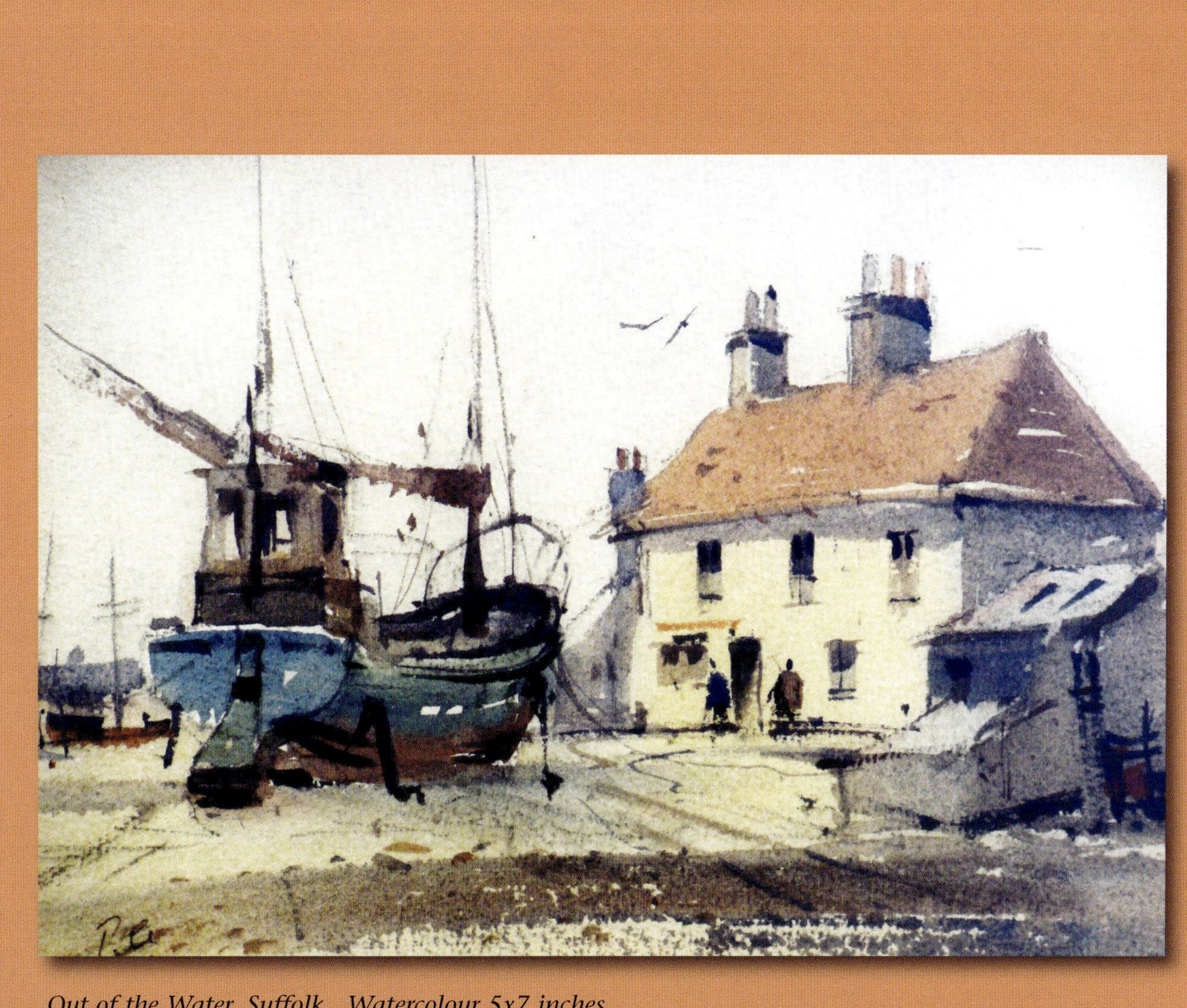

Out of the Water, Suffolk. Watercolour 5x7 inches.

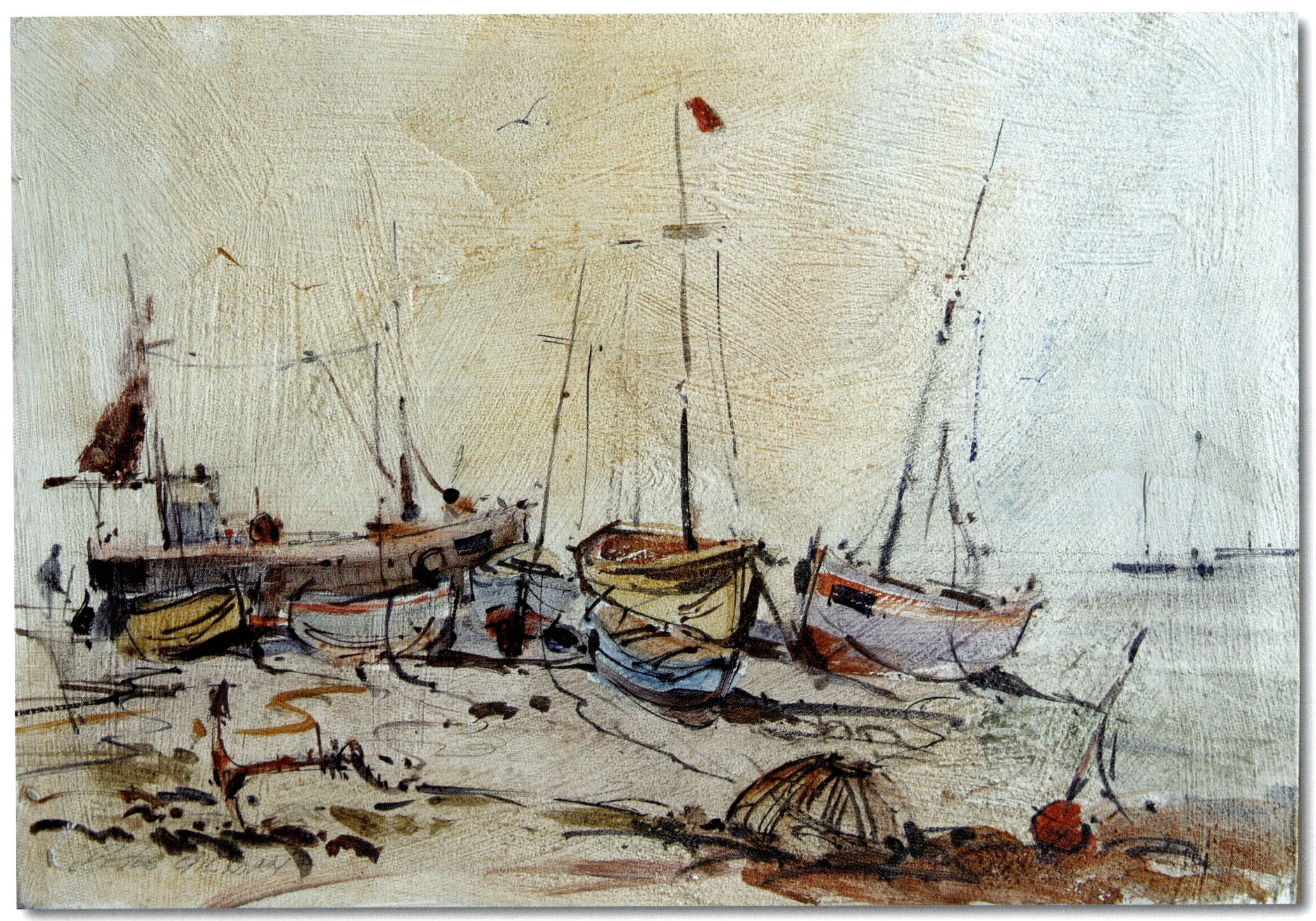

Southwold, Suffolk. (John Stillman Collection)

Opposite: Suffolk Landscape. Oil sketch. (John Stillman Collection)

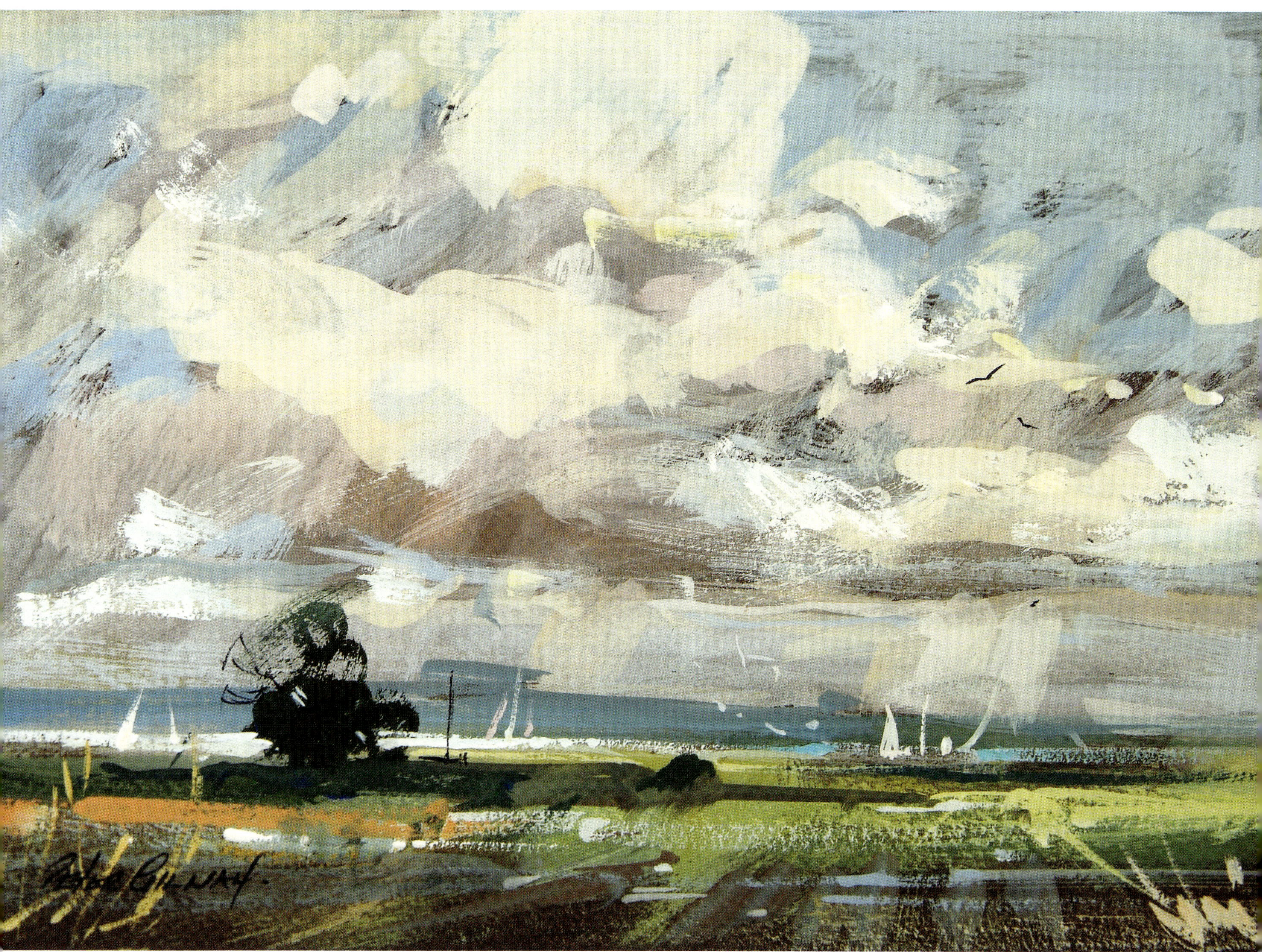

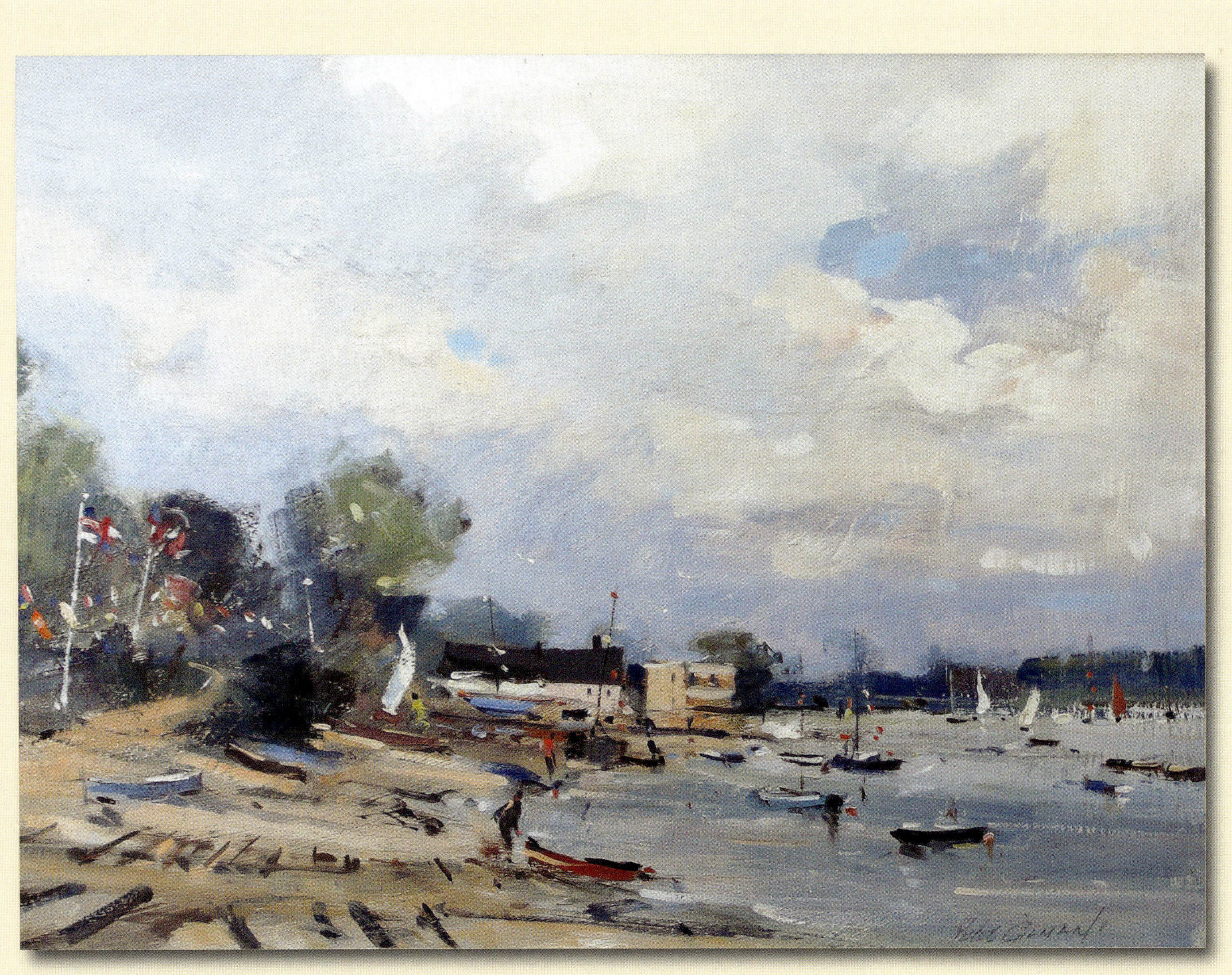

Waldringfield, Suffolk. Oil. (John Stillman Collection)

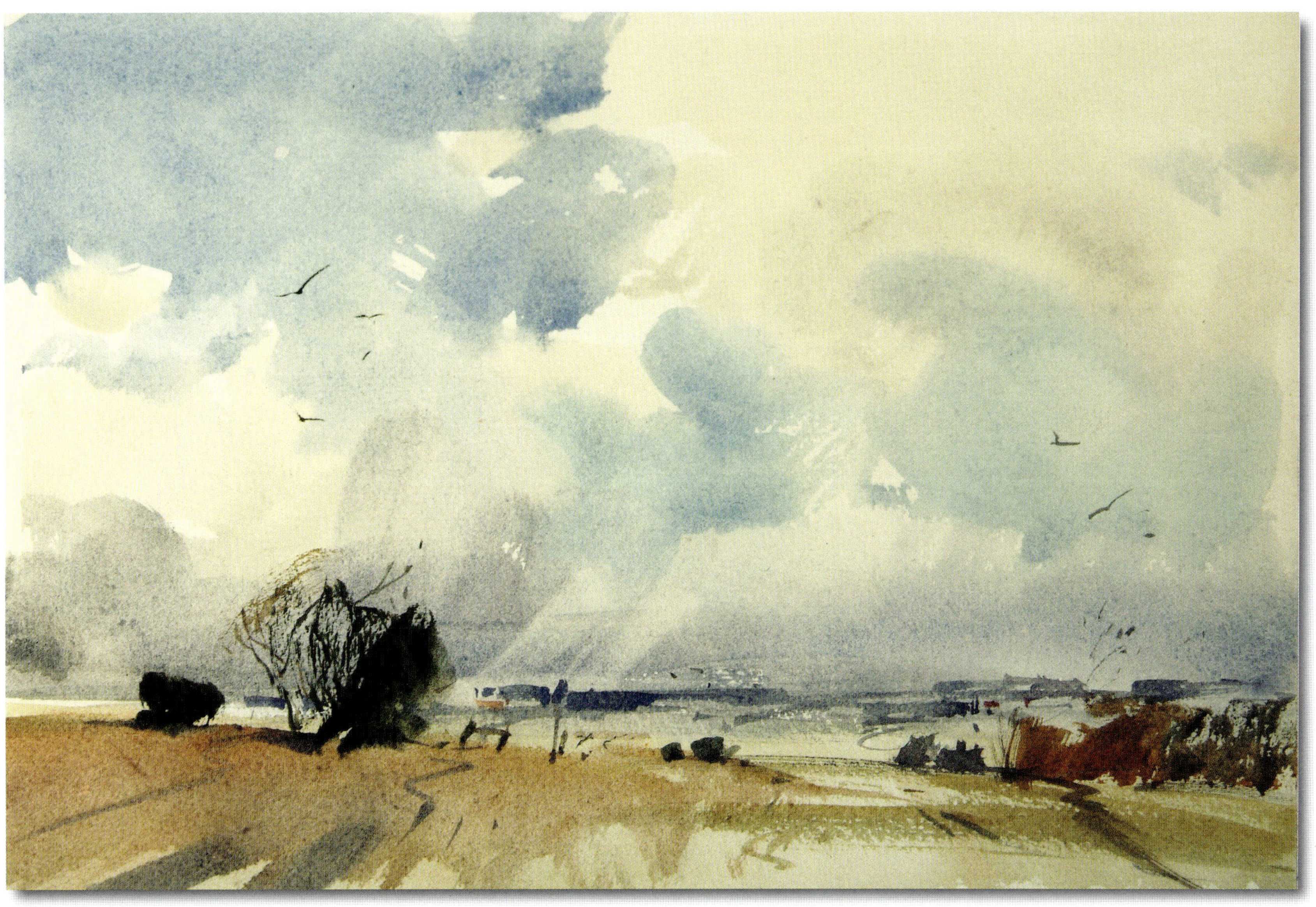

Suffolk Landscape II. Watercolour.

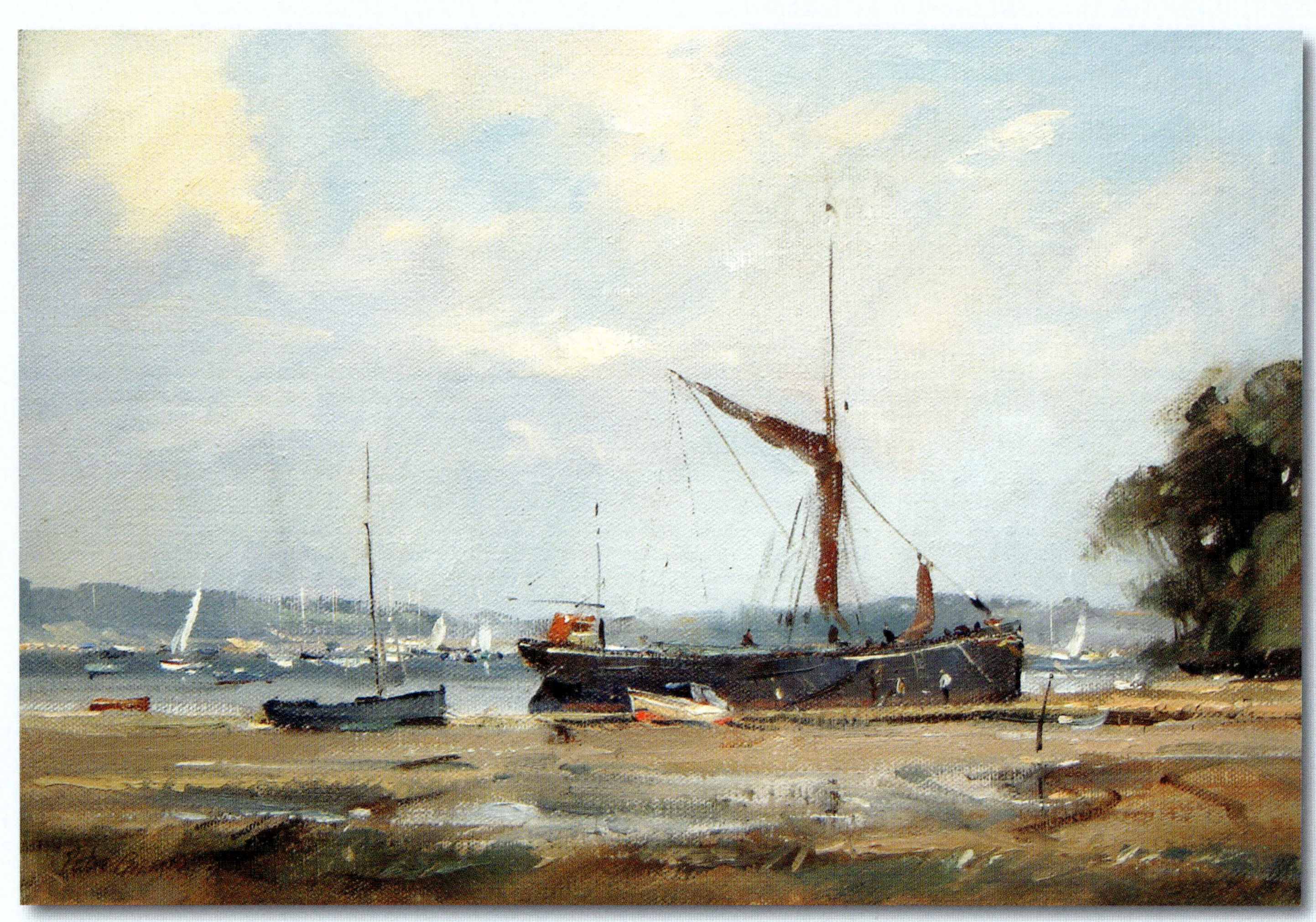

Pin Mill, Suffolk. Oil. (Michael Hill Collection)

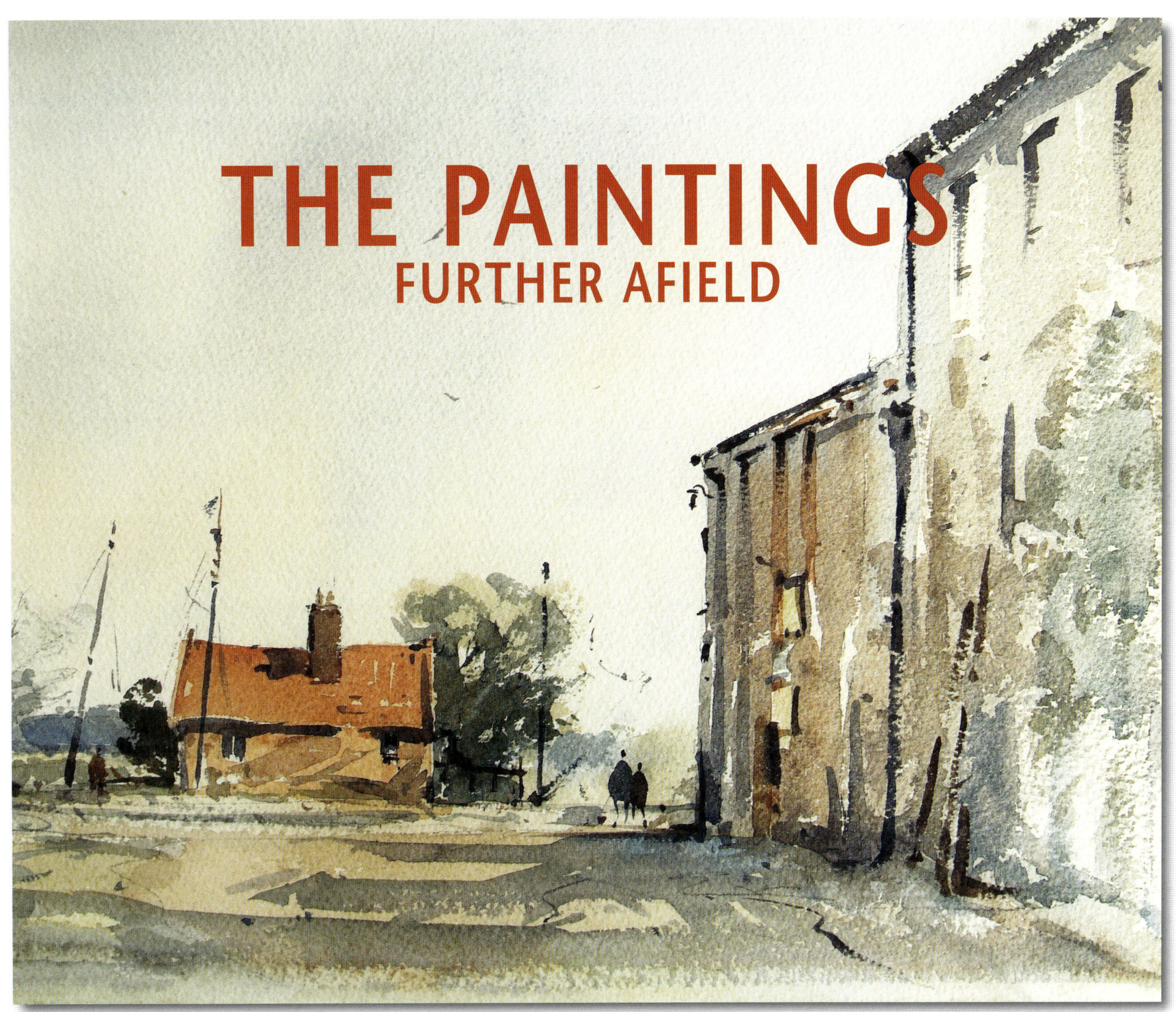

THE PAINTINGS
FURTHER AFIELD

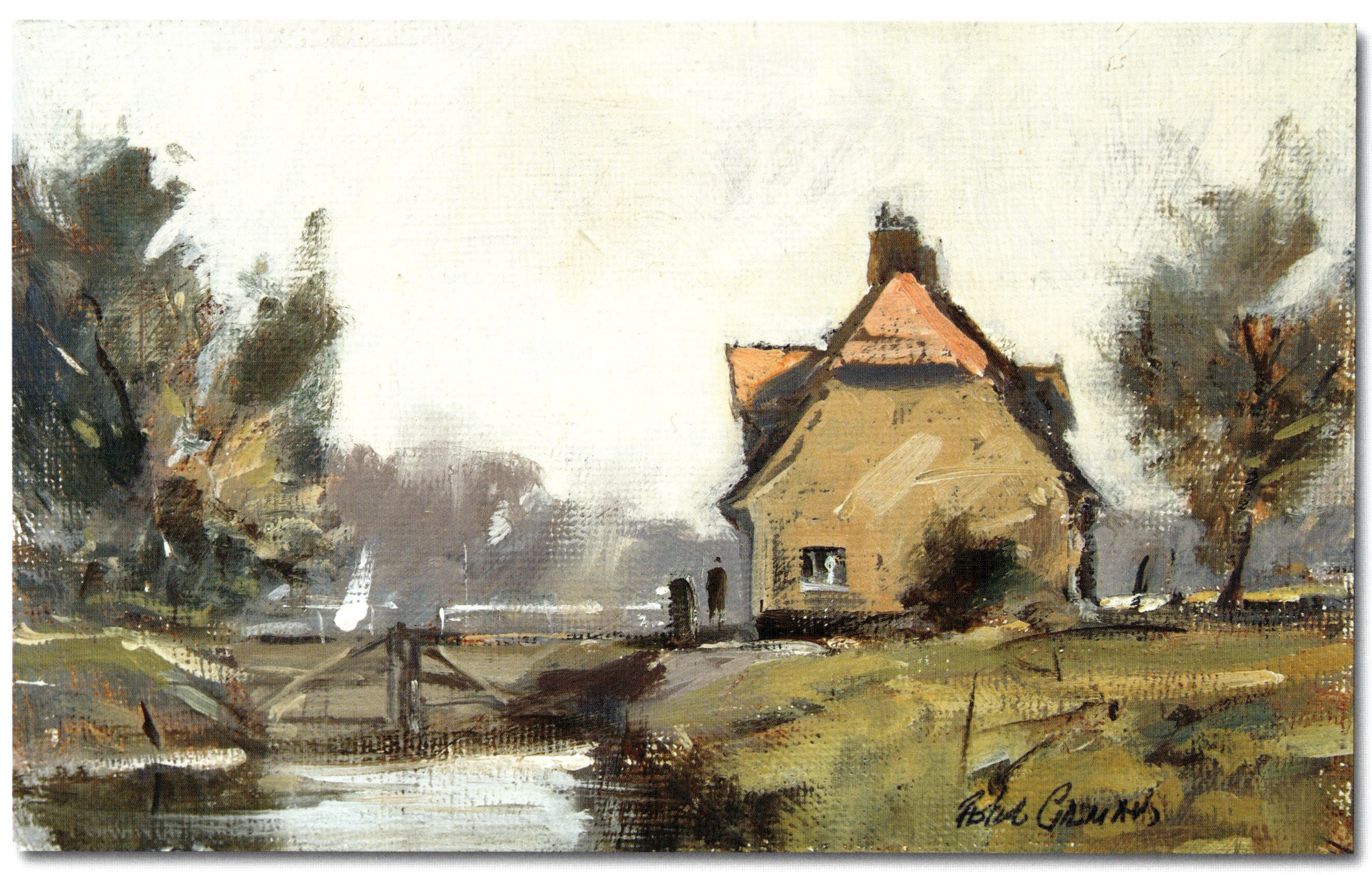

Abingdon Lock, Oxfordshire, October. Mixed media 18x11 inches.

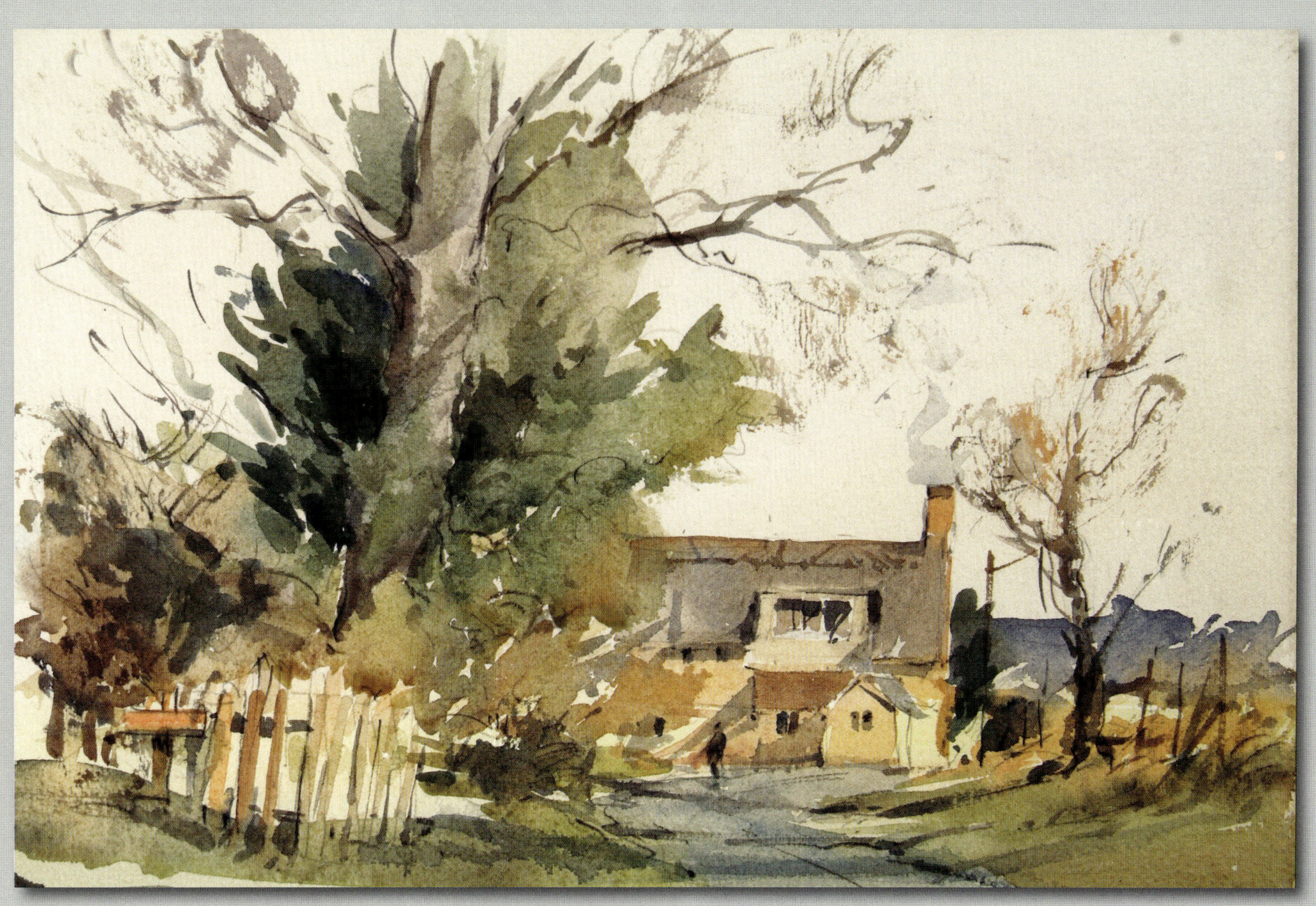

Hyde Mill Cottage, Ickleford, Hertfordshire, 1979. Watercolour 27.5x19 inches.

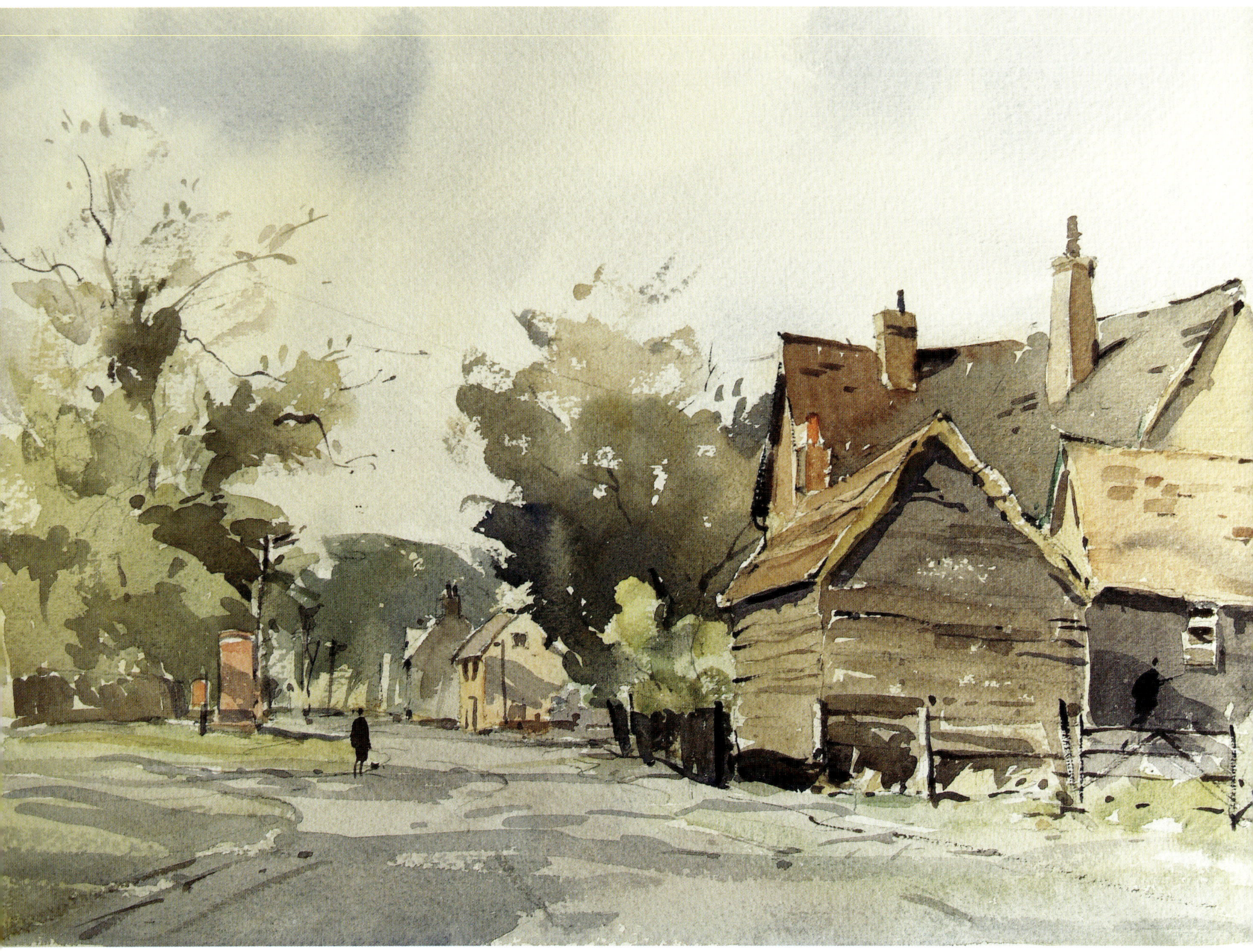

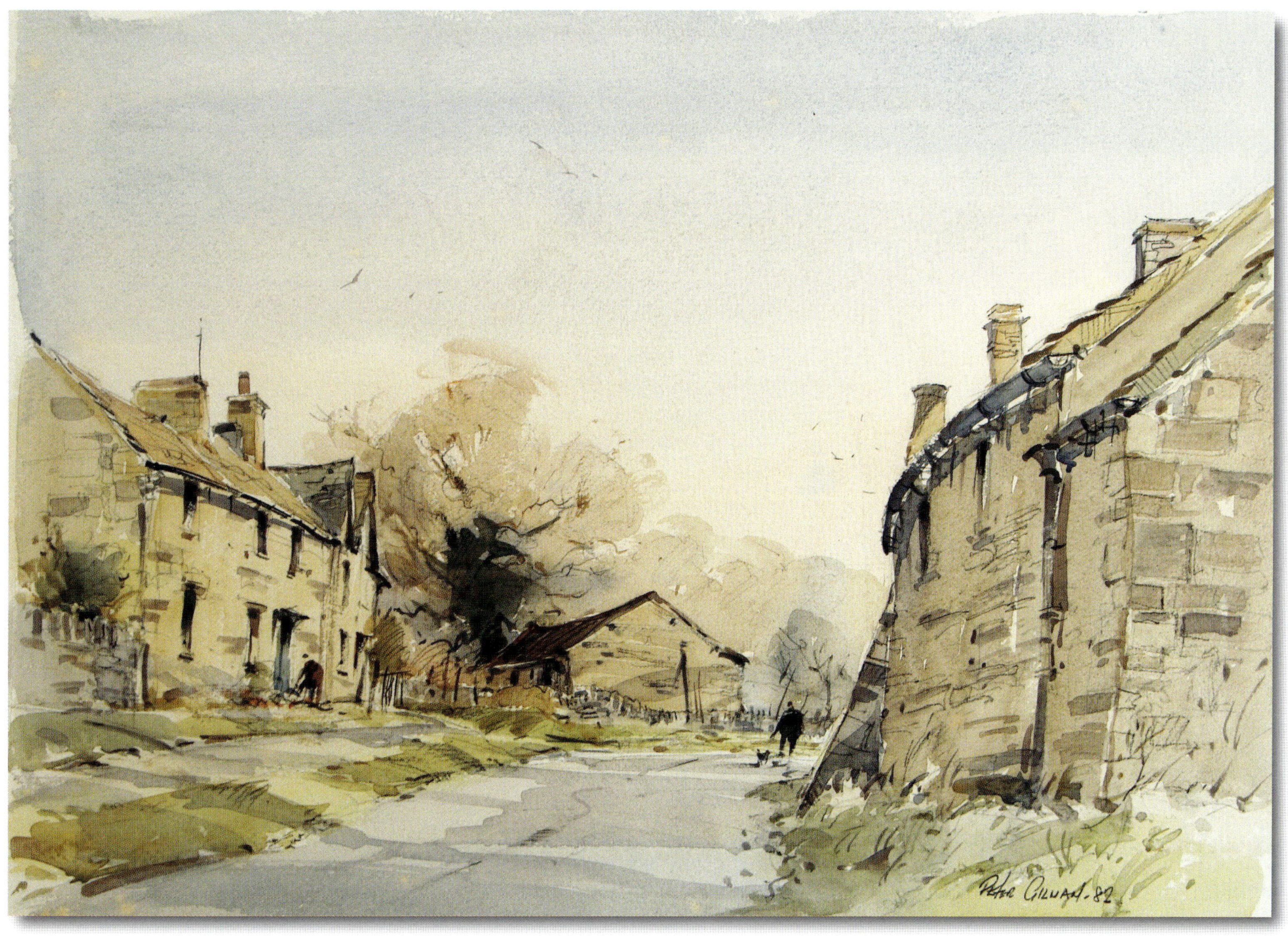

Village Scene. Watercolour 37x27 inches.

A Morning Stroll, Whittington, near Cheltenham. Watercolour 43x30 inches.

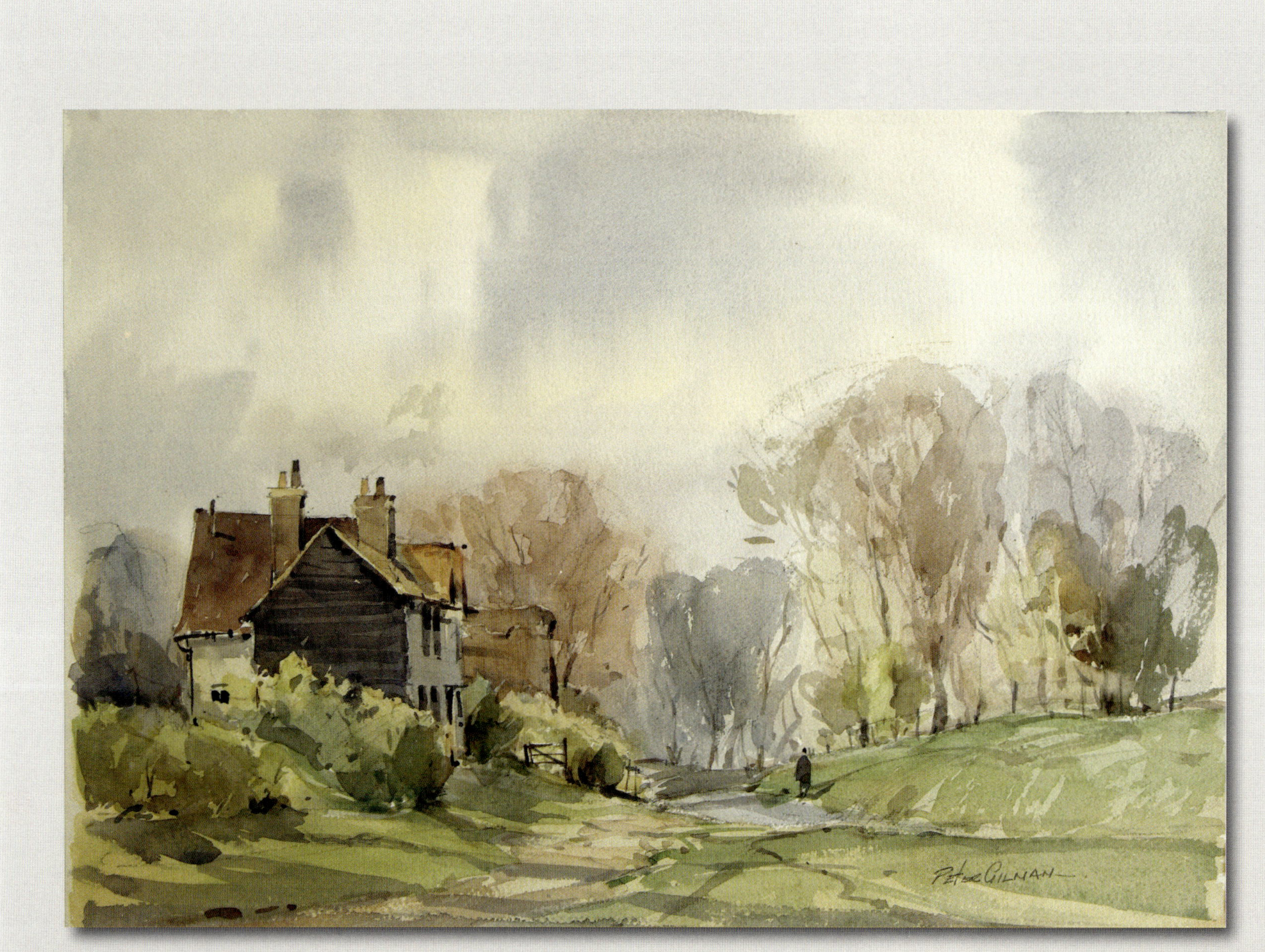

Cottages at Buntington, Hertfordshire, April 1984. Watercolour 39x29 inches.

Opposite: No Entry! Watercolour 38x28 inches.

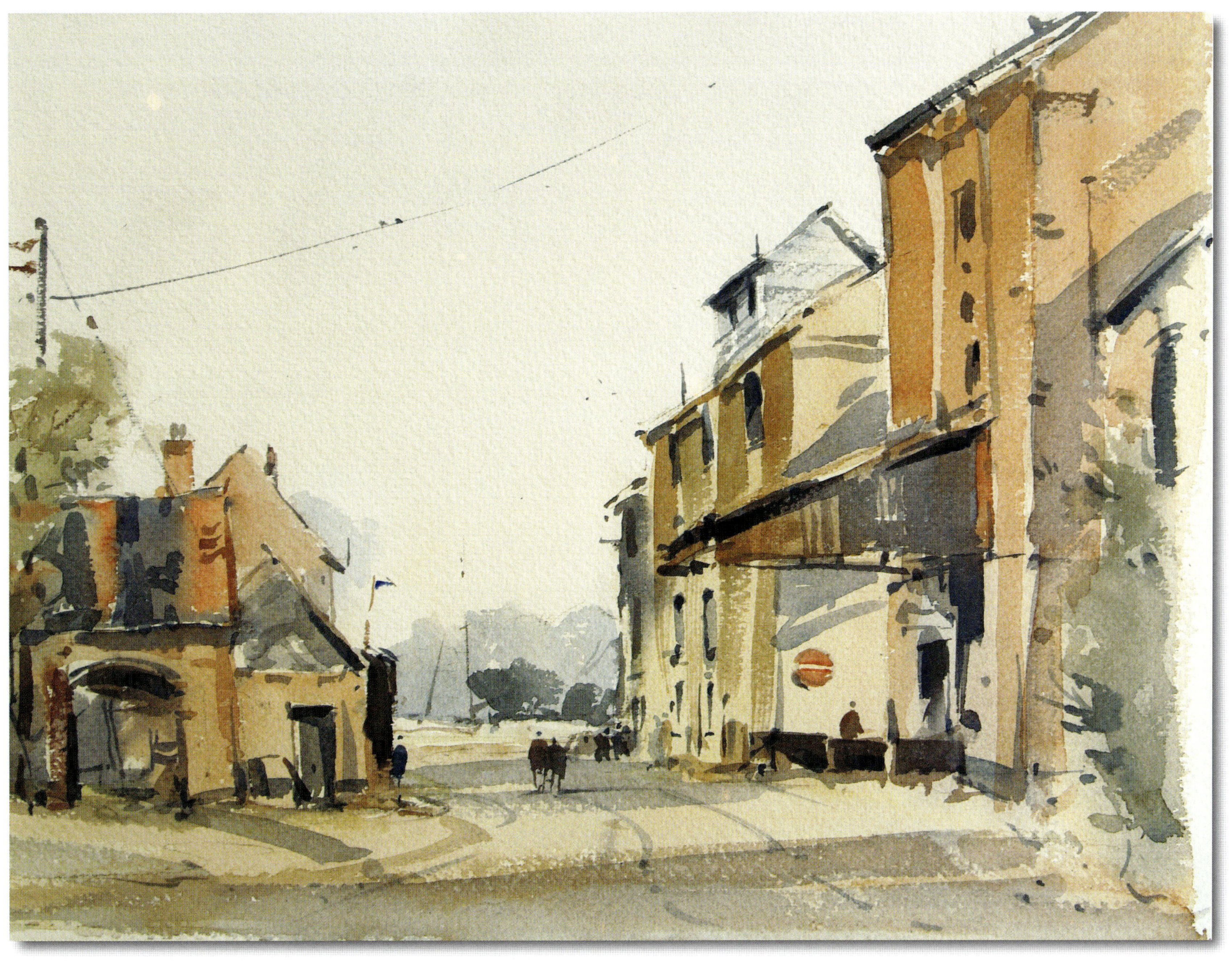

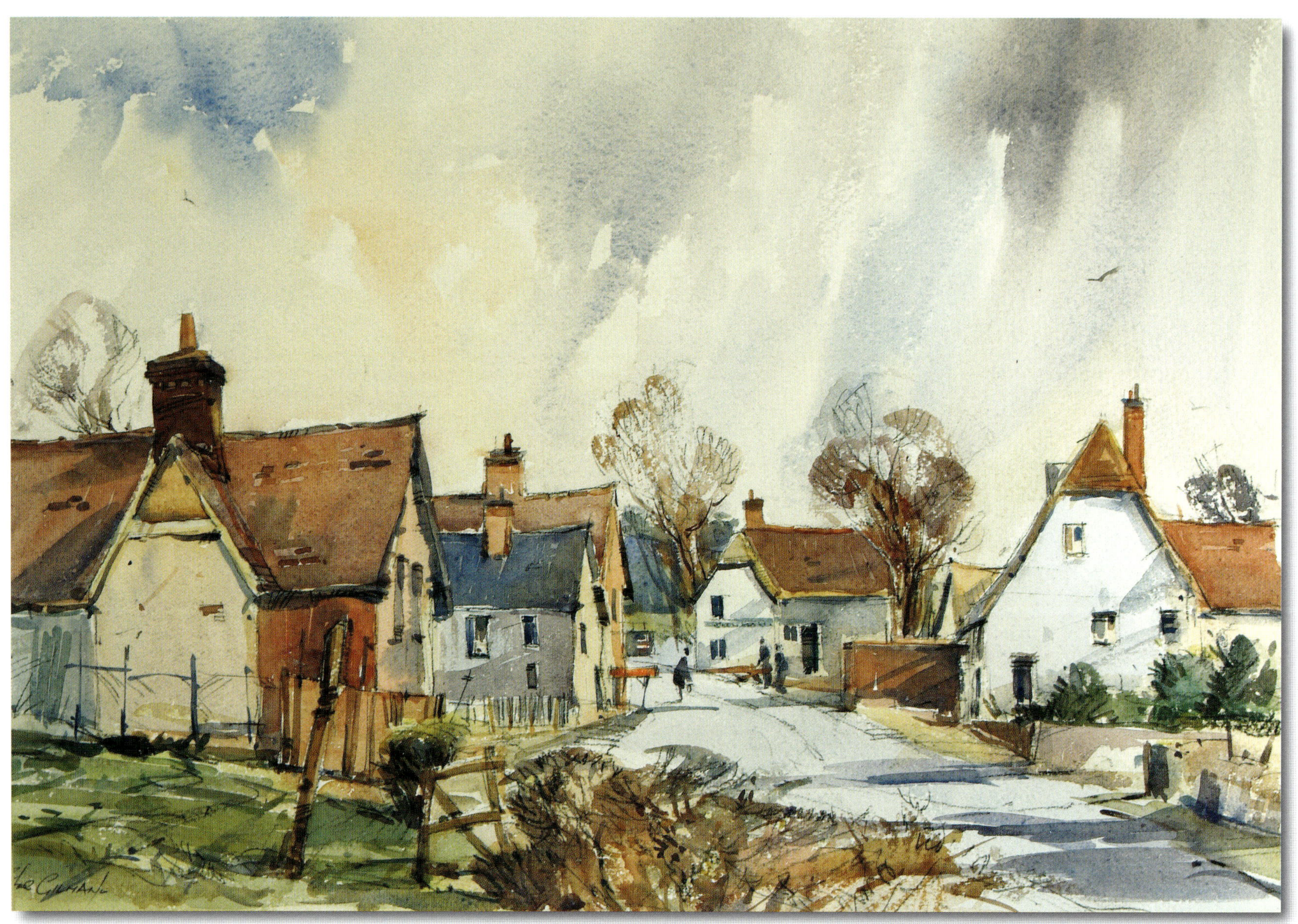

Lidlington, Bedfordshire. Watercolour 43x23 inches.

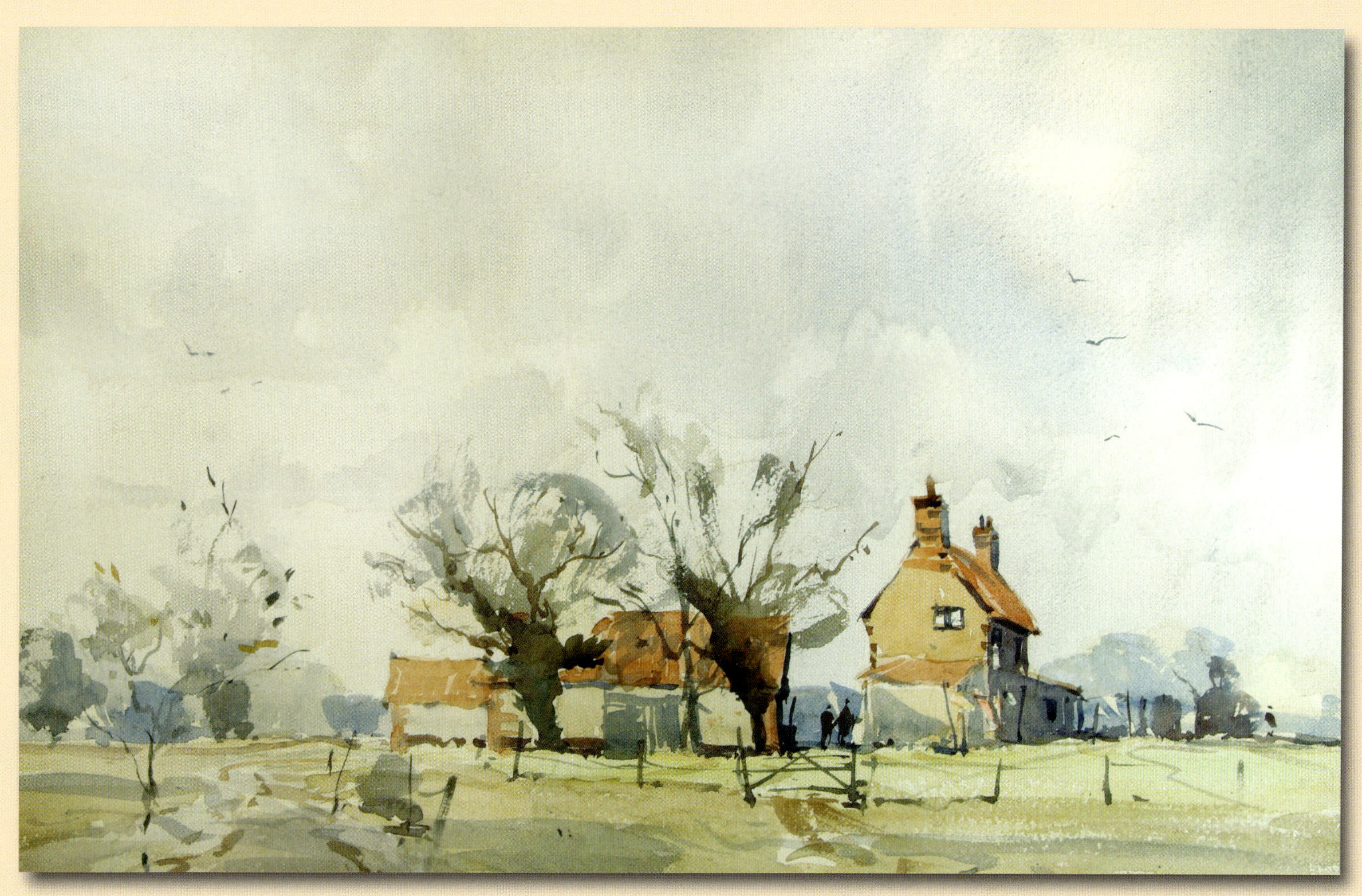

Red roofs. Watercolour 56x37 inches.

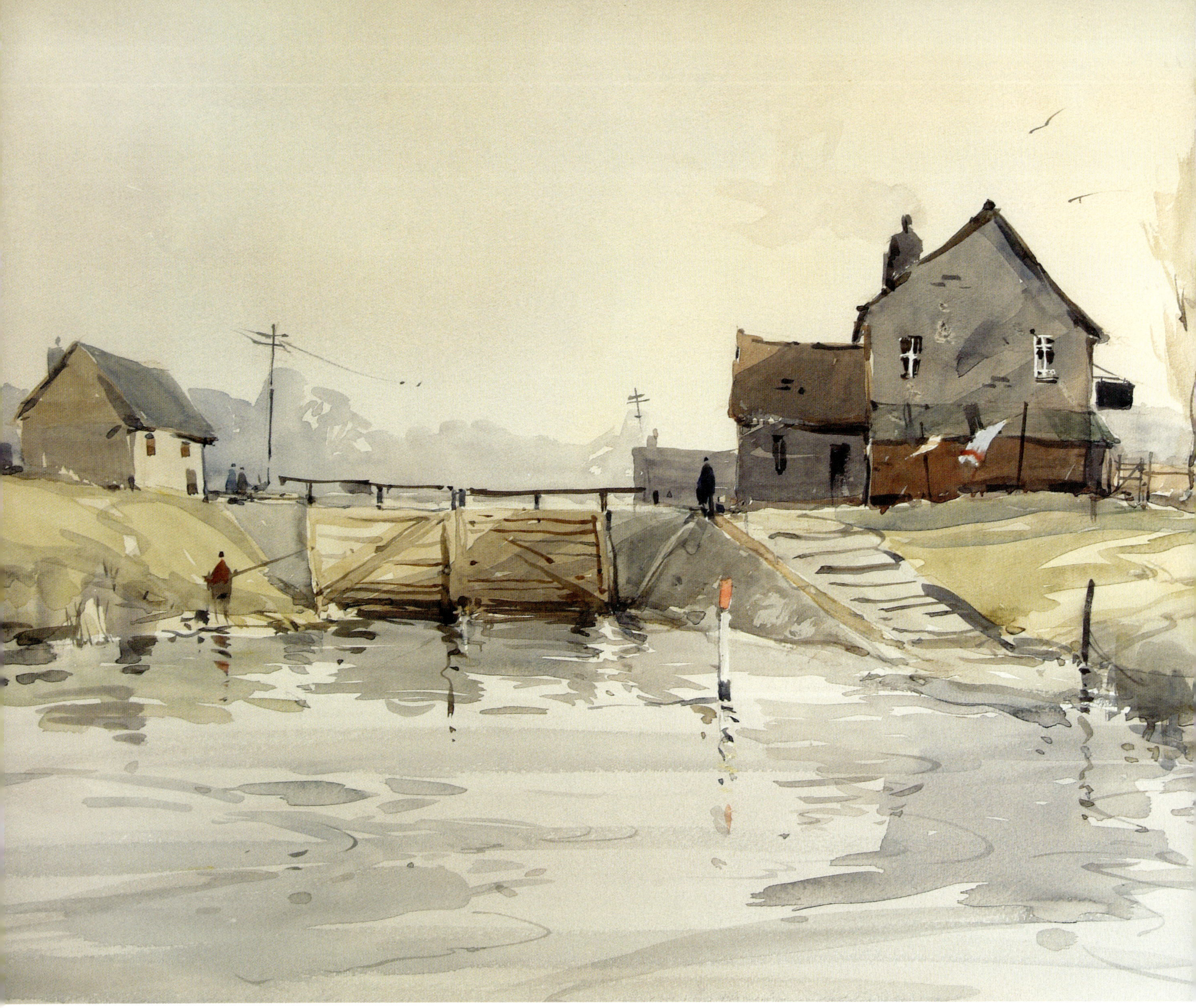

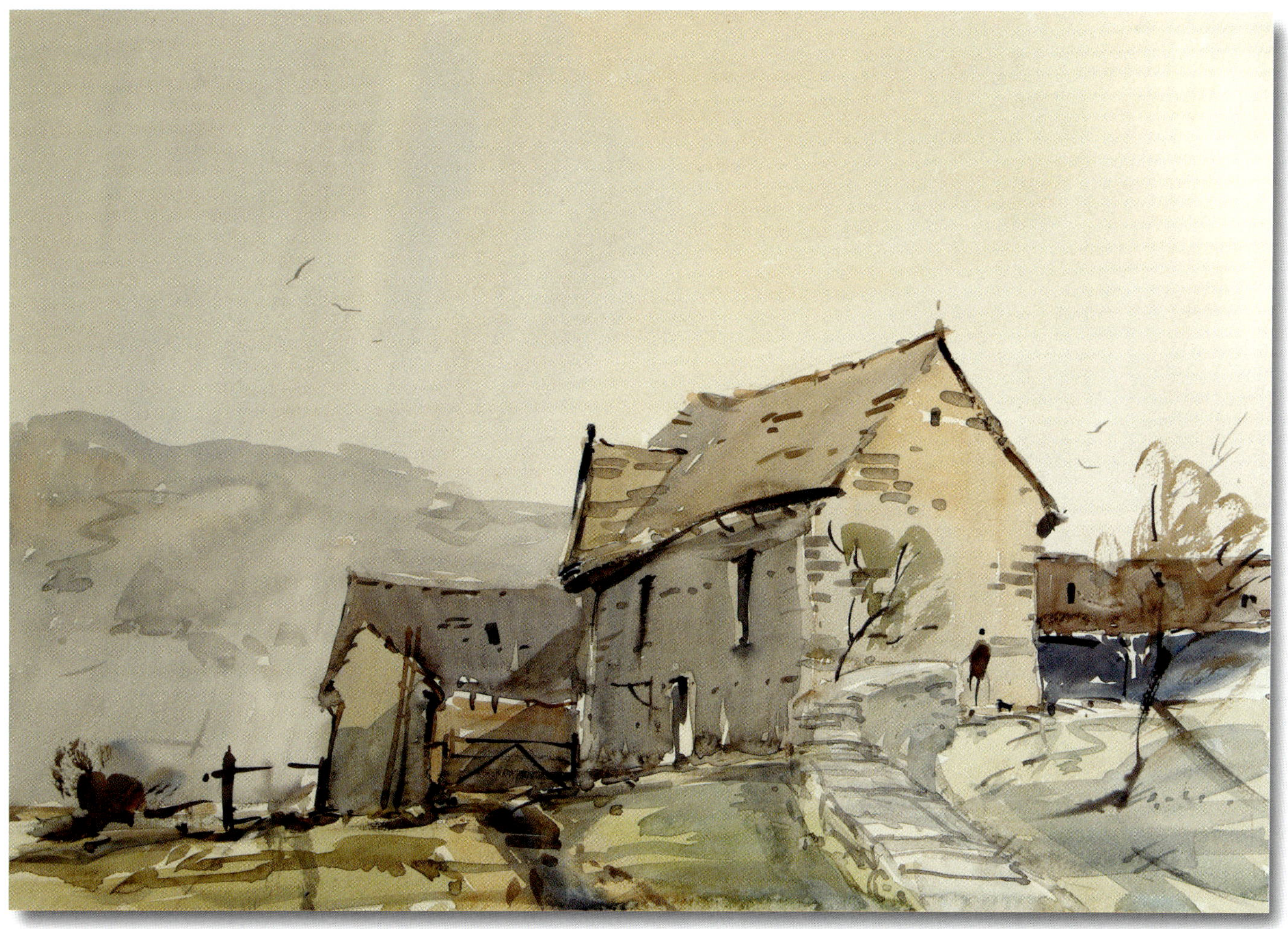

The Old Lock Gate. Watercolour 58x41 inches.

Upland Farm. Watercolour 53x38 inches.

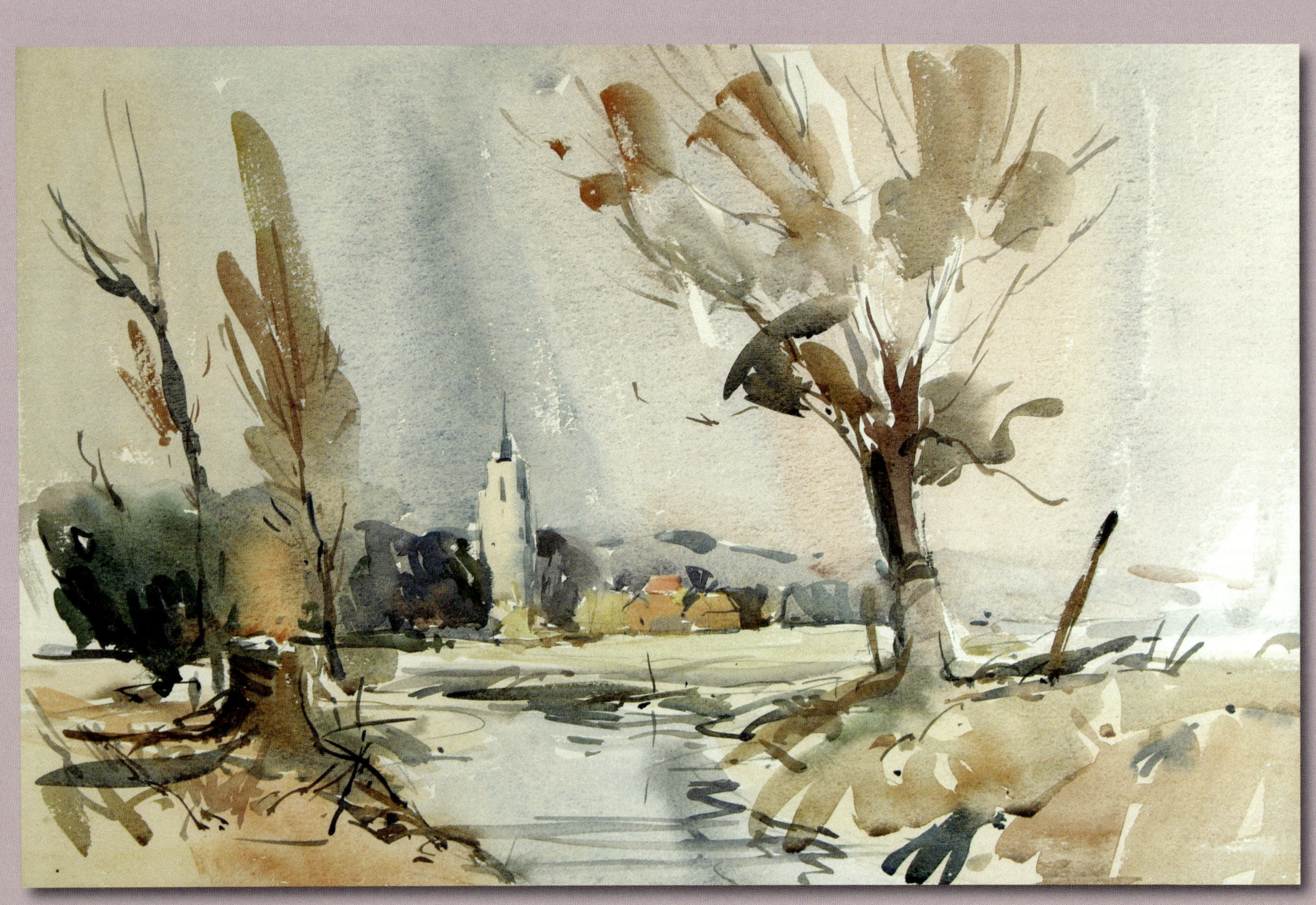

Autumn Afternoon, Ashwell, Hertfordshire. Watercolour 56x38 inches.

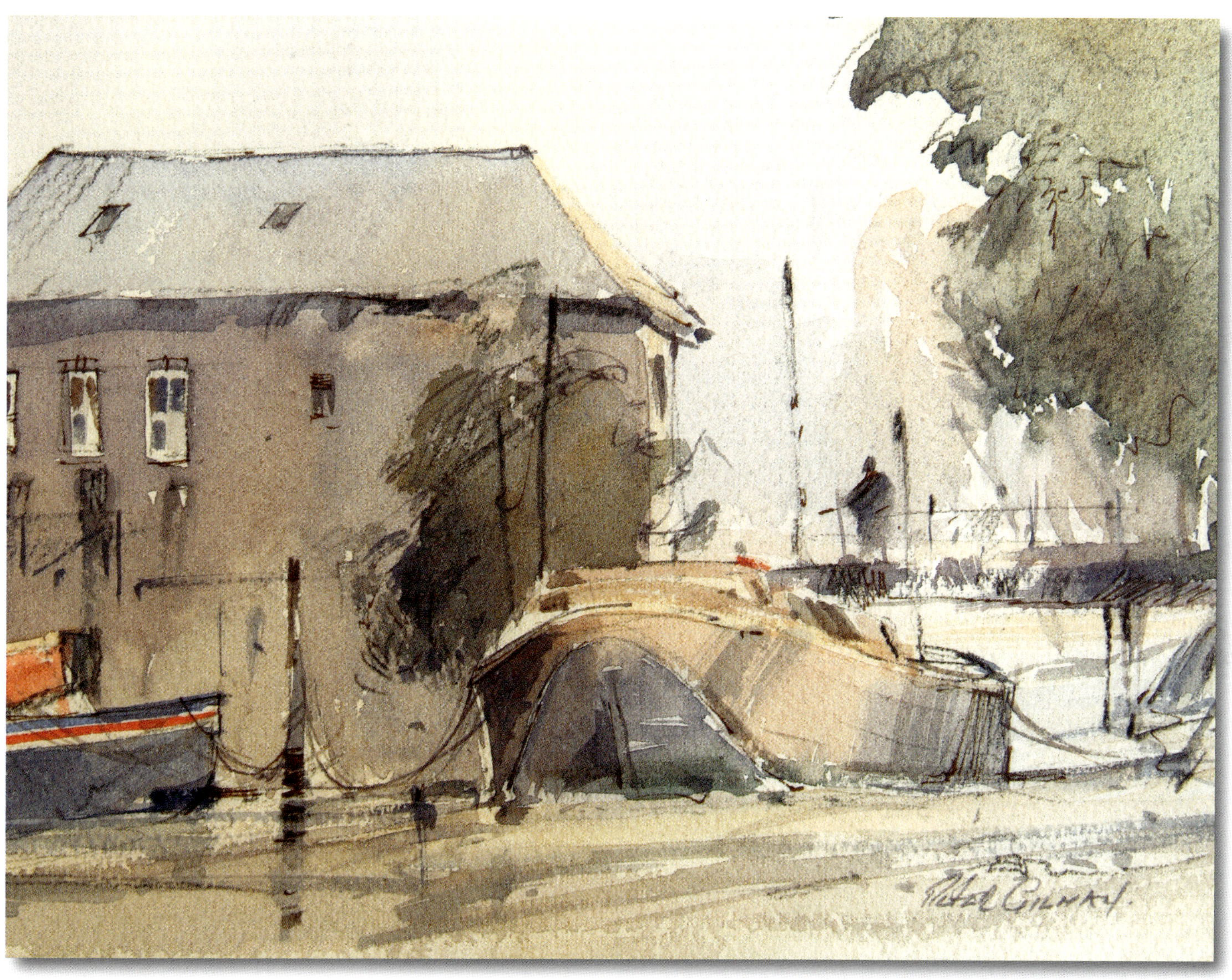

Barges on the Thames, 1980. Watercolour 17x13 inches.

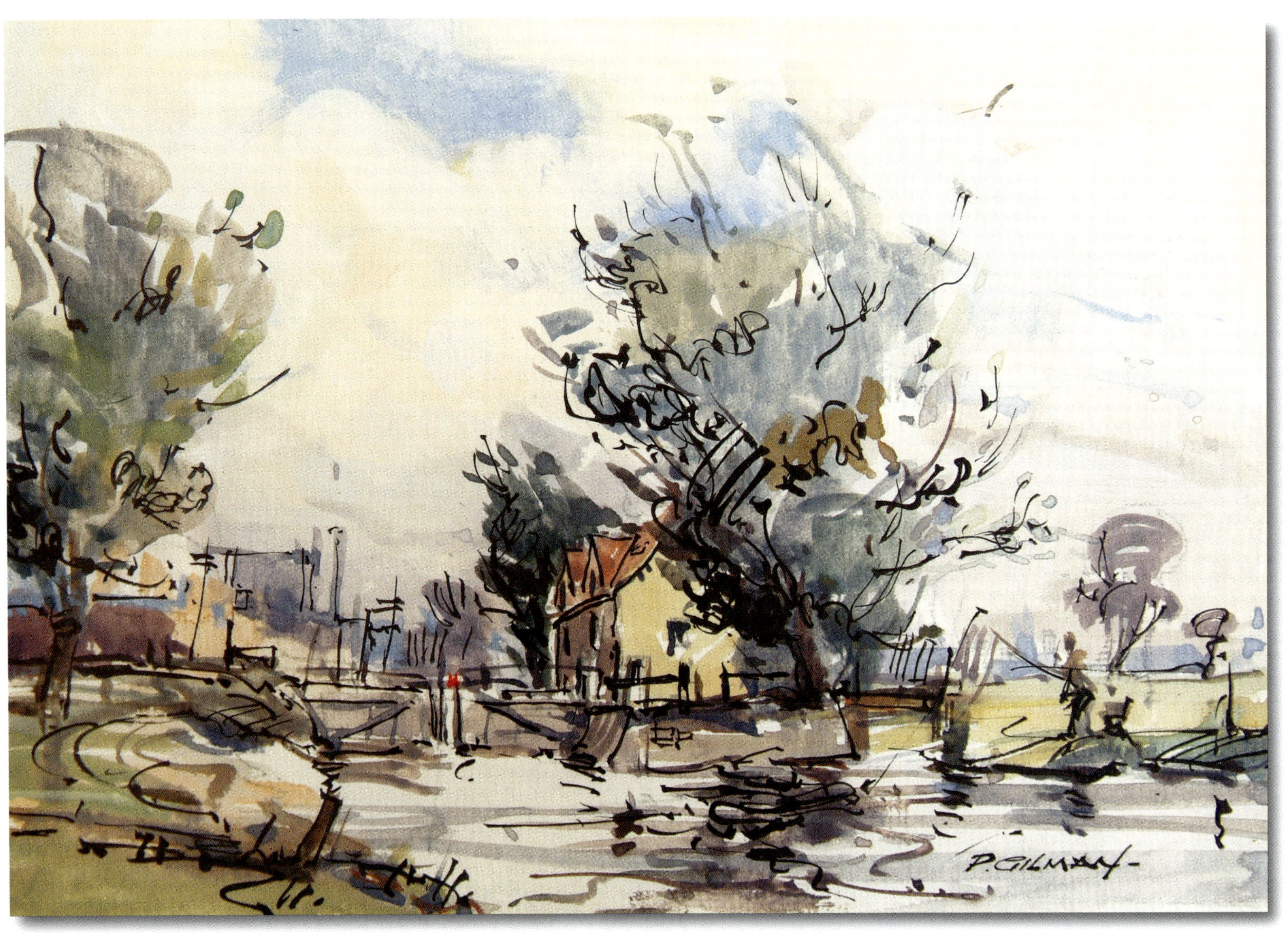

Fisherman at the Lock Gates. Watercolour 14x10 inches.

Opposite: The Village Pub. Watercolour 33x25 inches.

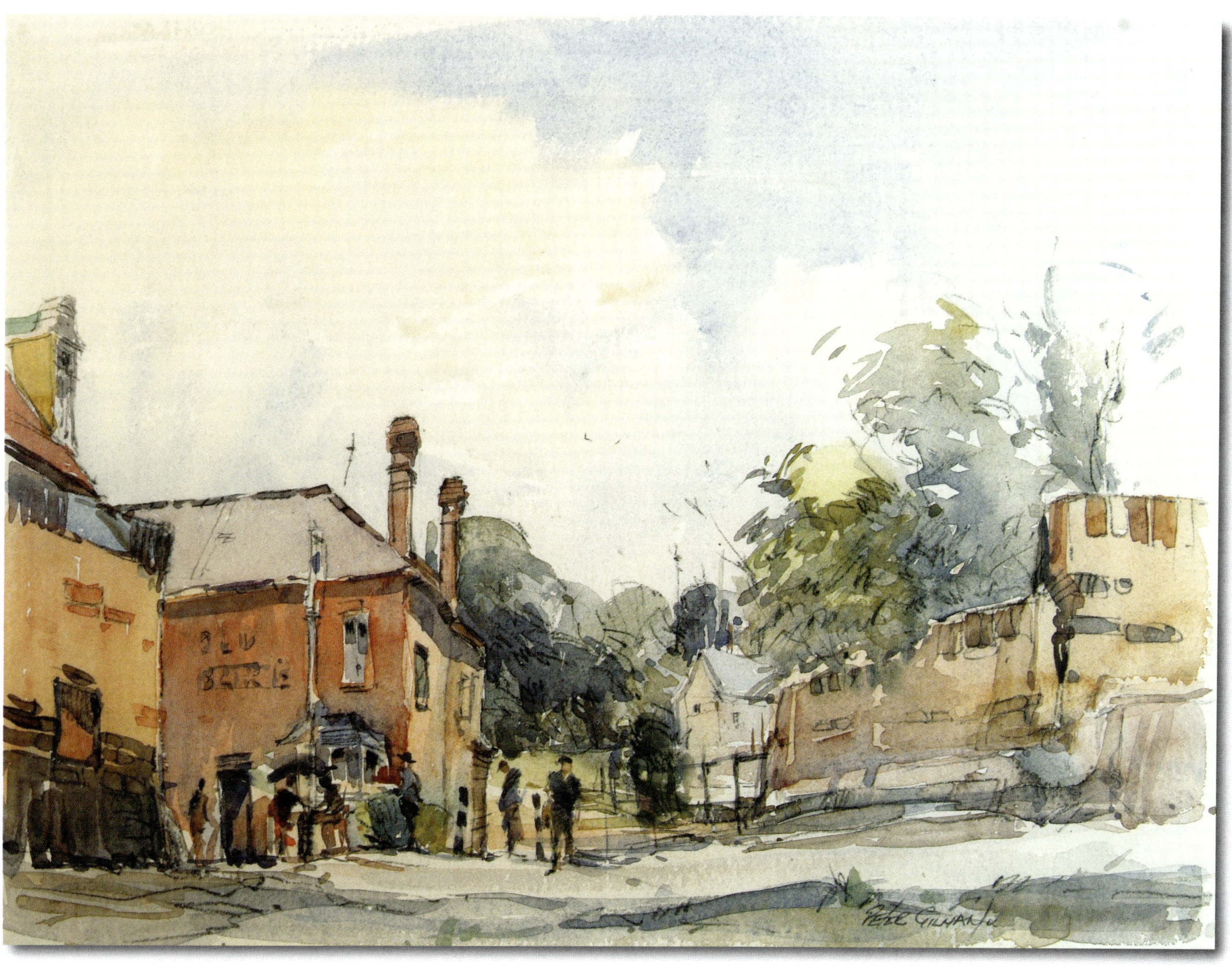

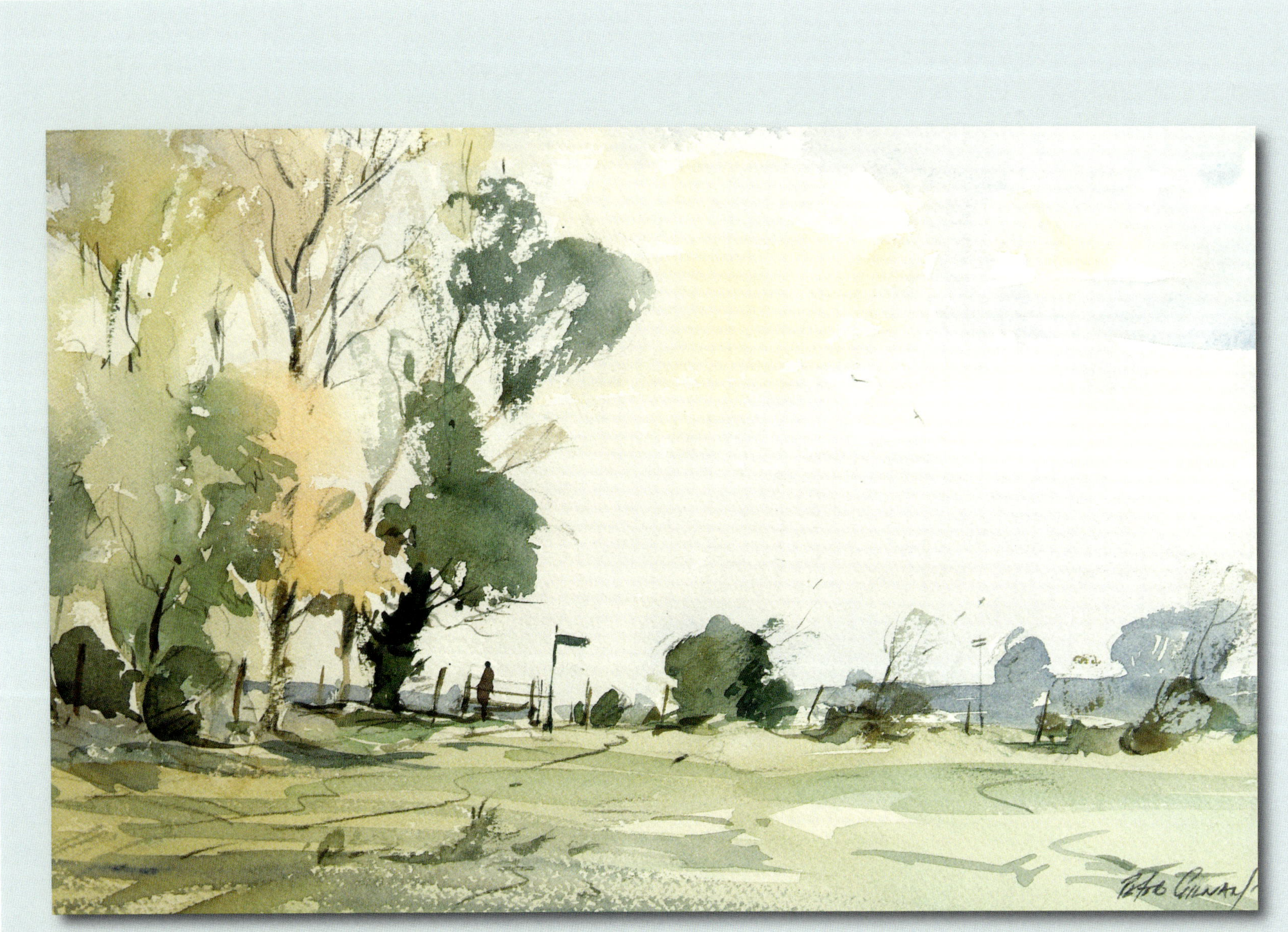

Footpath near Ashwell, Hertfordshire. Watercolour 30x20 inches.

Opposite: Stevenage Old Town North. Watercolour and ink 33x25 inches.

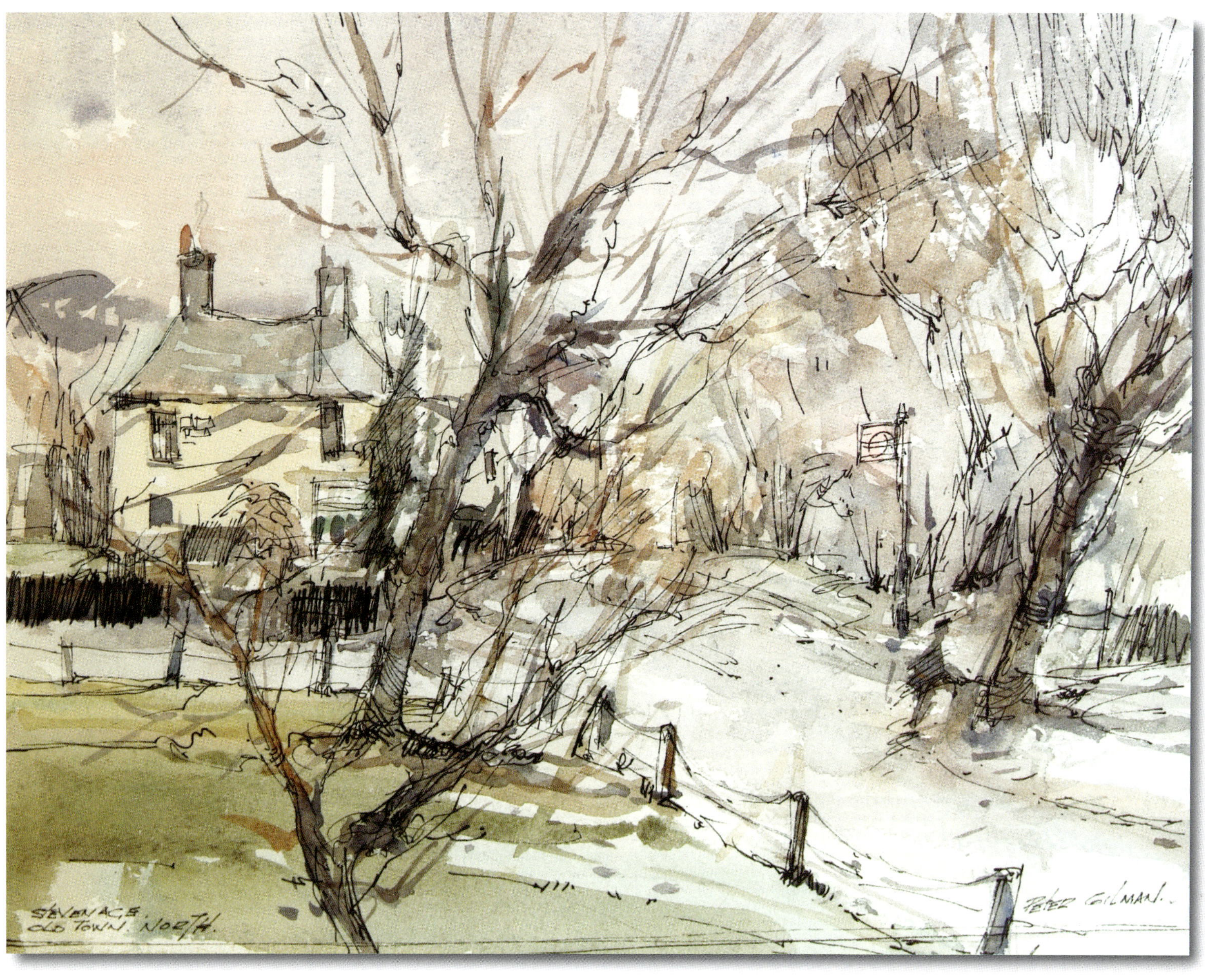
STEVENAGE
OLD TOWN. NORTH.
PETER GILMAN.

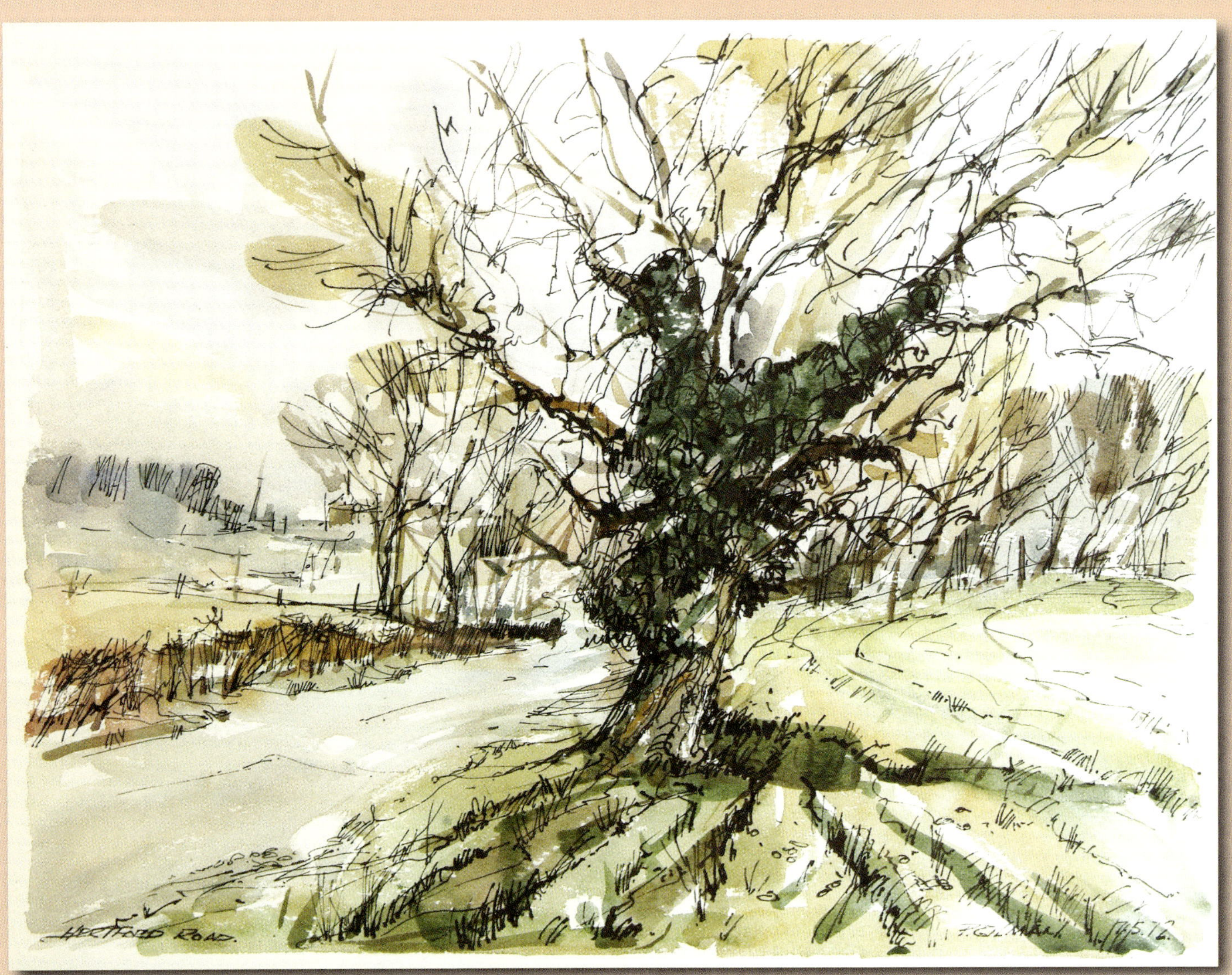

A Hertfordshire Lane, 1972. Watercolour and ink 33x26 inches.

Opposite: Creature Comforts. Watercolour and ink 33x26 inches.

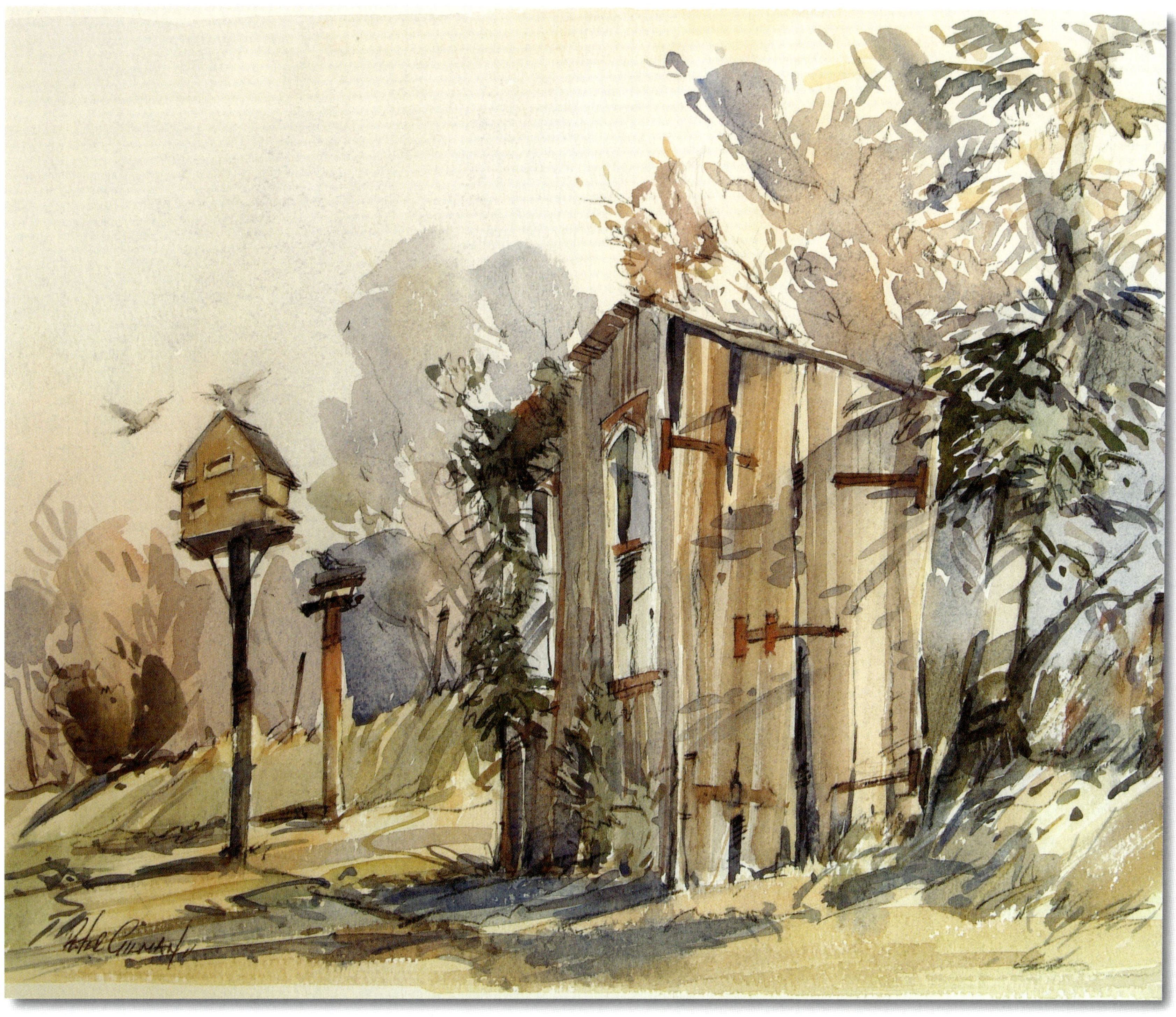

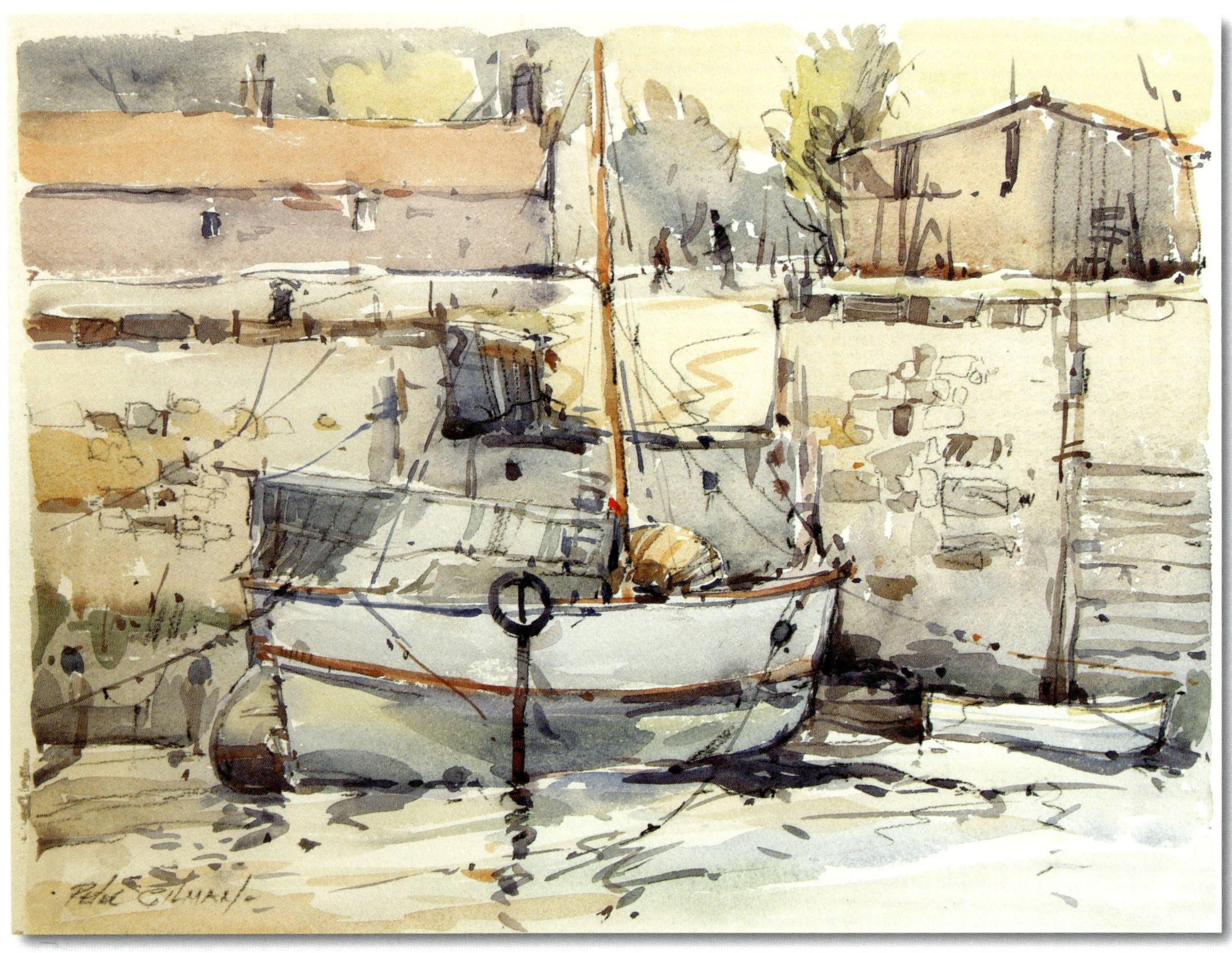

Porlock Weir, Somerset, June 1976. Watercolour 33x26 inches.

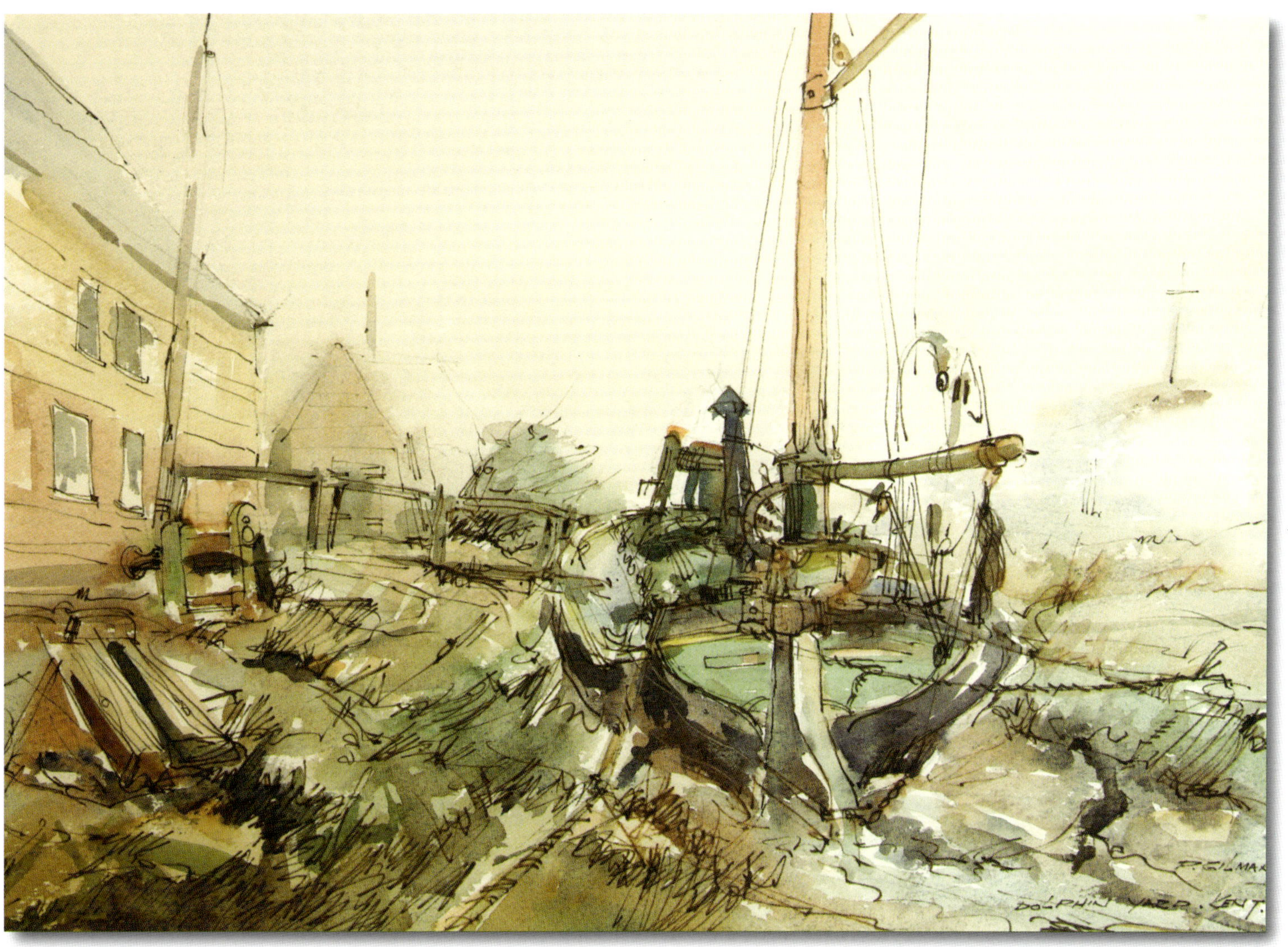

Dolphin Boatyard Kent, 1971. Watercolour 38x30 inches.

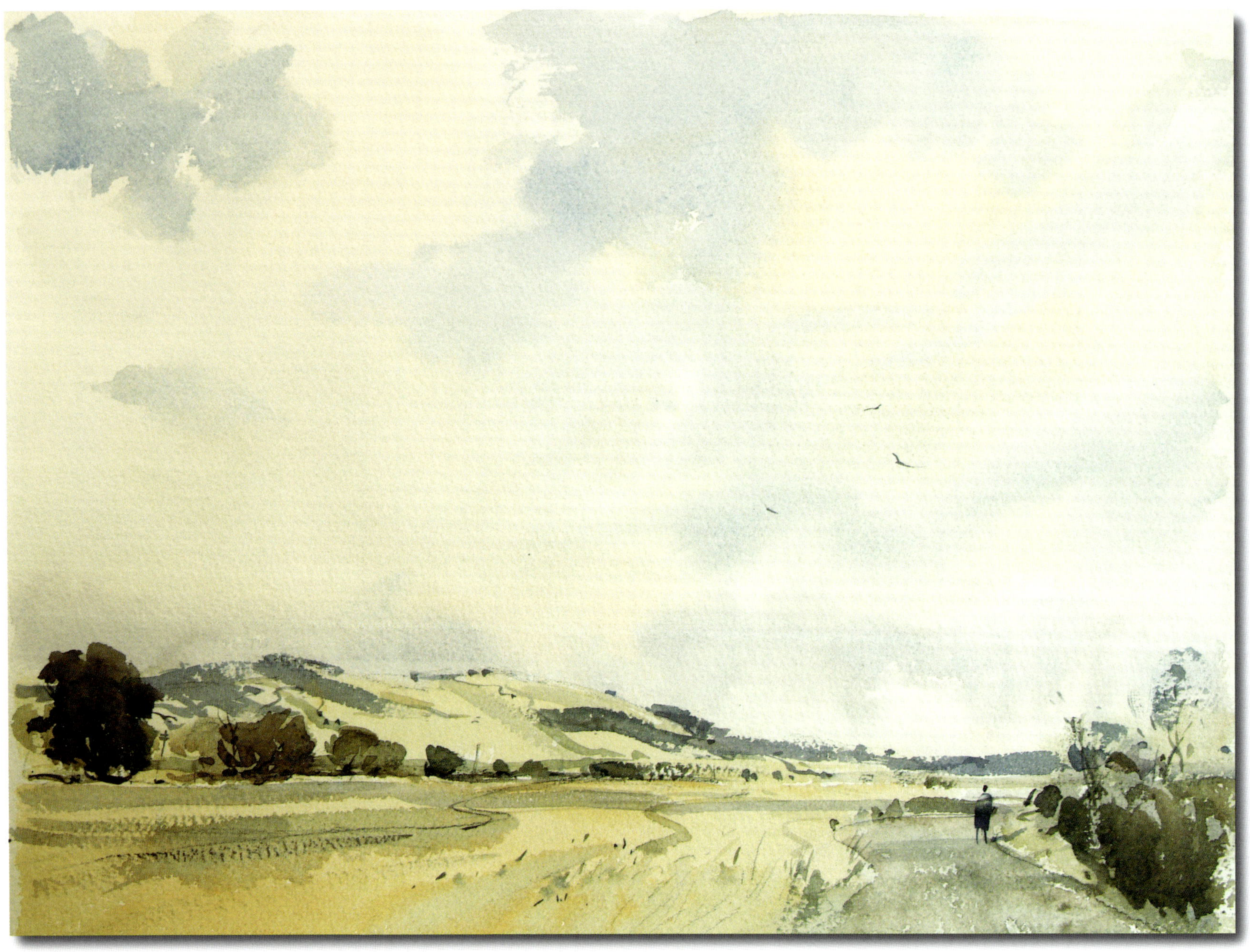

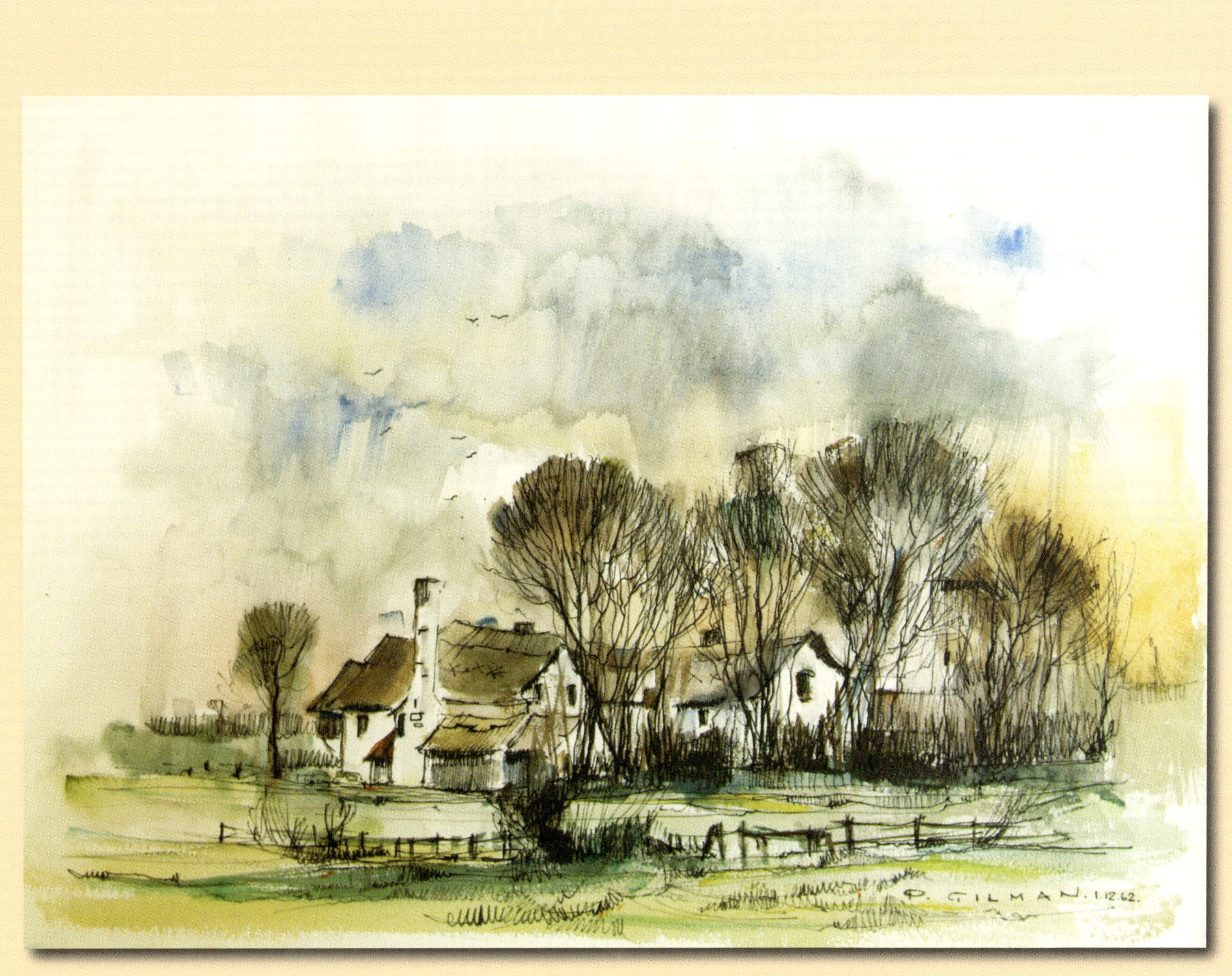

The Thatched Farmhouse. Watercolour and ink 39x28 inches.

Valley Walk. Watercolour and ink 38x30 inches.

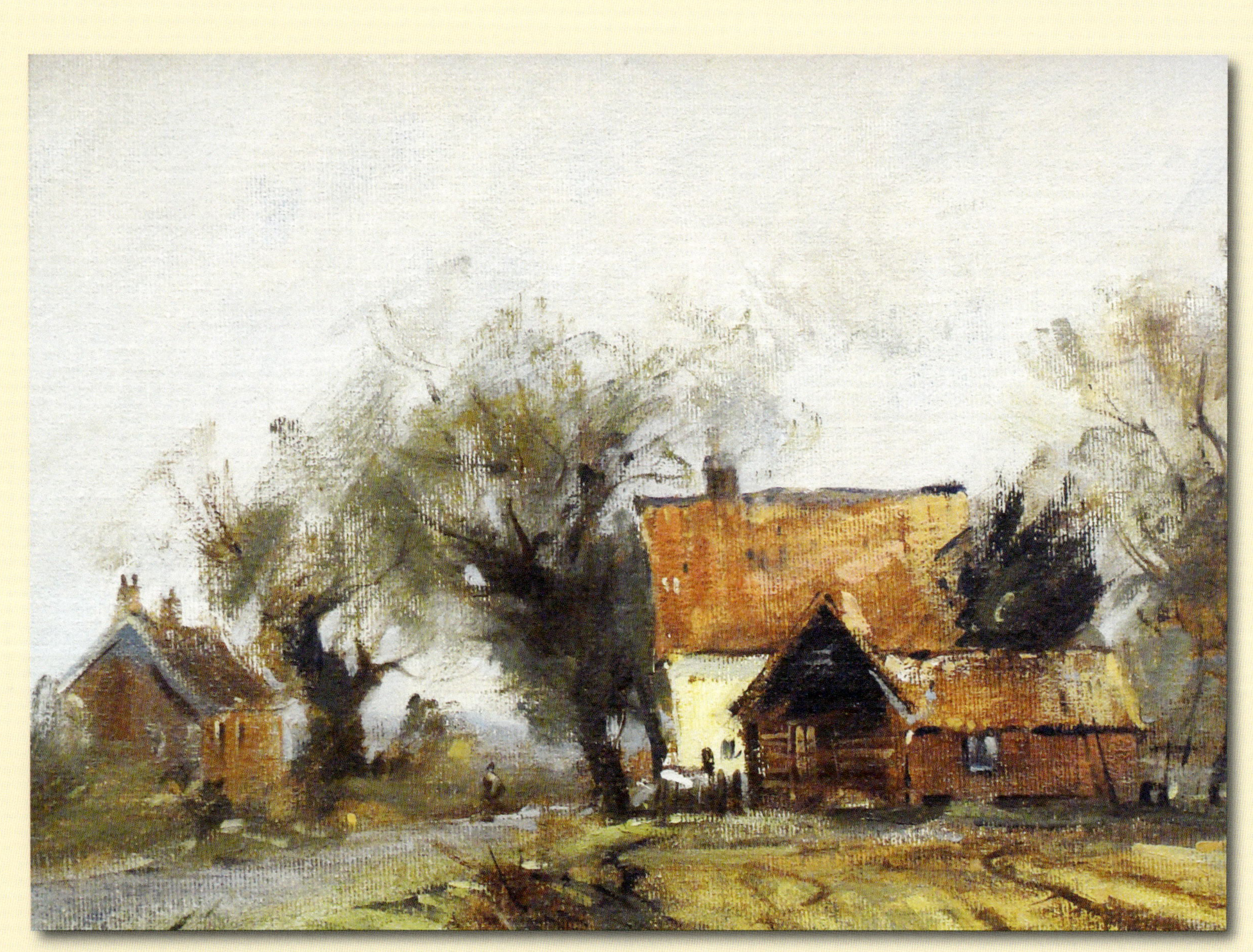

Cottages at Badingham, East Sussex. Oil.

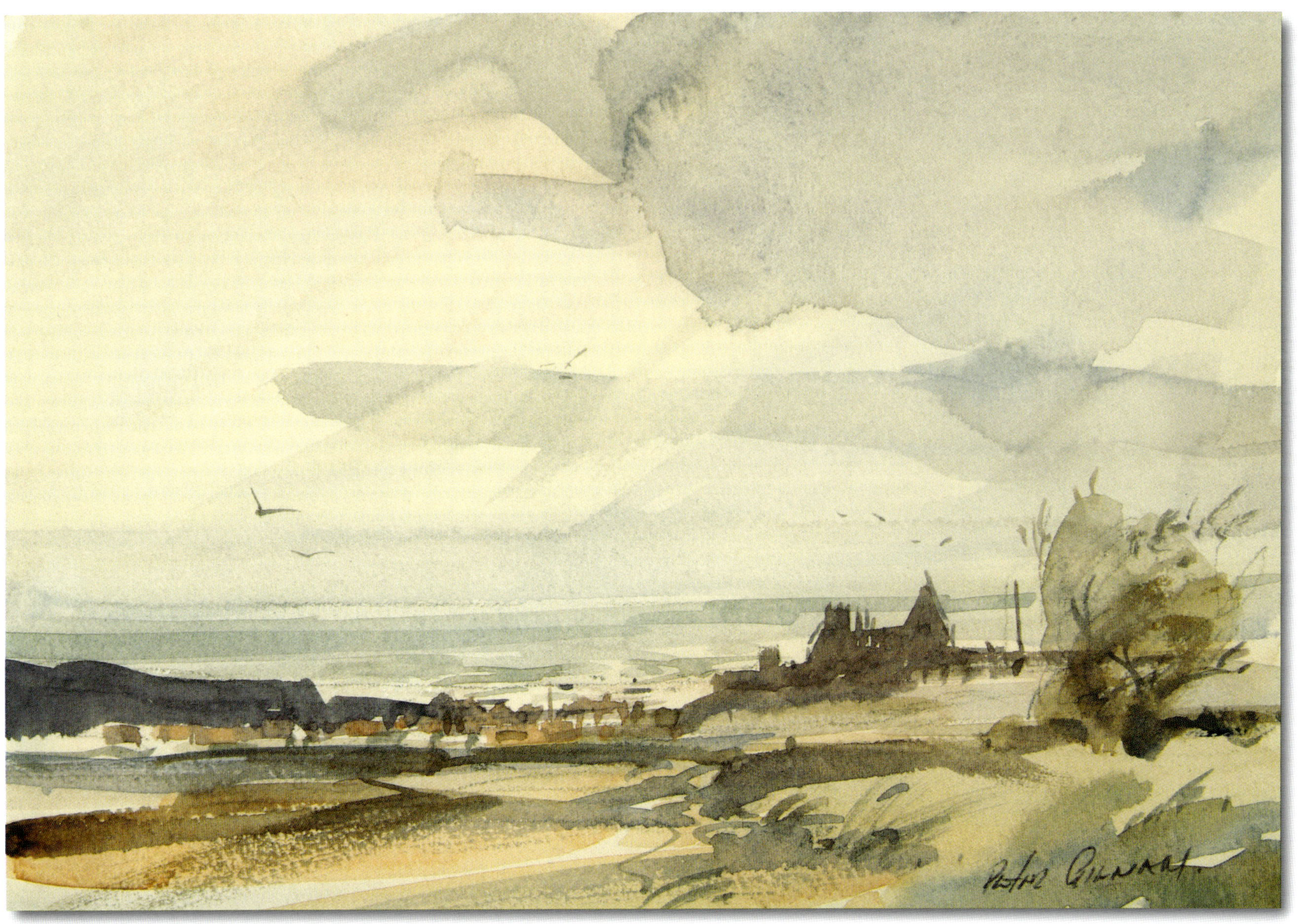

Towards Whitby from Robin Hood Bay, 1981. Watercolour 18x12.5 inches.

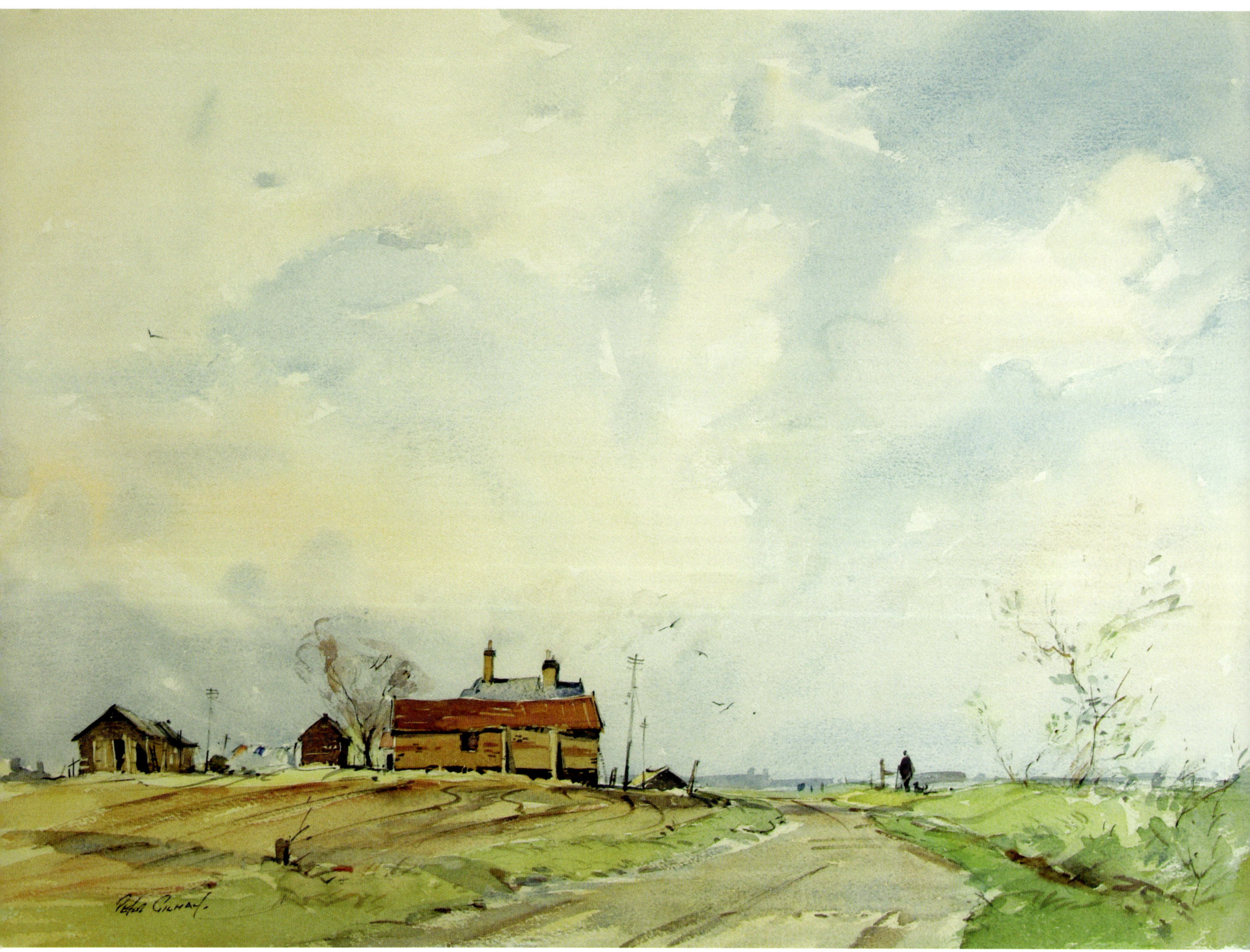

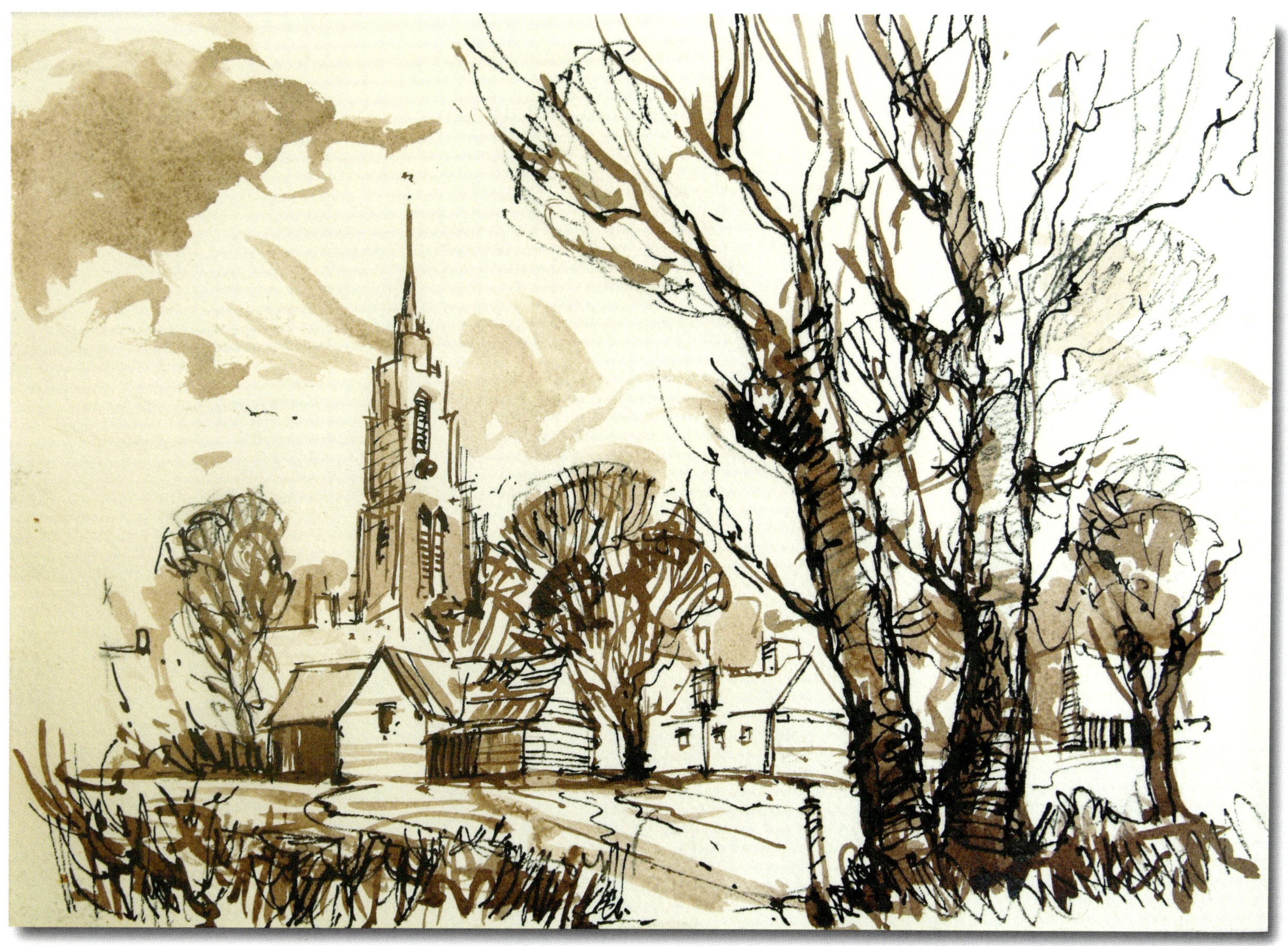

Winter Village. Ink and wash drawing 26x19 inches.

Opposite: April Morning, Blunham Bedfordshire, 1981. Watercolour 69x42 inches.

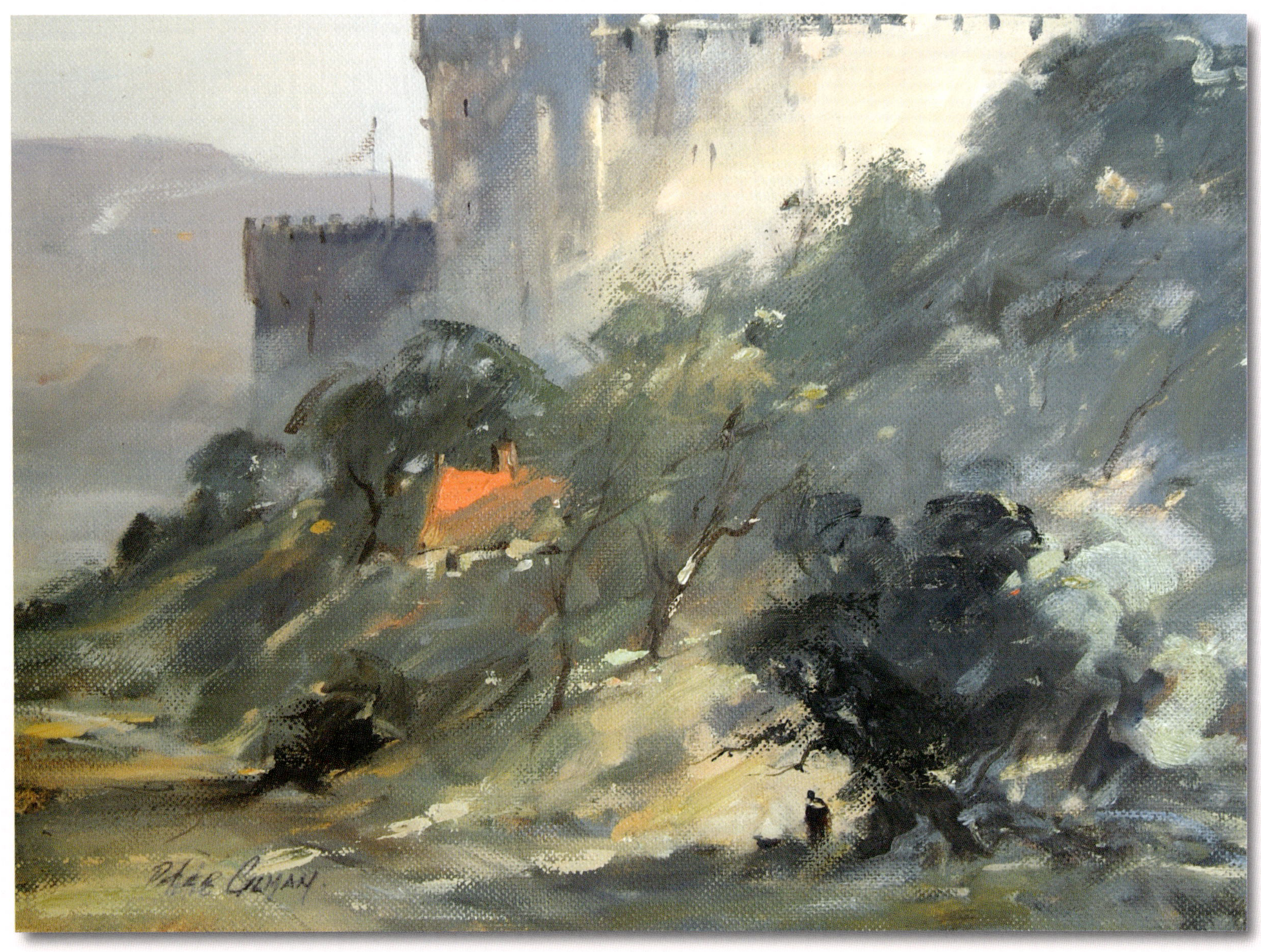

Durham Castle, September 1980. Oil 30x23 inches.

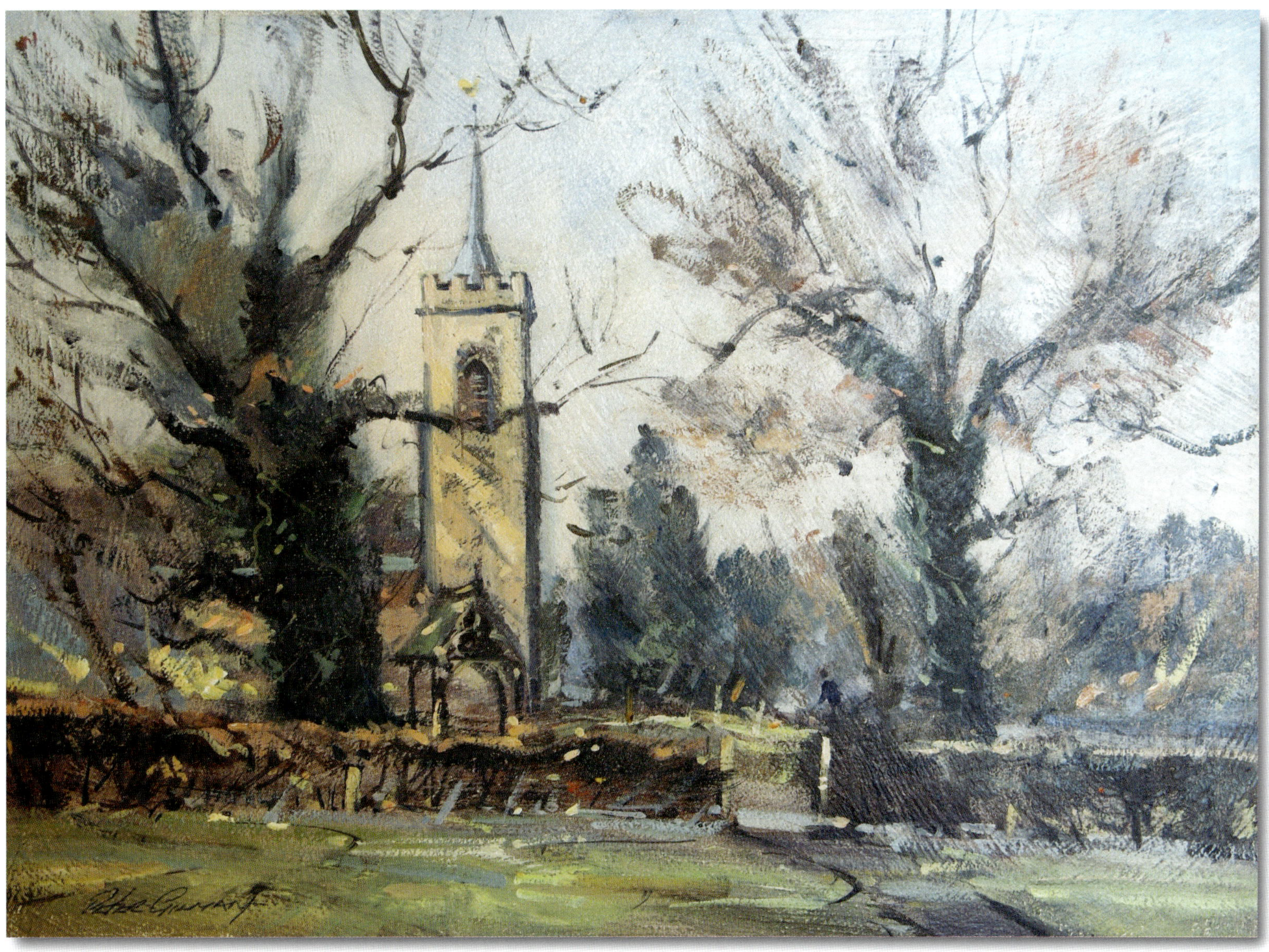

The Country Churchyard. Oil 30x23 inches.

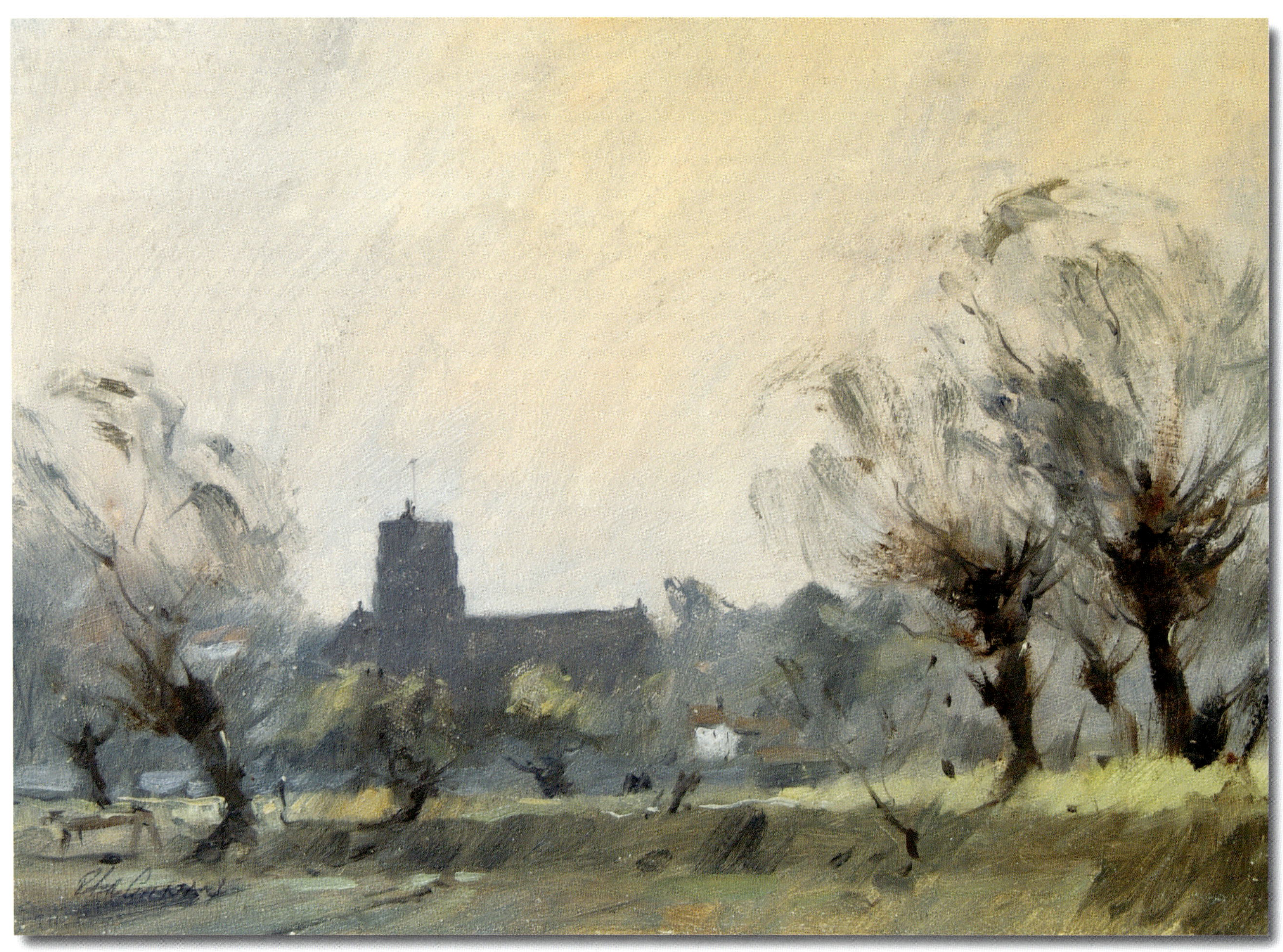

Tolls the Knell of Parting Day. Oil 30x23 inches.

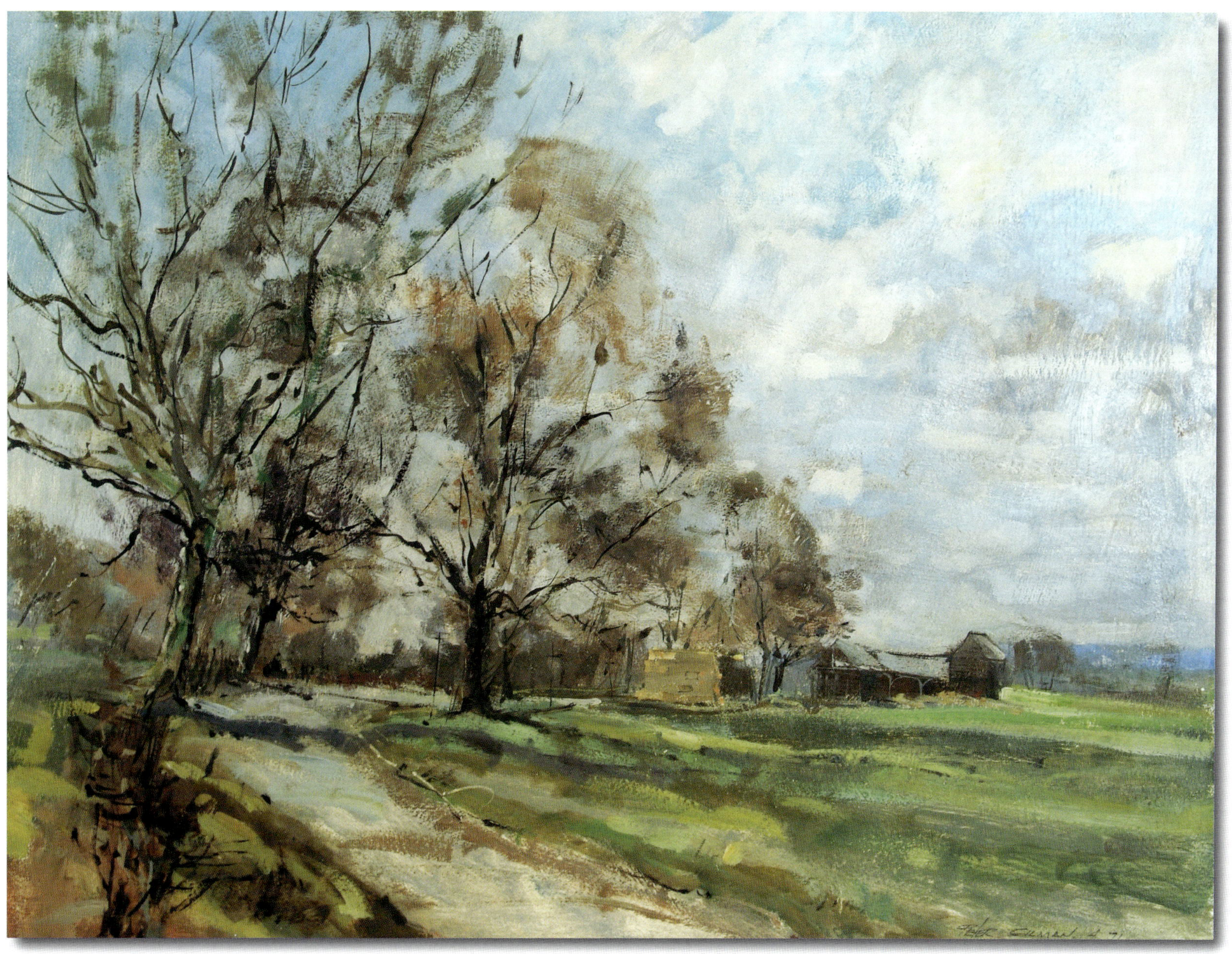

The Old Barn, Ashwell, Hertfordshire. Oil 51x40 inches.

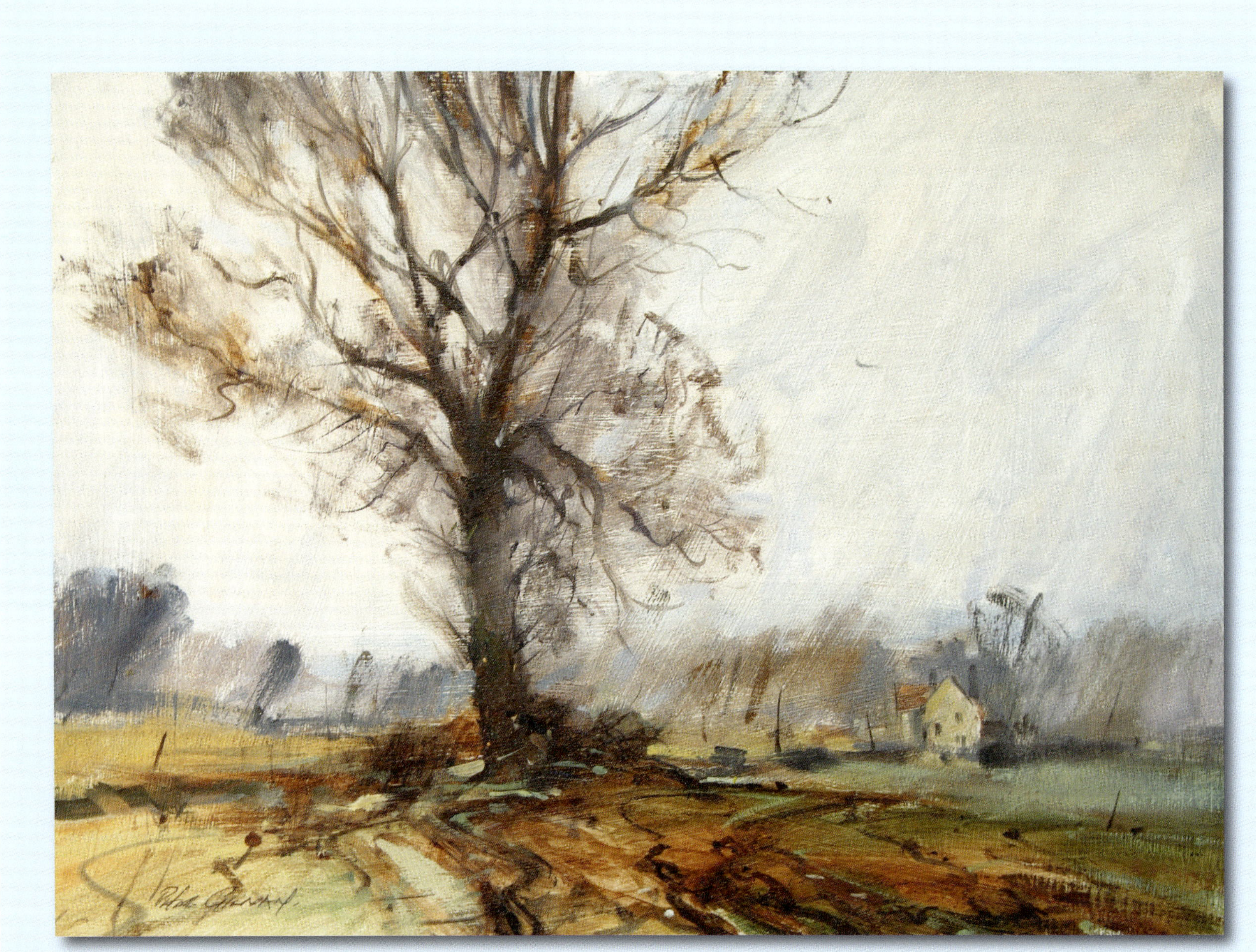

Ancient Elm in Winter. Near Hinxworth, Hertfordshire. Oil 30x22 inches.

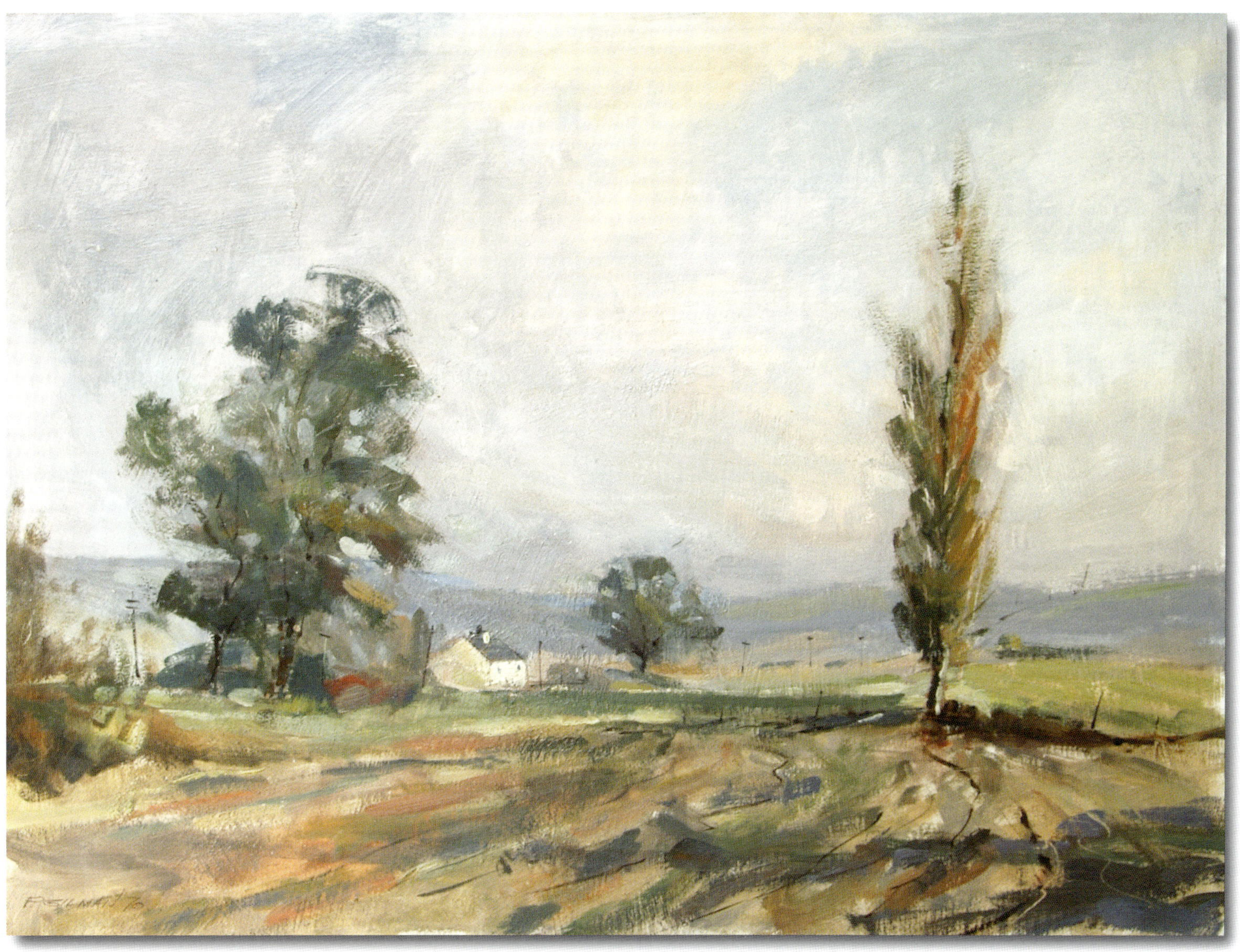

Late Summer, Newnham, Gloucestershire. Oil 51x40 inches.

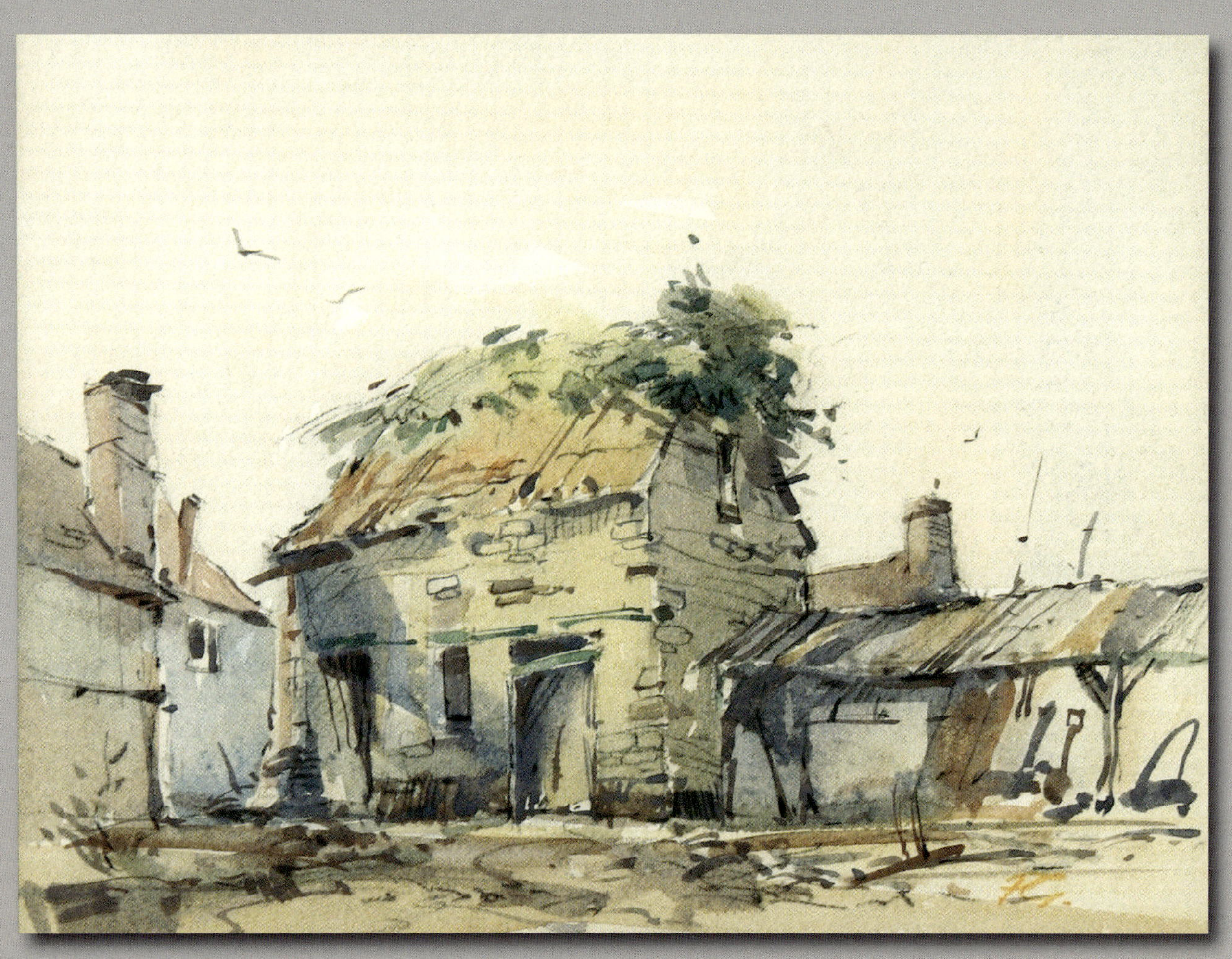

Ruins of the Old Surgery, Ashwell, Hertfordshire. Watercolour 14x11 inches.

Opposite: Bear House, Ashwell, Hertfordshire. Watercolour 38x28 inches.

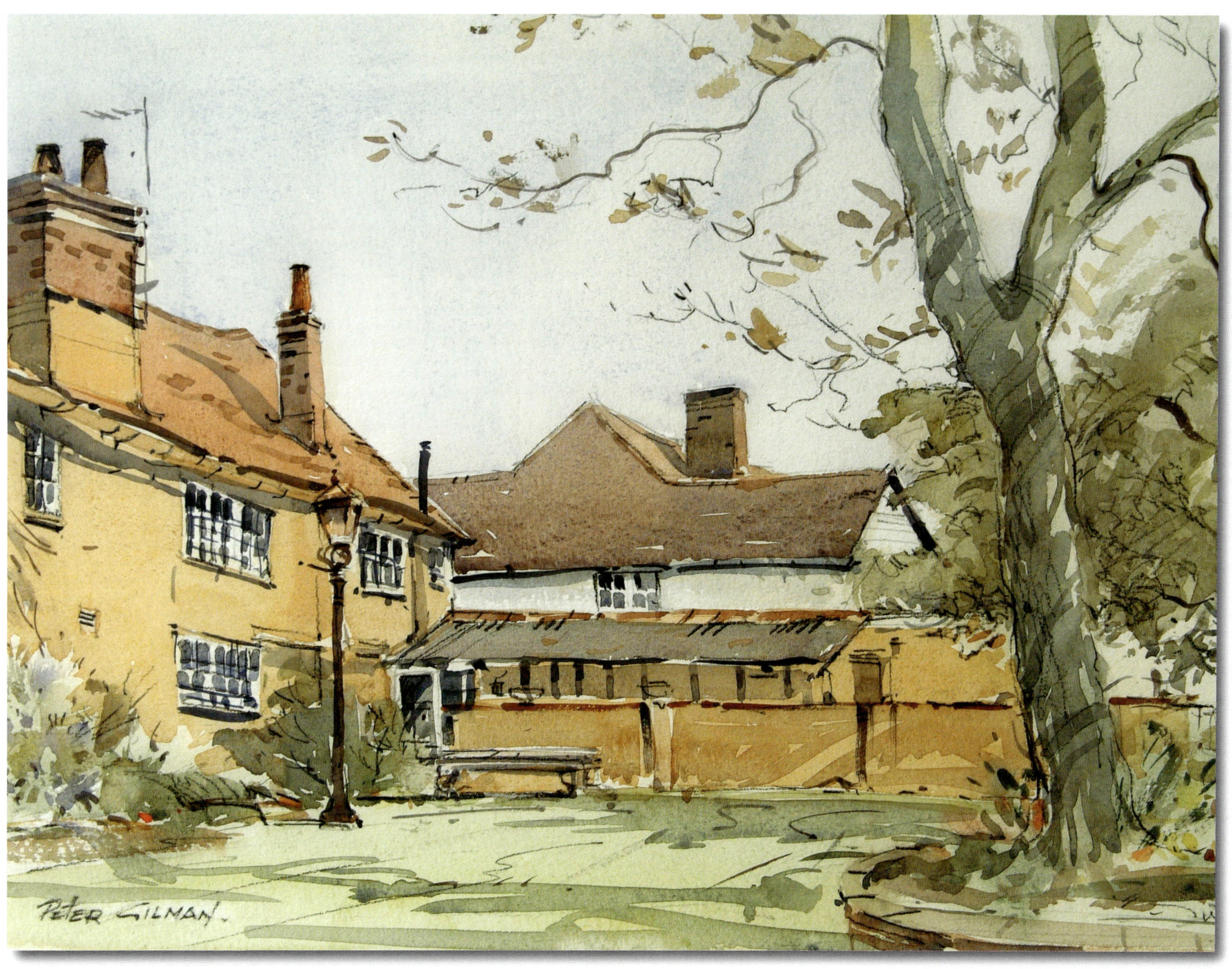

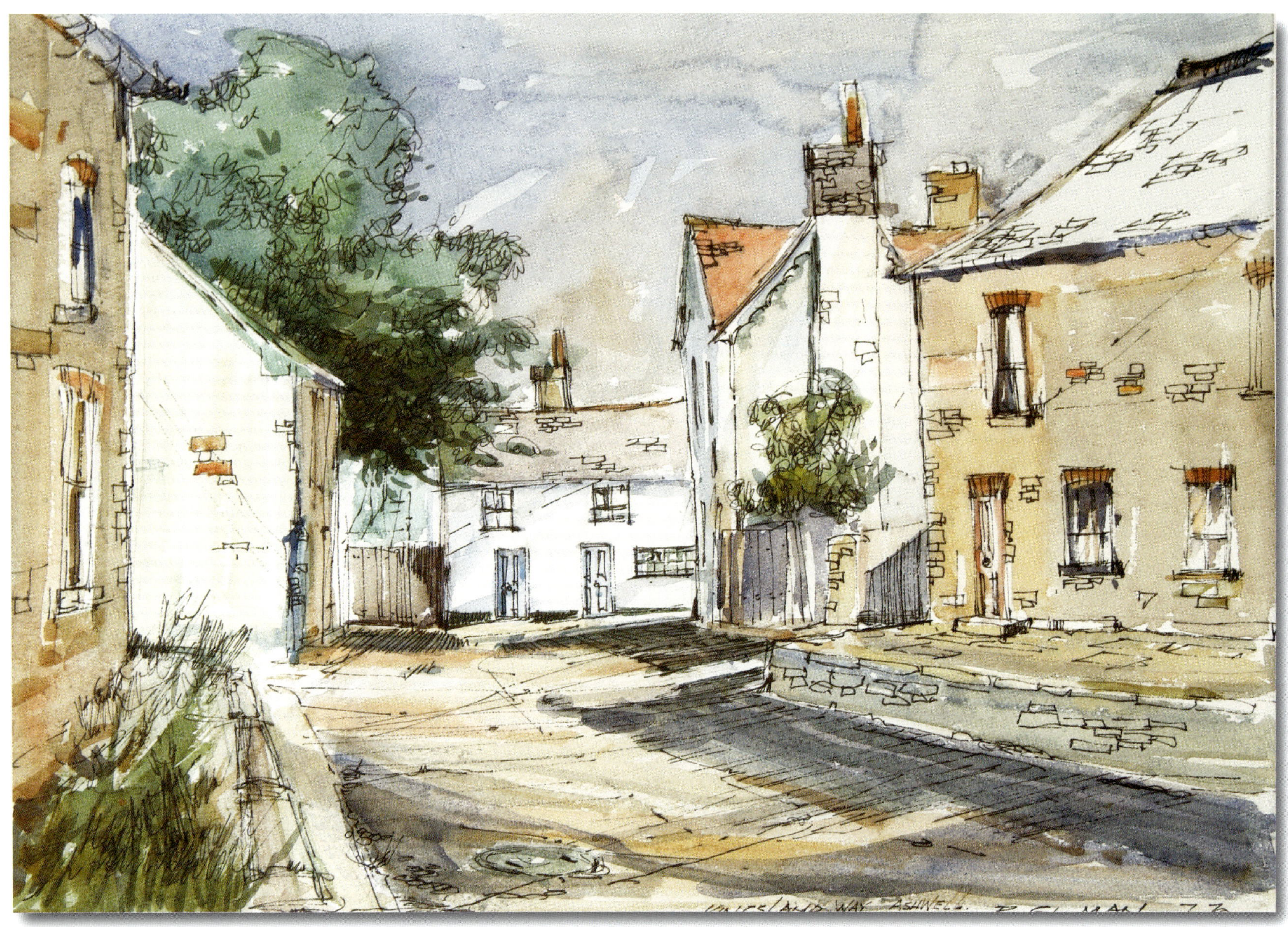

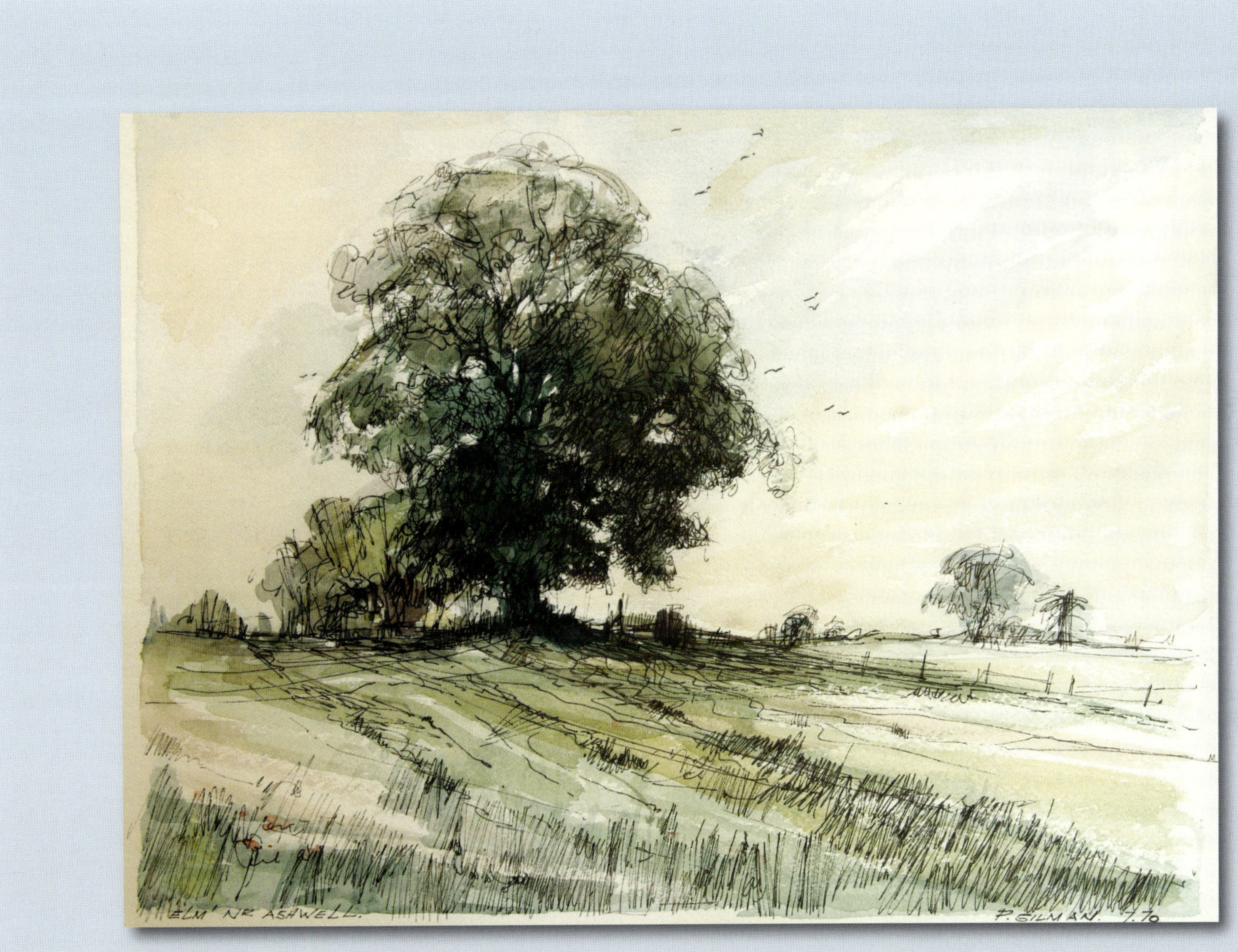

In Full Leaf. Watercolour and ink 33x27 inches.

Opposite: Kingsland Way, Ashwell, Hertfordshire. Watercolour 33x27 inches.

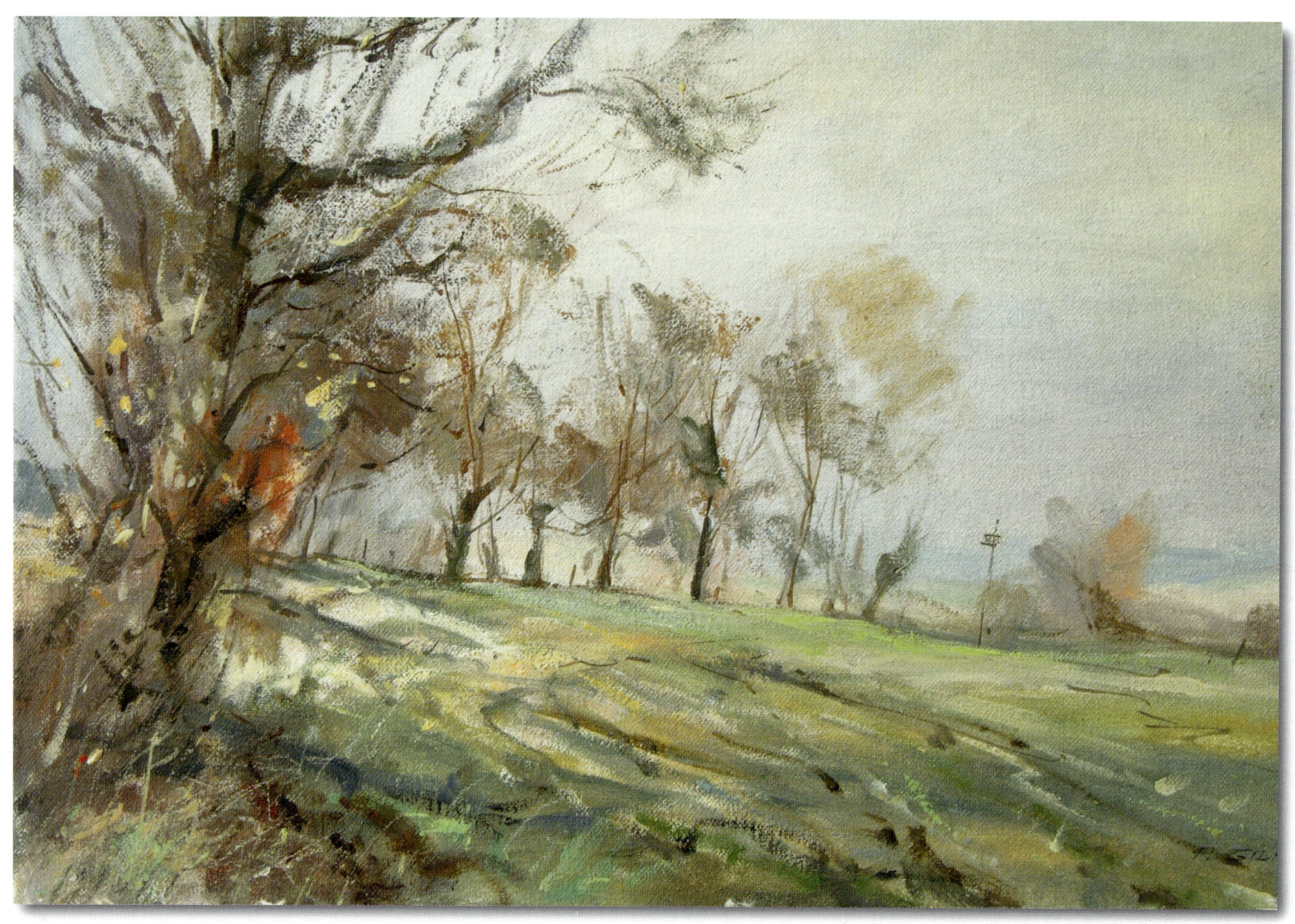

Morden Road, Ashwell, Hertfordshire, 1976. Oil 36x26 inches.

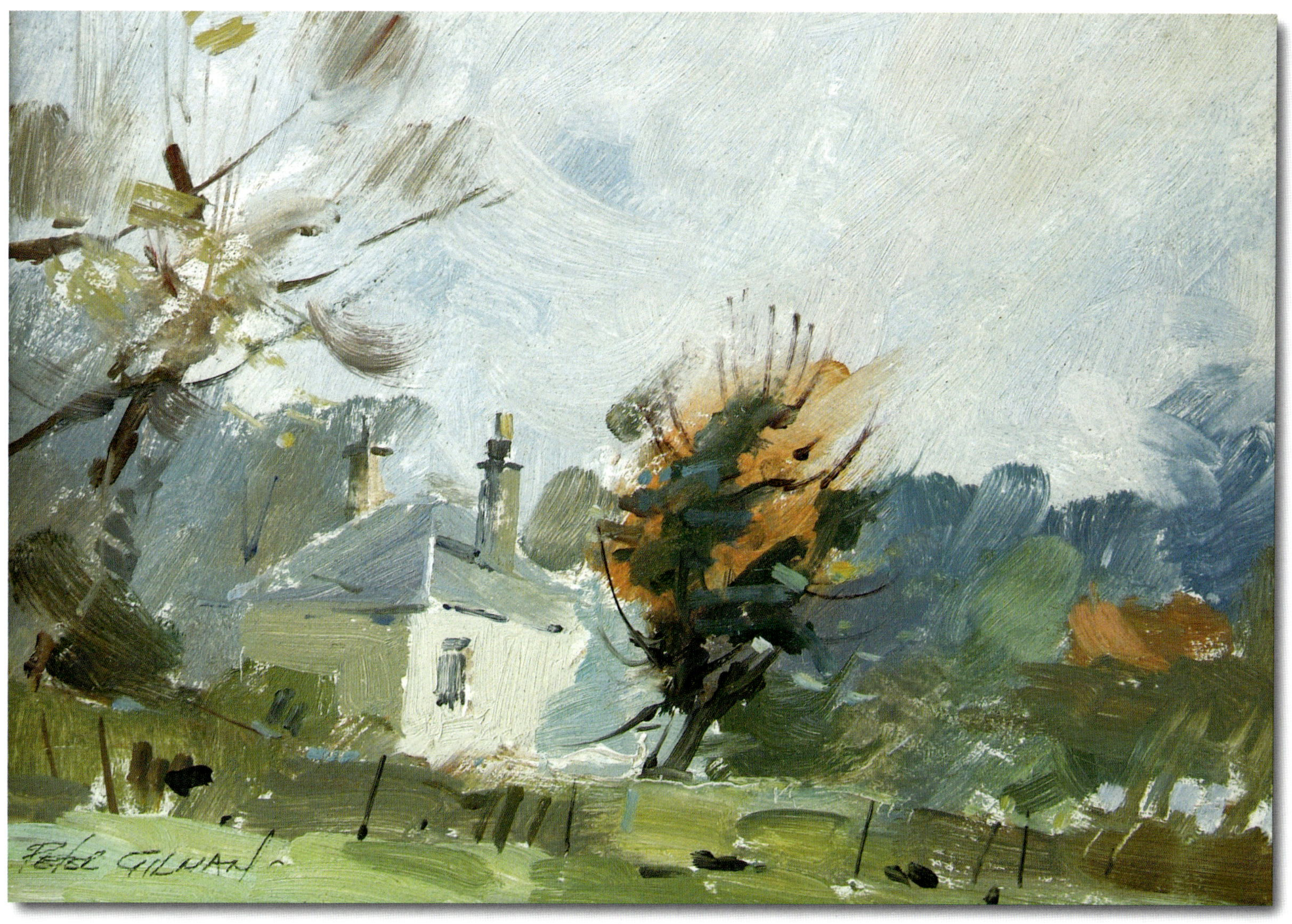

Near Ringstead, Ashwell, Hertfordshire, 1974. Oil 20x15 inches.

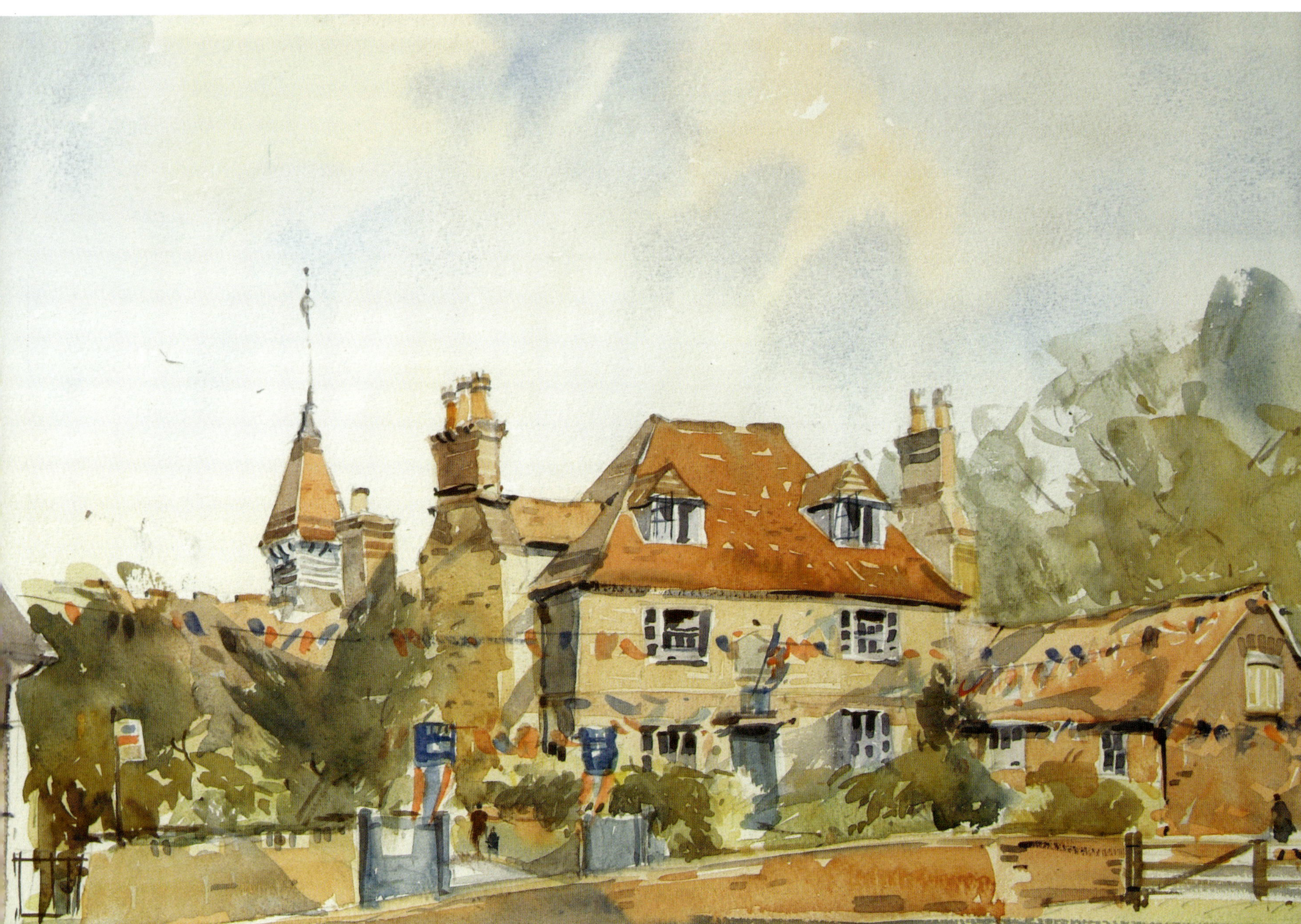

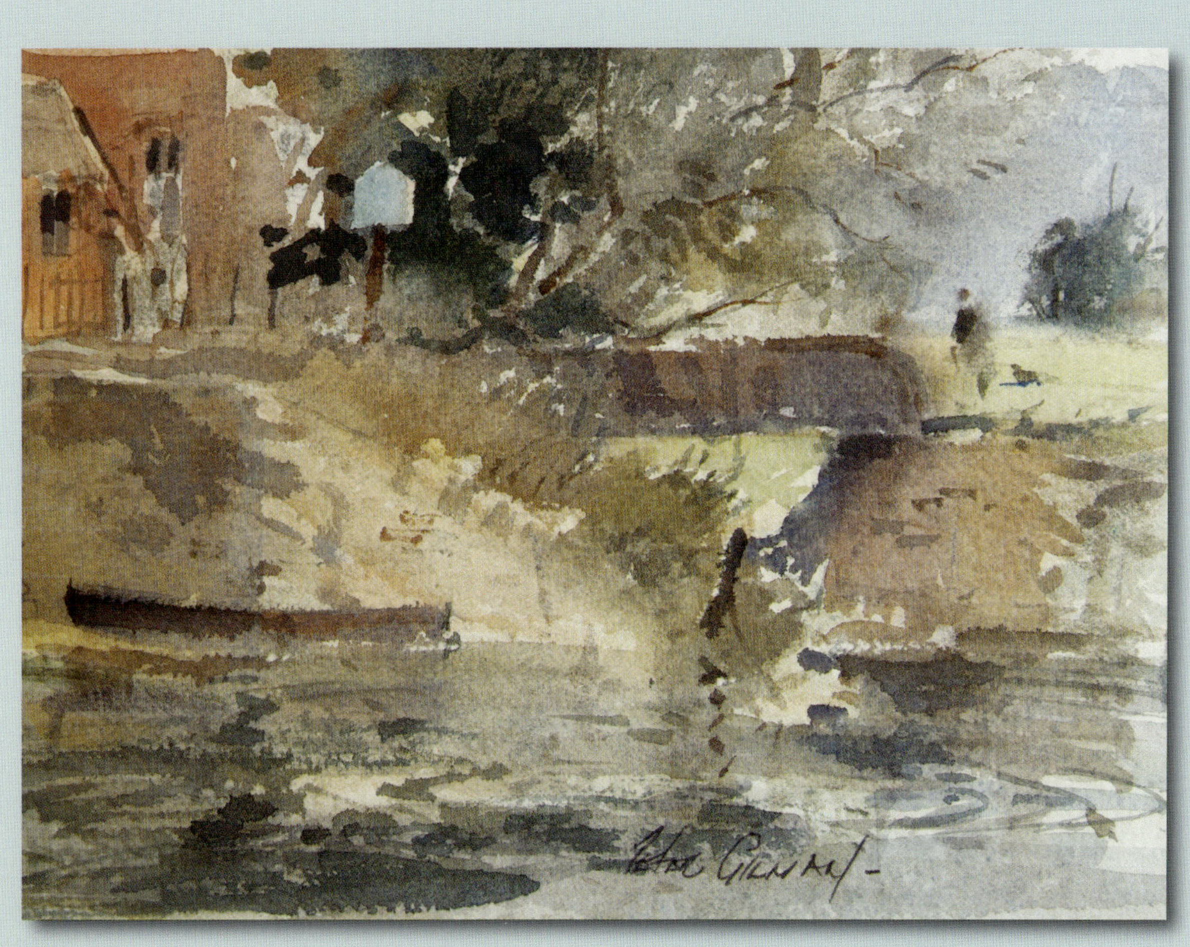

Hertford Lock, Summer Evening, Hertfordshire, 1980. Watercolour 17x13 inches.

Opposite: Kingsland Way, Ashwell, Hertfordshire. Watercolour 33x27 inches.

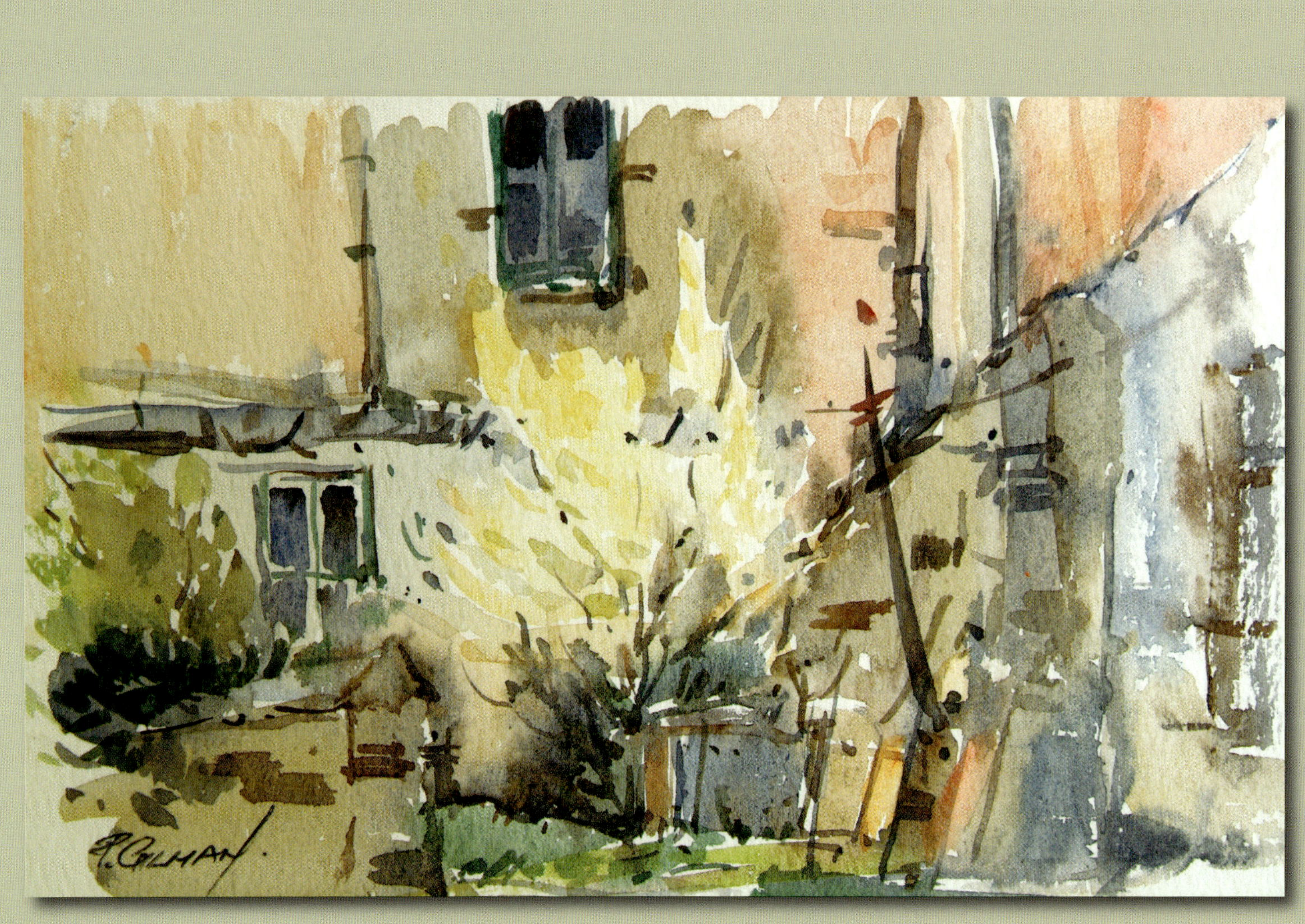

Spring Morning, Silver Street, Ashwell, Hertfordshire. Watercolour 33x27 inches.

Opposite: The Red Barn. Oil 5lx40.

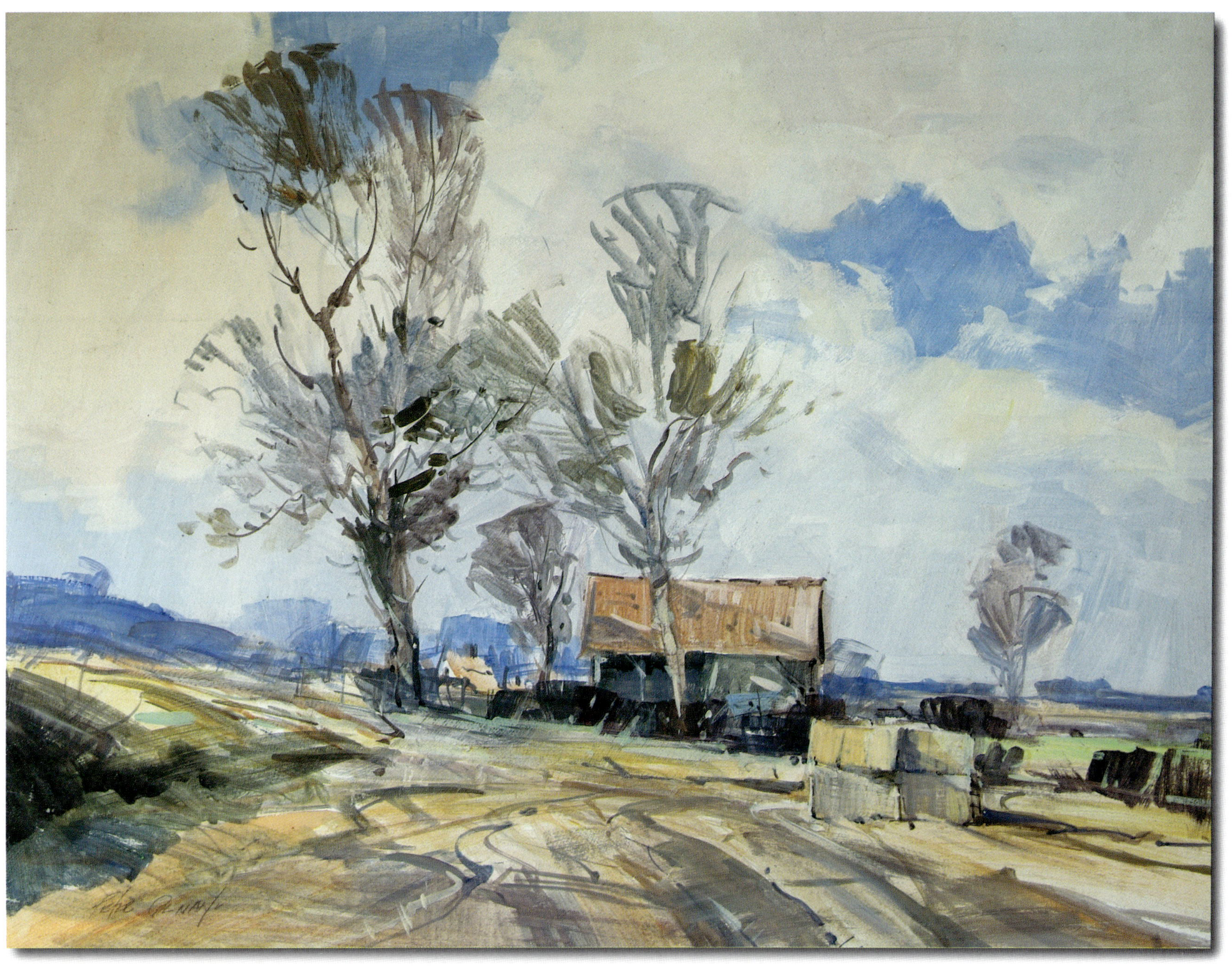

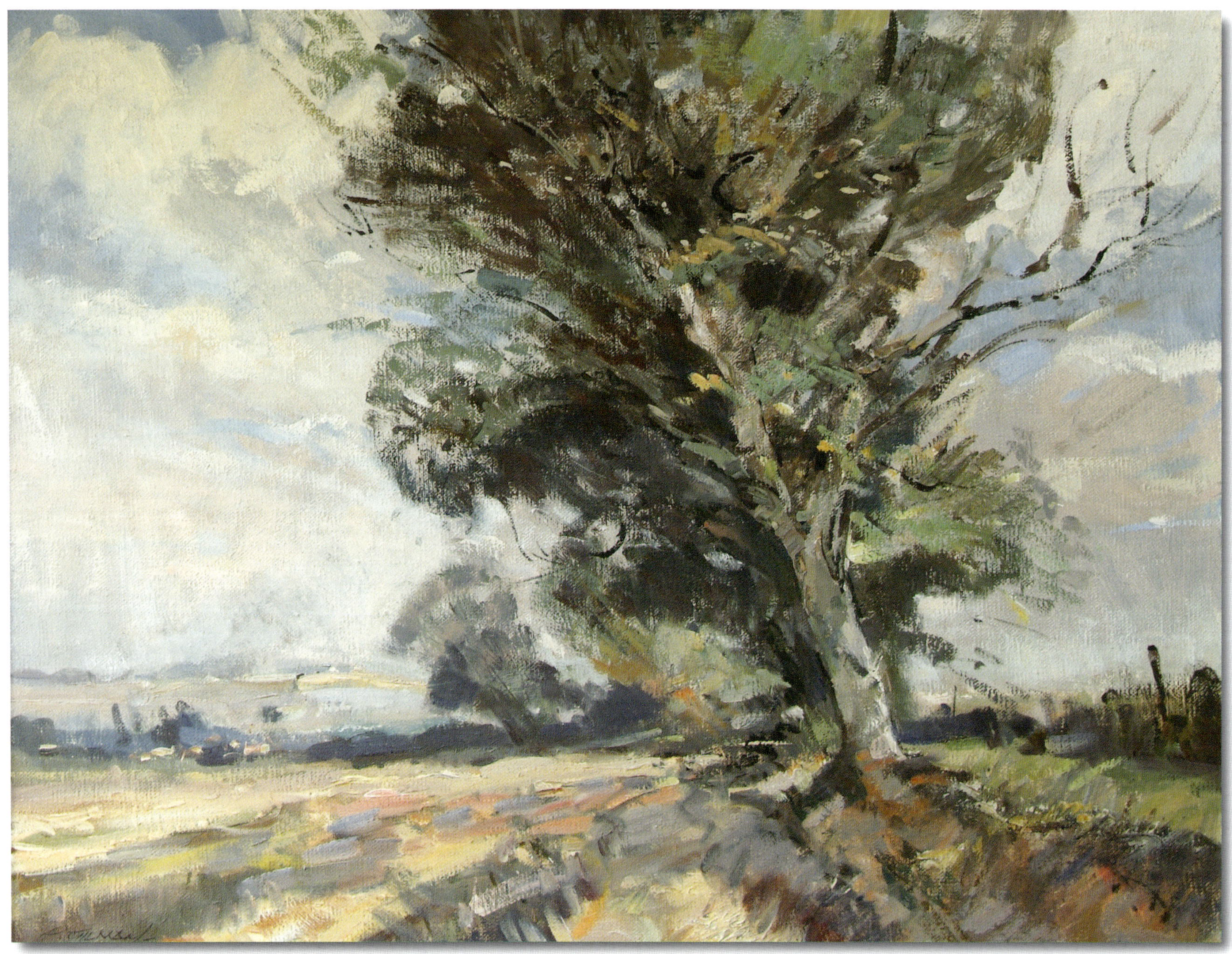

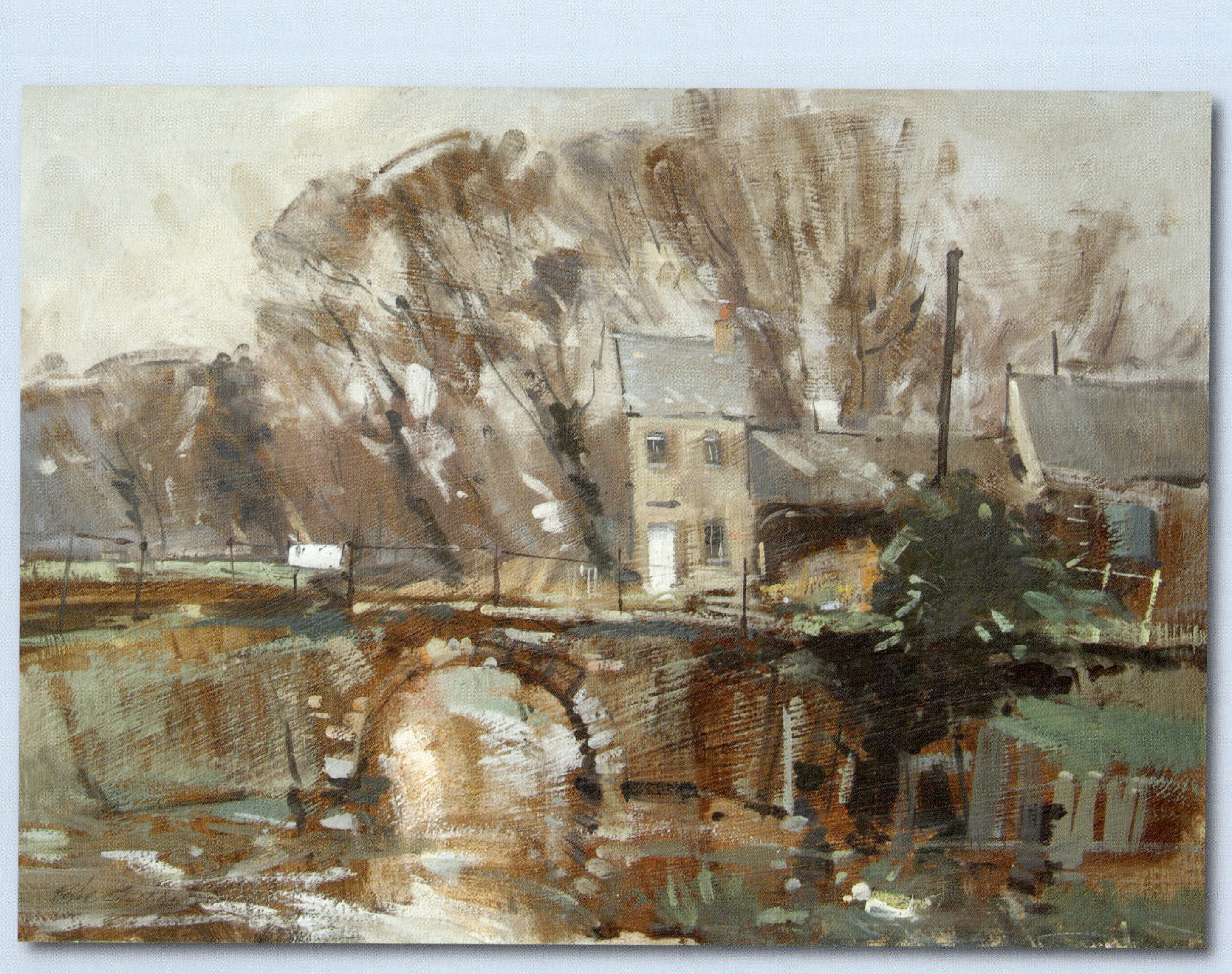

Tempsford, Bedfordshire. Oil 41x30 inches.

Opposite: Ashwell Elms, Hertfordshire. Oil 50x40 inches.

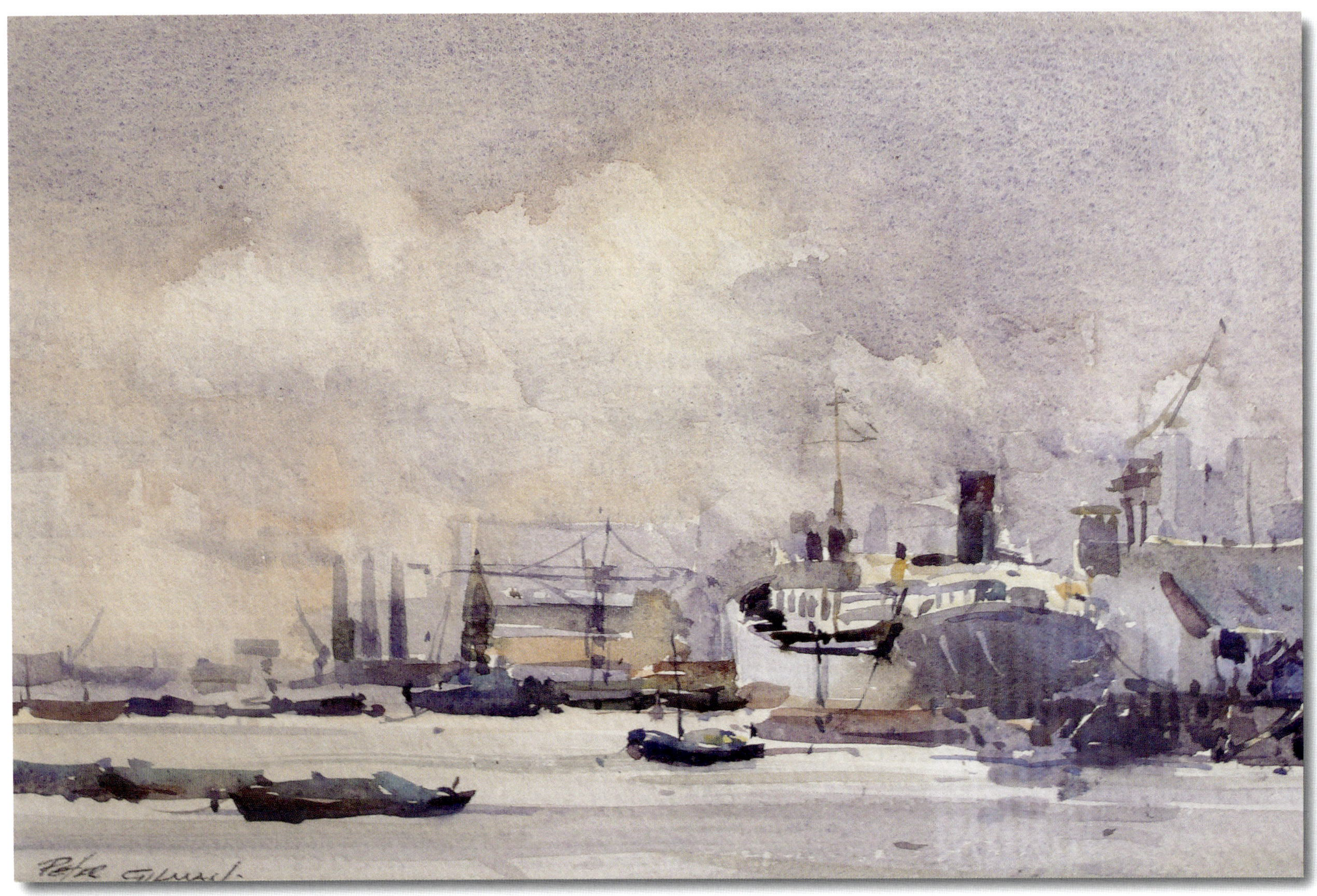

Scene on the River Thames. Watercolour. (John Stillman Collection)

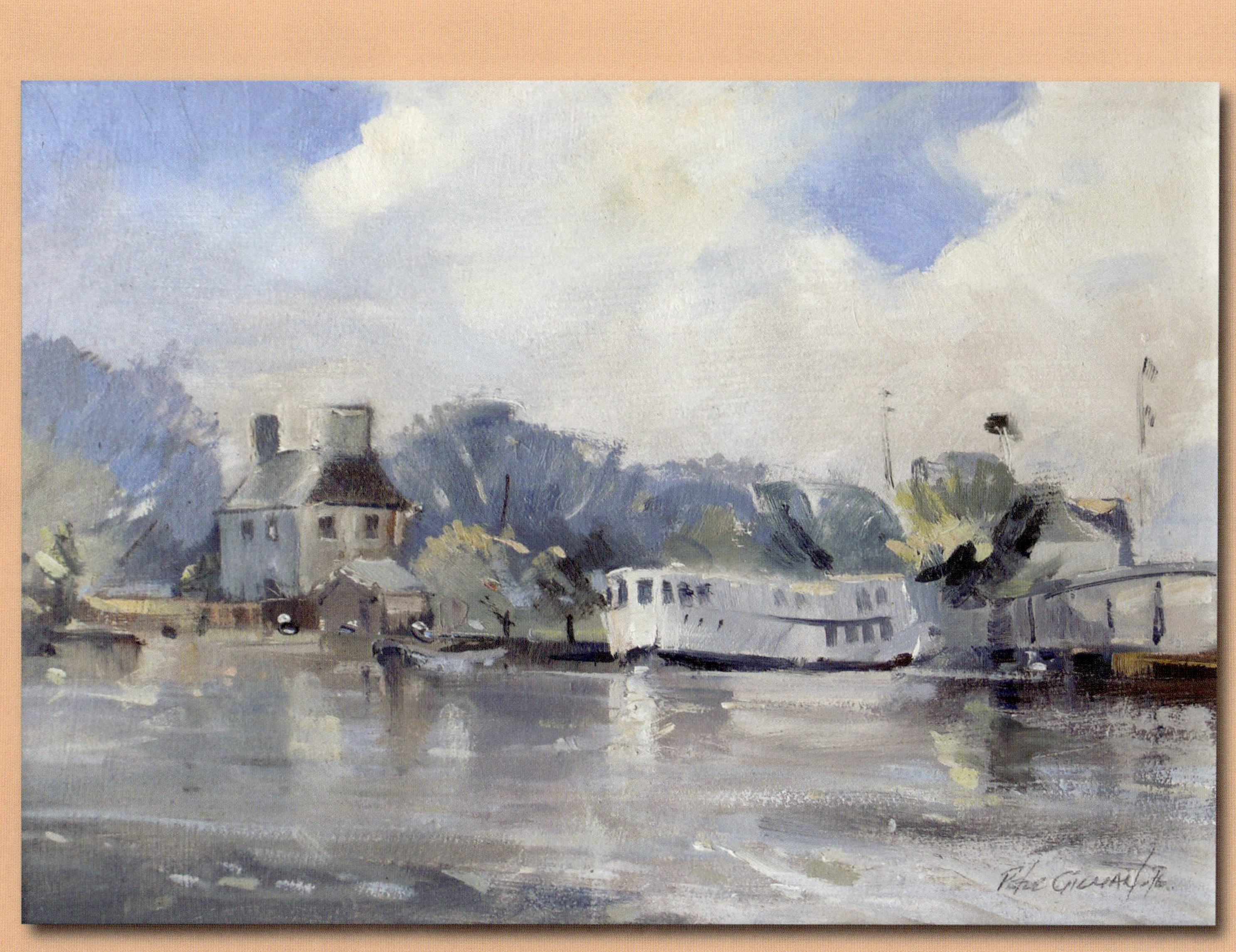

Thames Pleasure Cruise Boat, lying up. Oil. (John Stillman Collection)

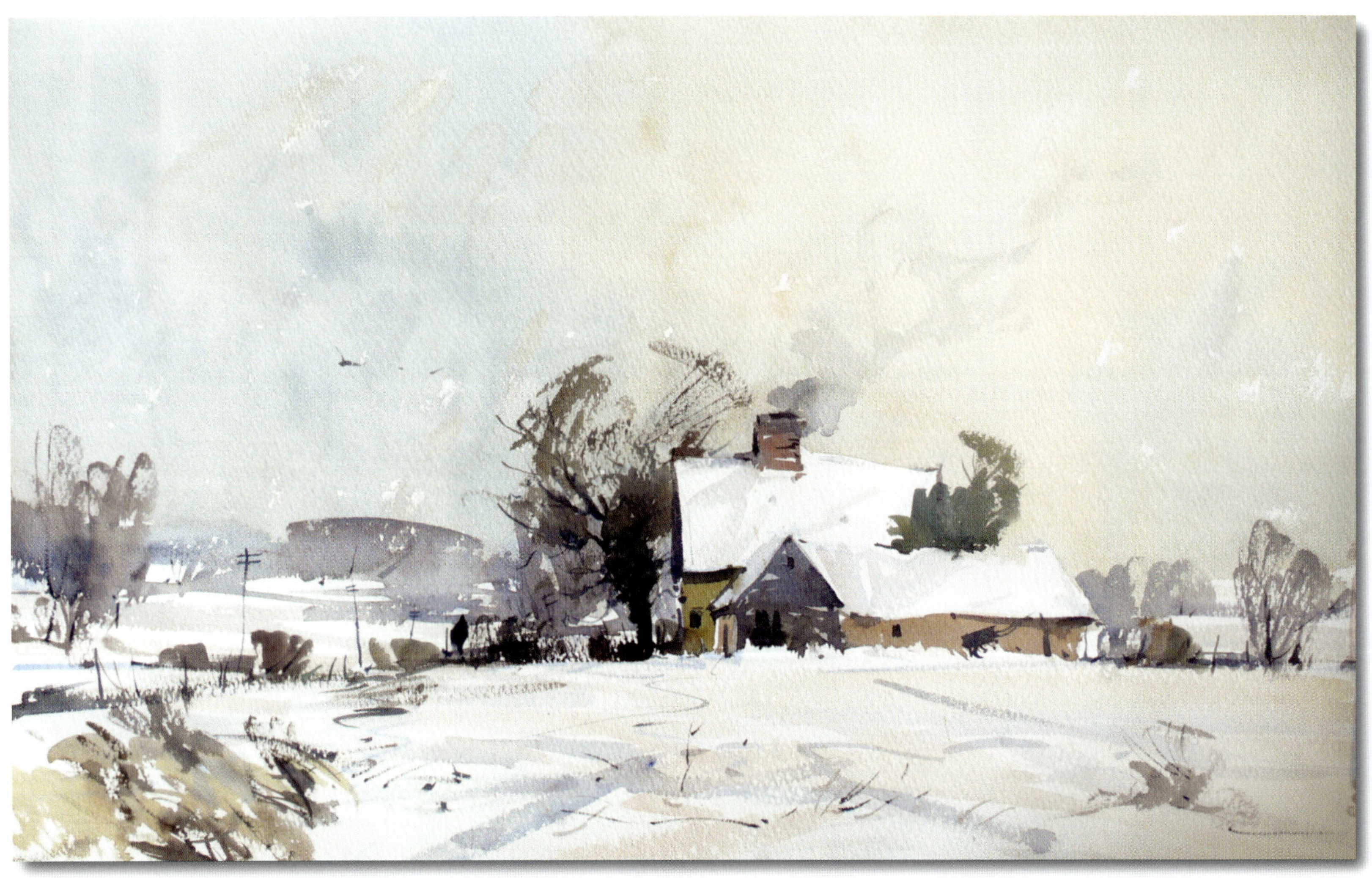

Cottage in Snow. Watercolour. (John Stillman Collection)

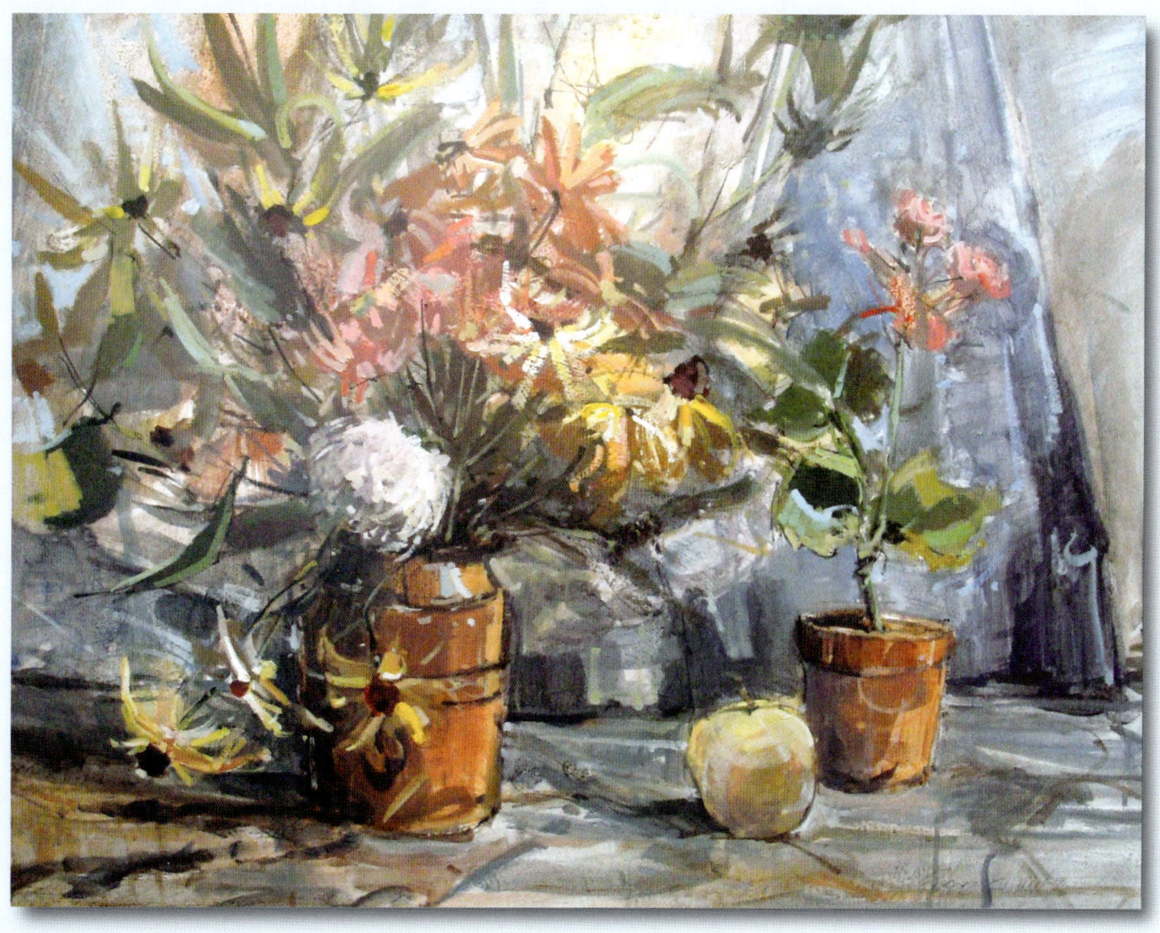

Still Life with Flowers. Oil.

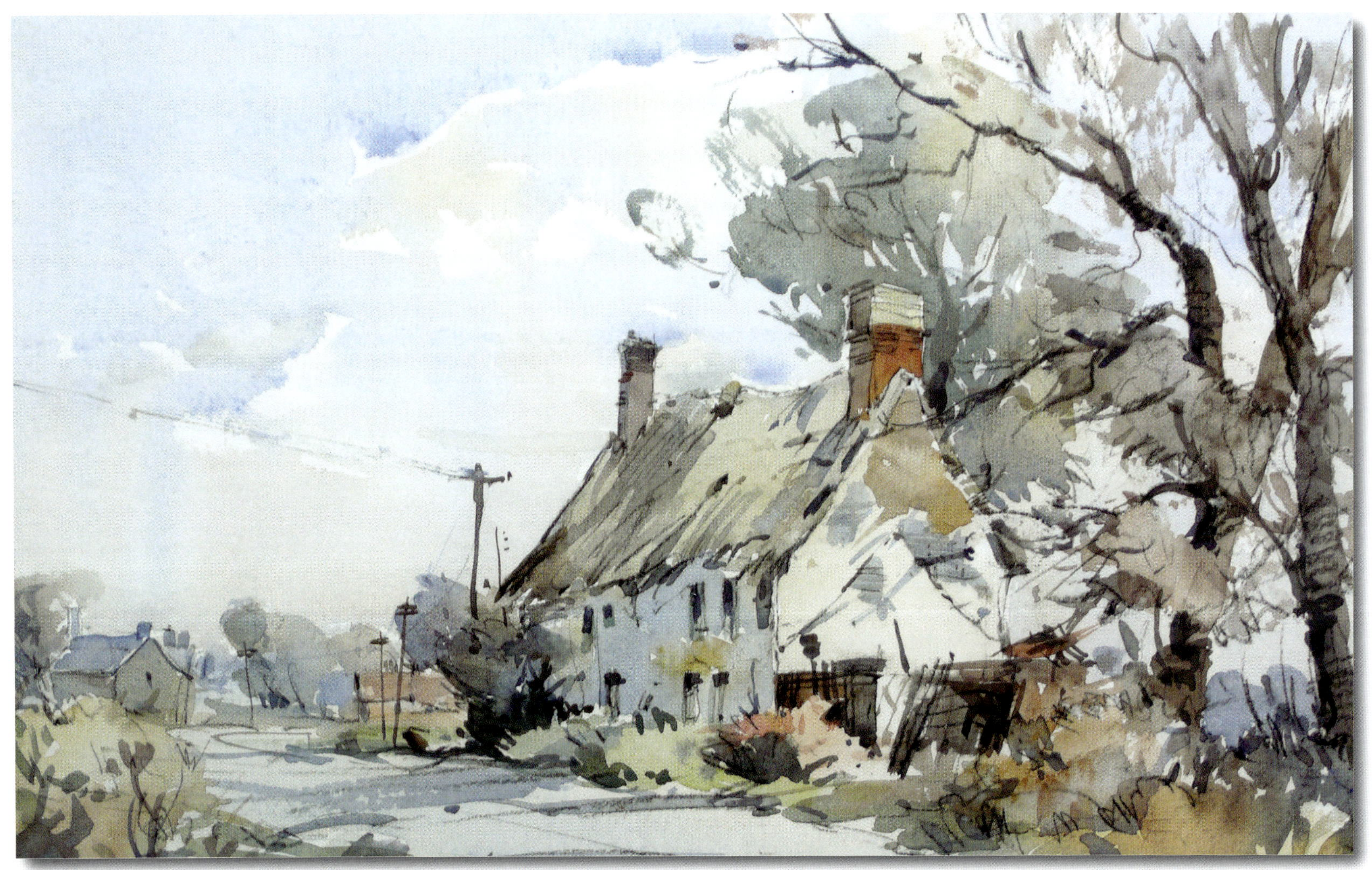

Old Cottage near Guilden Morden, Hertfordshire. Watercolour (John Stillman Collection).

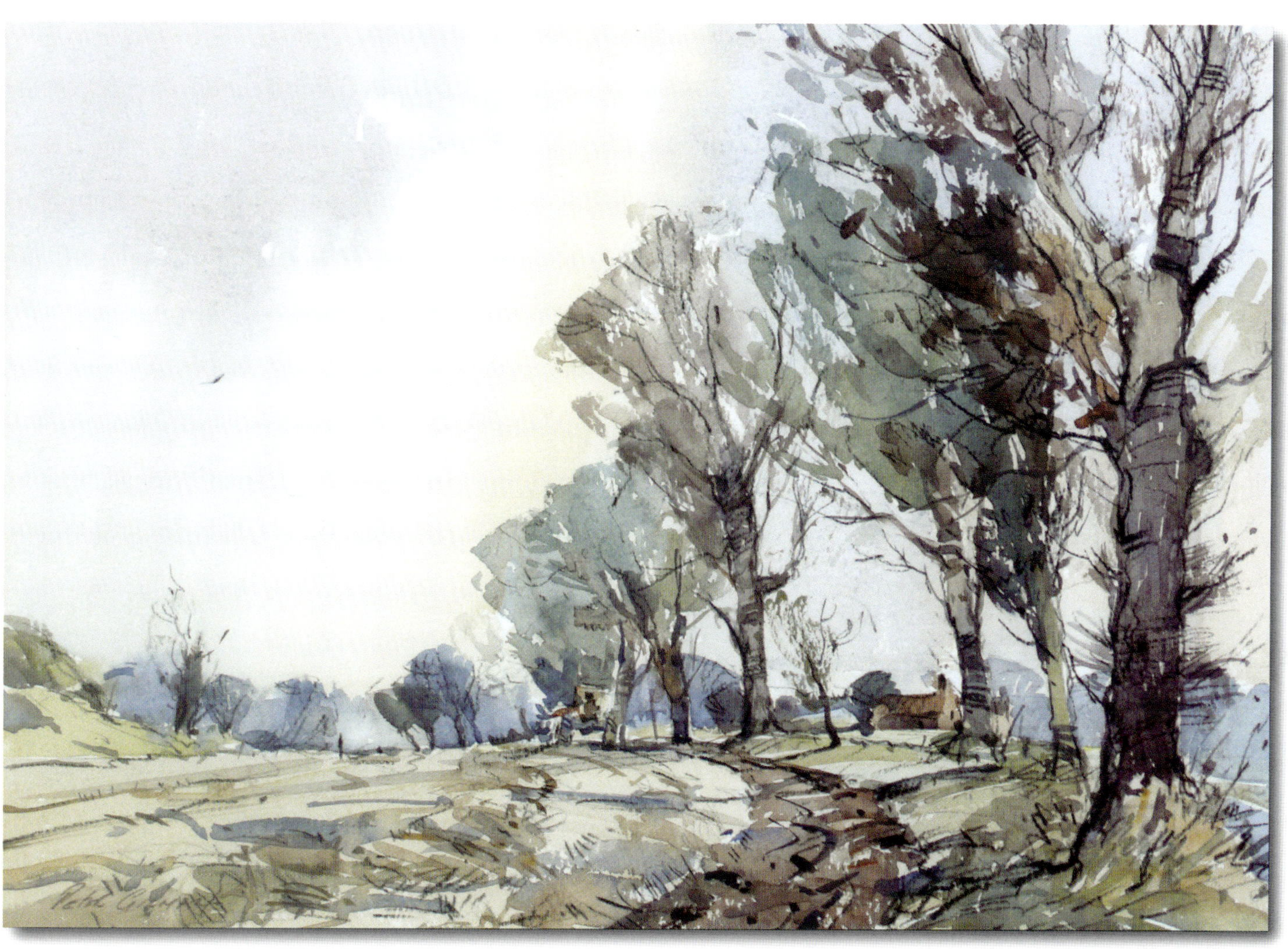

Turning in the Stubble, Hammer Hill, Bedfordshire. Watercolour. (John Stillman Collection)

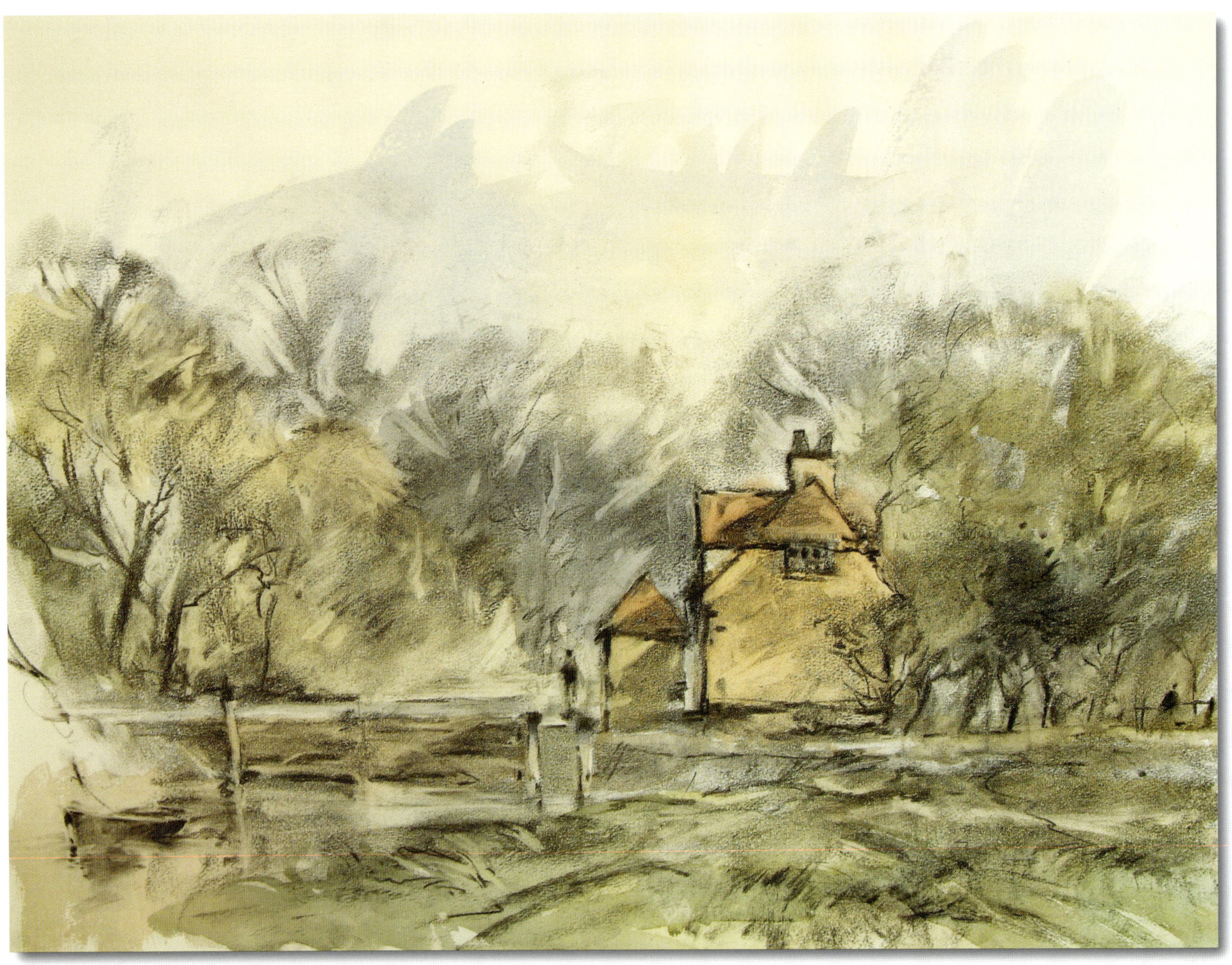

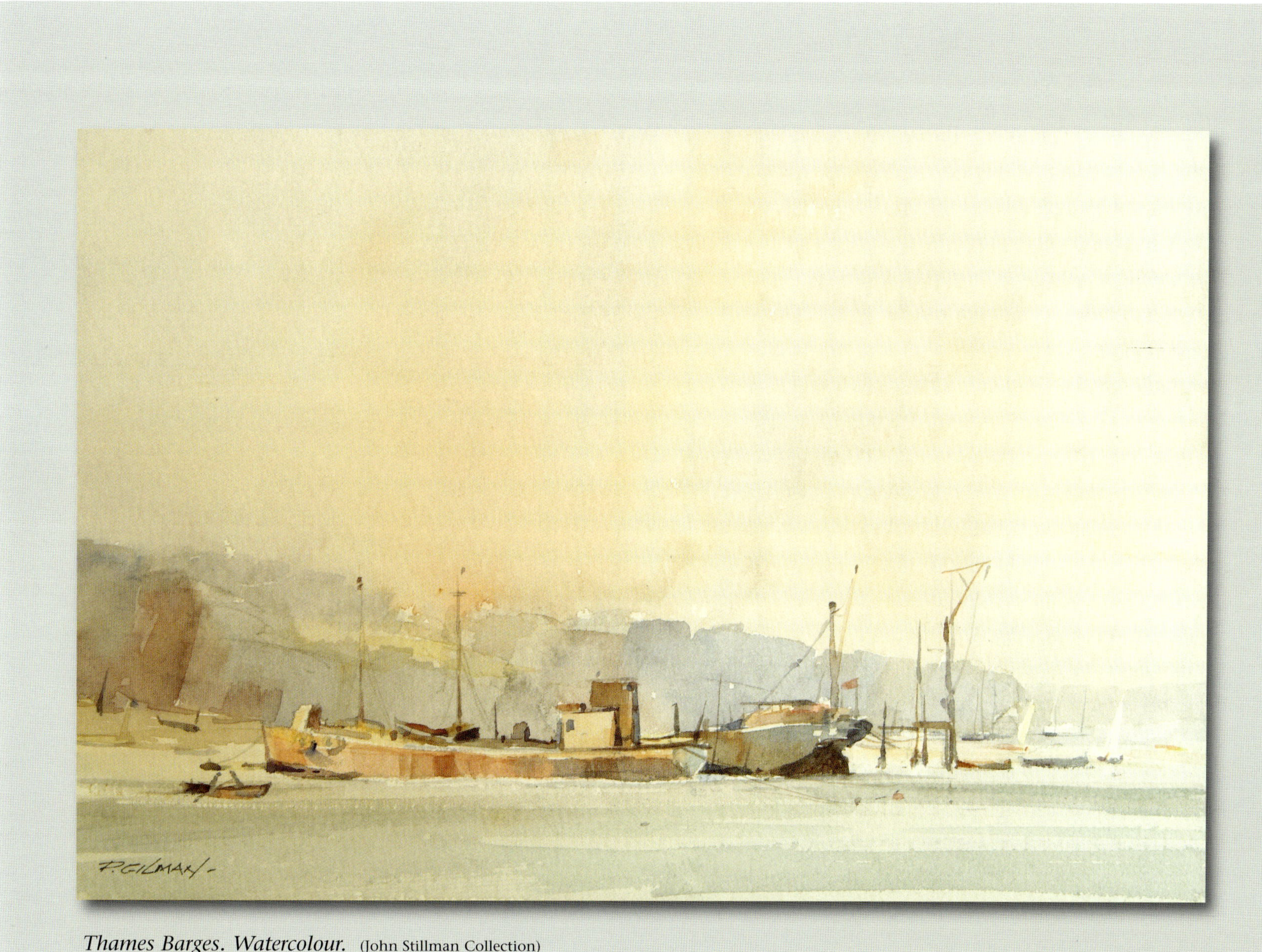

Thames Barges. Watercolour. (John Stillman Collection)

Opposite: The Lock-keepers Cottage. Watercolour and charcoal. (John Stillman Collection)

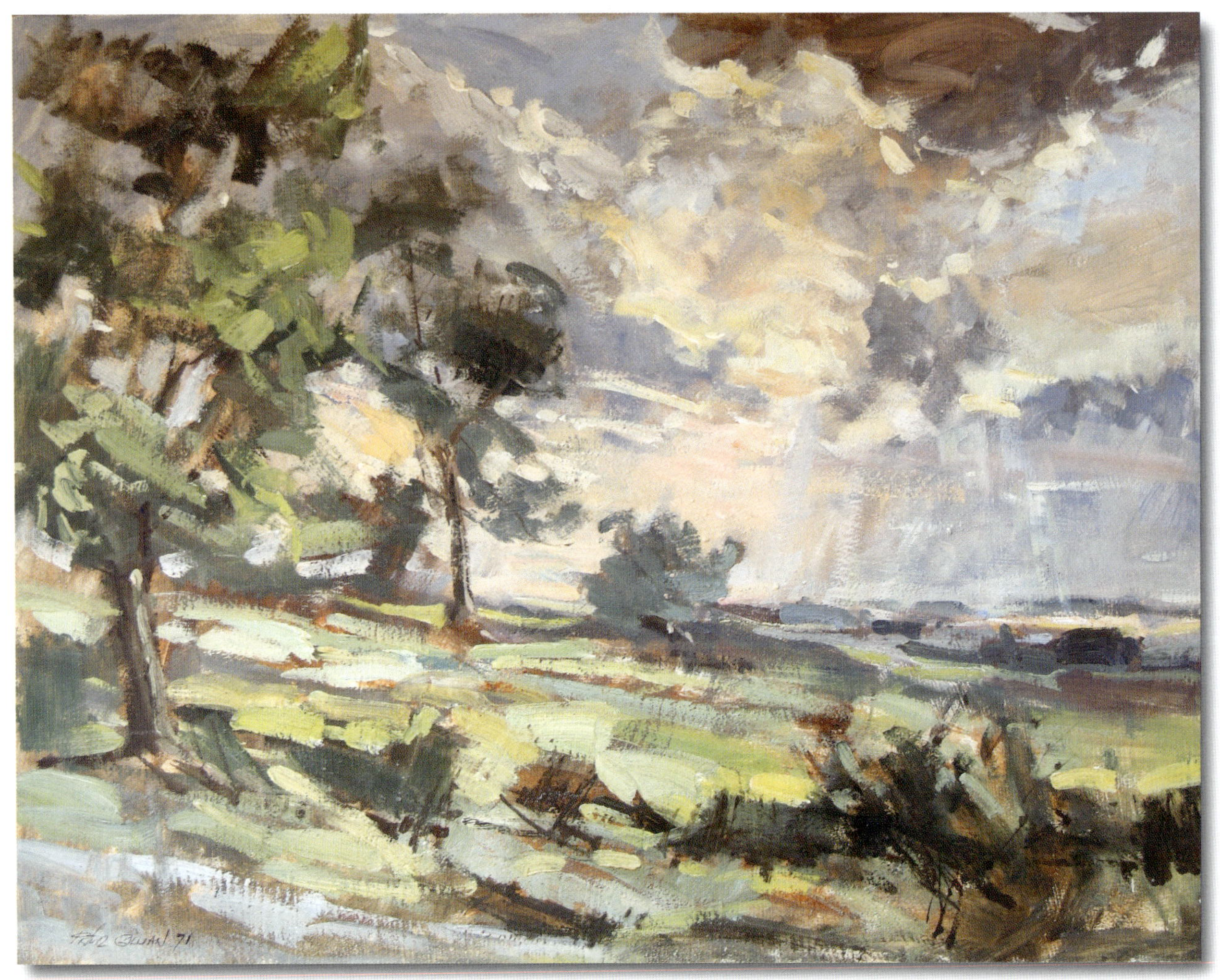

Sunlight Through Evening Clouds. Oil.

Opposite: Summer Fields. Oil.

Overleaf: At the End of the Day. Oil.

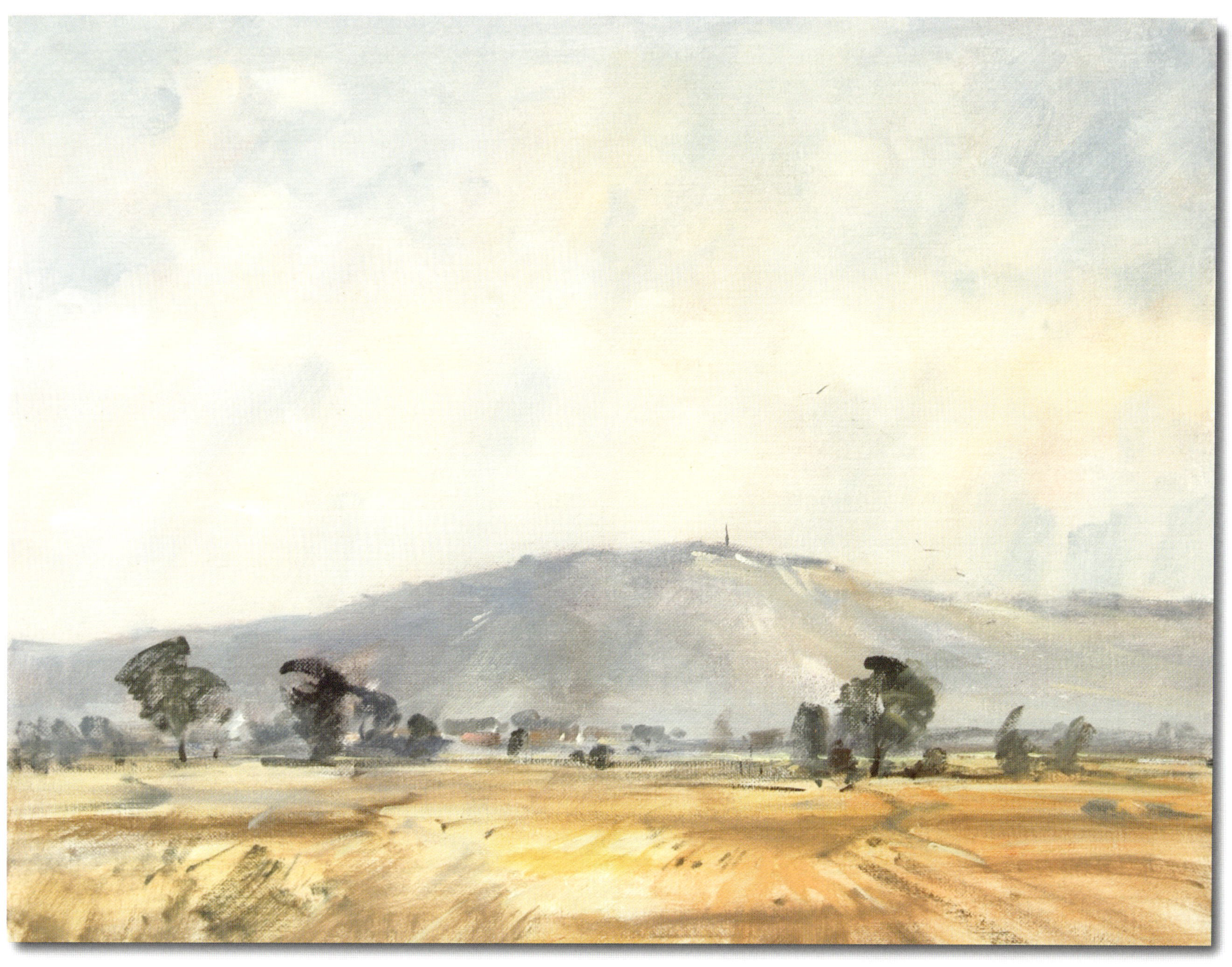

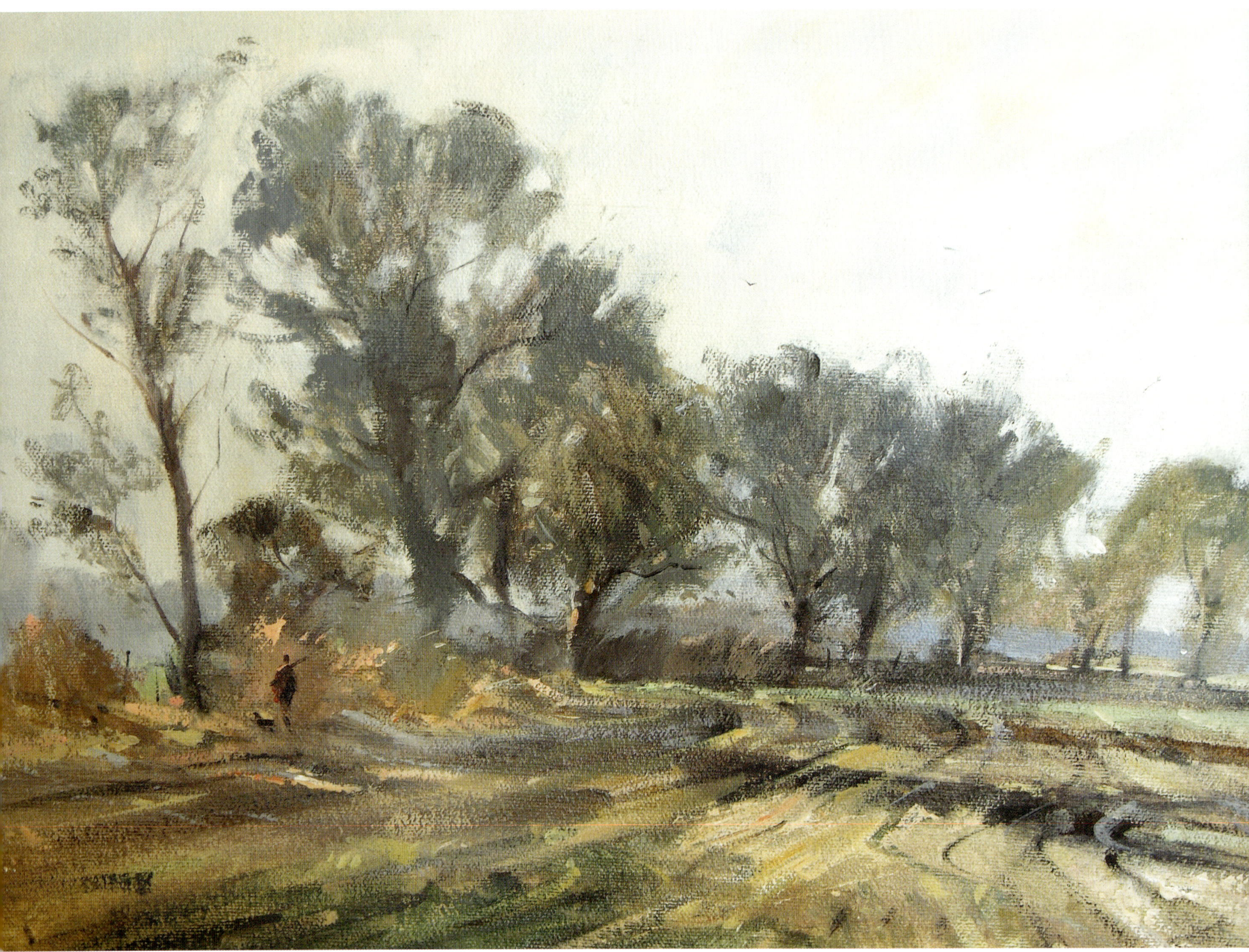

PERSONAL MEMORIES OF PETER GILMAN

MAXINE GILMAN

Of course, much has been written of Peter Gilman, the artist, but it must not be forgotten that he was also a much-loved father. It was common knowledge that Peter idolised his daughter Maxine, indeed his life revolved around her, so it is most fitting that the editorial of this book should contain her recollections.

'As the daughter of Peter Gilman, growing up, I never really thought of him as an artist. He was just my dad who happened to paint a lot. I took the pictures on the wall for granted and the fact that dad was always in his studio in the garden, or itching to get back into his studio, as commonplace.

When I was six we moved to the picturesque village of Ashwell in Hertfordshire. I can only assume this move was partly influenced by the painting opportunities it would create. We lived in a house that was built on the site of the Old Bull pub on the High Street. What would have been the garage of the pub was situated in the back garden and turned into a studio space. If dad was not out painting somewhere, this is where you would find him. He found it hard not to paint. On

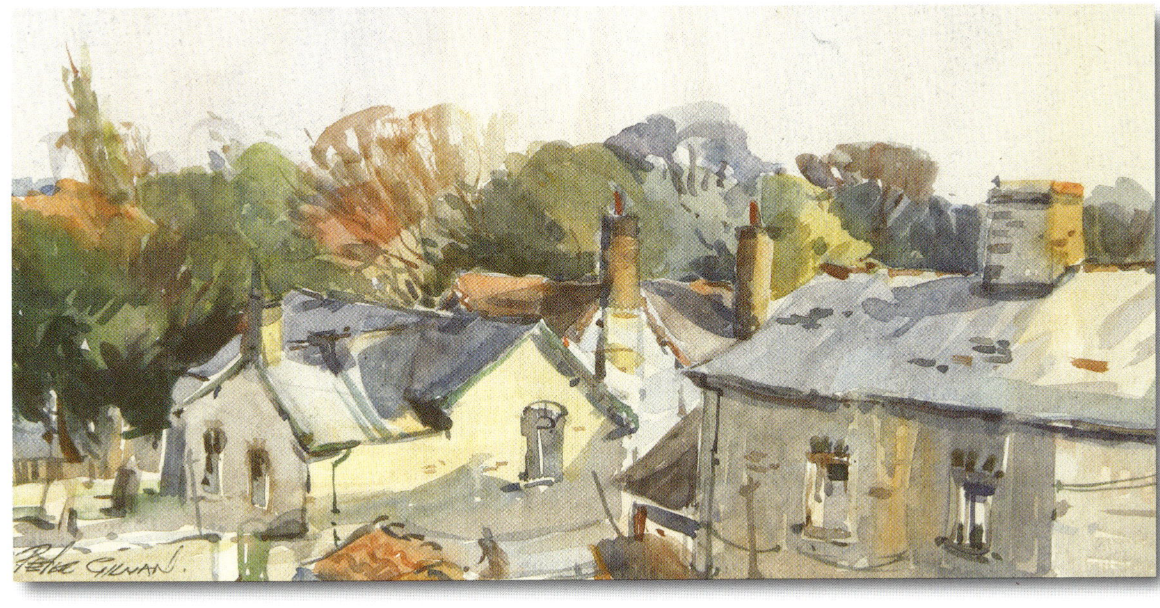

A Summer's Morning, Kingsland Terrace, Ashwell, Hertfordshire, 1975. Watercolour 33x27 inches.

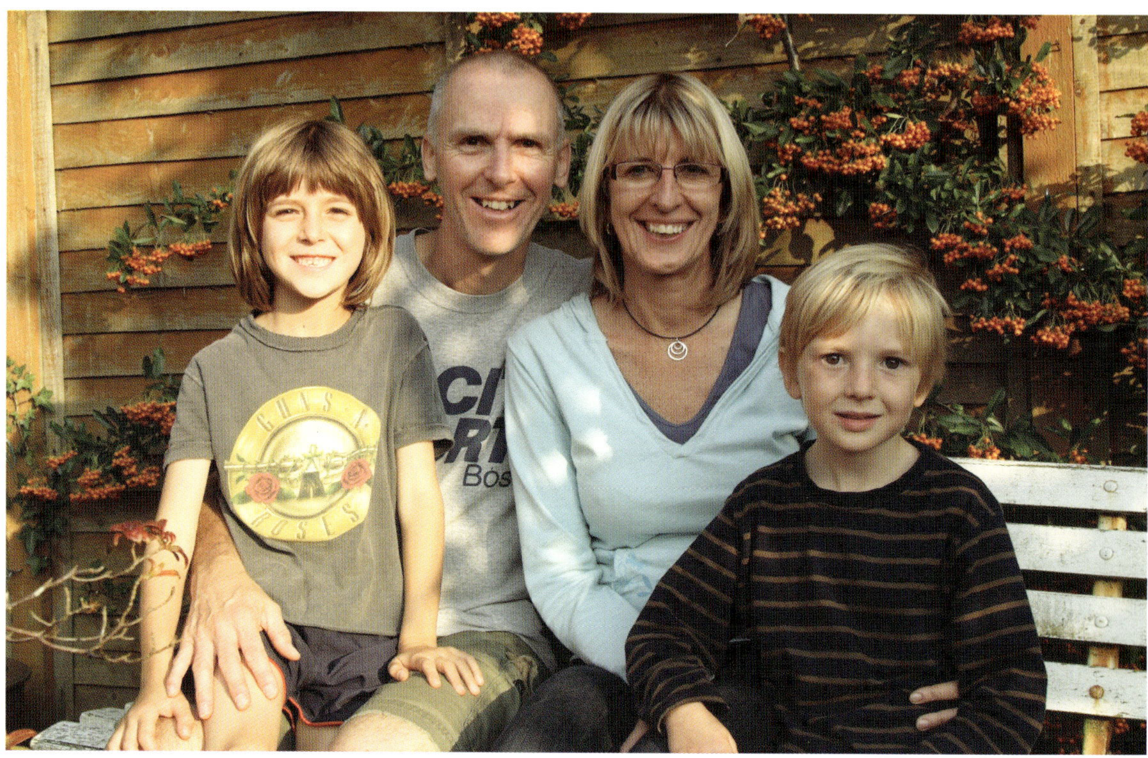

special occasion he would make an effort to stay out of the studio but we could tell the next painting was going on in his head.

I would sometimes spend time in the studio with dad. He would encourage me to paint by giving me a board, an easel and some oils, but he never put pressure on me to follow in his footsteps. He would encourage any of my friends who took an interest in art, giving them serious, constructive advice if they asked for his help.

One of the fond memories I have of time spent with him is wandering through the Sunday art market along the Edgware Road, stopping off while on a journey to visit family in London. We used to view the paintings tied to the railings of the park, with dad giving me a critique of the artwork. He would point out what he liked, occasionally stopping to talk to an artist. Sometimes, if I were lucky, he would buy me something from one of the craft stalls.

At secondary school, I am ashamed to say I was rather embarrassed by dad's profession. I wanted people to think he had a "proper job". If I were asked what my father did for a living, I would answer that he was a painter in the hope they would think he was a painter and decorator.

After leaving school I went to work in a hotel in Gibraltar for the summer. One day I got talking to a couple who were on holiday. From chatting we soon discovered we came from the same Letchworth area and shared an interest in art. The lady was very pleased to tell me she knew a well known local artist who lived in Ashwell. I was very amused, but proud when she mentioned dad's name. It was a bit of a revelation to me as to how dad was viewed by others. Not just a dad who painted, but a well respected artist.'

ADRIAN HILL – DIRECTOR PICTURECRAFT GALLERY, HOLT

Regrettably, I never had the pleasure of meeting Peter Gilman. My task in assembling an account of his life and to provide examples of his paintings has involved many pleasurable hours of research and I have been tremendously enlightened through listening to many stories from his family, friends and painting colleagues.

Clearly he was a man of two seasons, for he appears to have been quite a different man to his family compared to those times when he was encapsulated in his world of painting. However, it is obvious that he was a man who was greatly loved and held in the very highest esteem by all those privileged to know him.

Peter Gilman inspired and motivated so many people during his short life. How appropriate that the legacy of his work, in teaching, writing and painting ensures this will continue. However, I believe that Peter Gilman's greatest gift was in self-motivation. When he stood before an easel he became released from his self-imposed formality and allowed himself to become wonderfully expressive. Perhaps, when painting, Peter was truly at peace.

But I leave the paintings in this book to tell their own story. Peter Gilman's tragic and untimely death on 11 July 1984, just six weeks before his first one-man exhibition, denied him the knowledge to appreciate just how much his work was admired, and the phenomenal success that it proved to be, for this show resulted in every painting being sold and gained him the highest respect that he so richly deserved as a professional artist.

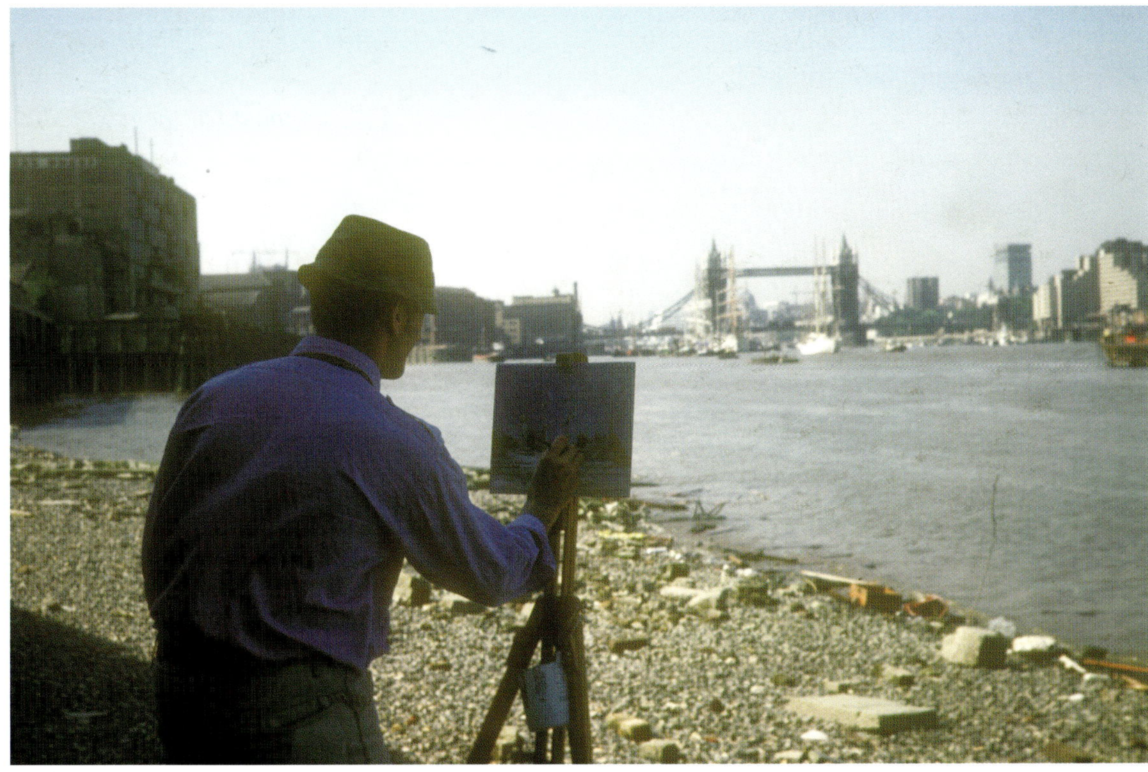

Peter Gilman painting the view of Tower Bridge on the River Thames, London.

JOHN STILLMAN
Member of The Wapping Group of Artists
'How Peter Gilman's paintings influenced my career'

The first original painting I ever bought was by Peter Gilman entitled, 'Thames Barges at Pin Mill', an iconic view. I remember seeing the painting standing on the floor of a gallery, propped up against the wall with other pictures around it. Instantly attracted, and after following a little negotiation, I was to happily leave the gallery as the proud owner of my first Gilman painting. It remains a very special painting to this day, and continues to receive tremendous admiration from visiting friends.

The purchase of that painting started me wishing to learn more about Peter and a desire to try and find more examples of his work. Over the following years I was able to build a picture of Peter's life through talking to various artist's who had known him and to some who had actually painted with him. Whenever there was an opportunity I would sing the praises of Peter's pictures.

In 2008, I was most fortunate in having the chance to meet with Peter Gilman's daughter Maxine at her home in Somerset. It proved to be an incredible time for me as I could finally ask all the questions that I needed to know in order to fill in the blanks of his life, and to try and understand a bit more about this sensitive man who had provided me with so much inspiration. Not only did the meeting reveal a goldmine of information but it enabled me the chance to see a selection of pictures from her private family collection.

Although I never had the pleasure of meeting Peter Gilman he has undoubtedly been a major influence to me, through the development of my own paintings and in my career as an artist. Though Peter is sadly no longer with us, his pictures continue to inspire me and I am sure this will be the case for many more artists in the future.

So, looking back to that very first purchase of a painting propped up against a gallery wall, to date, I now have over twenty Peter Gilman pictures, each and every one having a very special place in my home.

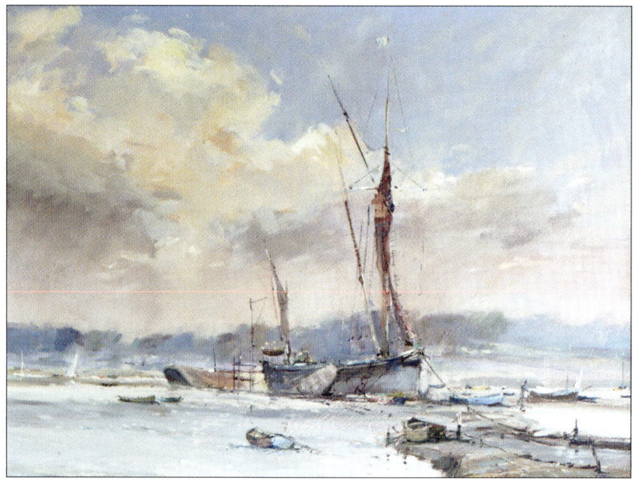

Pin Mill, Suffolk. Oil.
(John Stillman Collection)

THE WAPPING GROUP OF ARTISTS

The Wapping Group had its origins in 1939, when members of the Artists Society and the Langham Sketching Club, meeting at the 'Prospect of Whitby' public house in Wapping, decided to spend the summer months sketching together by the river Thames. The Second World War then intervened, but the same artists met again in 1946 to formally found The Wapping Group. The first President was Jack Merriott.

The maximum number of members was set at twenty-five, and the Group was dedicated to painting together outdoors, exhibitions being a secondary consideration. The painting season was from April to September, just as it remains today. In early years the Group was closely associated with the Port of London Authority, where the first three annual exhibitions were held at the PLA headquarters. Exhibitions were then moved to the Royal Exchange Gallery, where they continued to be held for the next thirty years.

In 1981 the venue was moved to St Botolph's Church, Aldgate, where annual exhibitions were staged until 2002. From 2003 annual exhibitions have been held at the Mall Galleries, in London. Other occasional exhibitions are held elsewhere, usually at the invitation of other galleries and institutions. Recent venues include The Henley River and Rowing Museum, and The Guildhall.

Originally the location for members to paint was concentrated between Westminster and Gravesend, but this area has steadily widened over the years. Today it ranges from Henley, up-river, through London and out to the Rivers Medway, Crouch and Blackwater. The Group also arranges occasional painting trips further afield, in recent years to locations that have included Bruges, the Loire Valley and Normandy.

A number of traditions have been acquired over the years, such as the Whitebait Suppers which start and finish the painting season, and the annual raffle of paintings, but the Group is proud to have remained exactly what it first set out to be: a small association of fellow-artists, appreciating each other's company while painting outdoors together, in all weathers.

Almost incidentally, The Wapping Group has recorded the changing face of London and the River Thames for over sixty years.

To mark the 25 years of the tragic passing of Peter Gilman, members of The Wapping Group decided to participate in the commemorative exhibition staged at the Picturecraft Gallery, Holt, Norfolk in November 2009, at which the following artists were to exhibit original paintings.

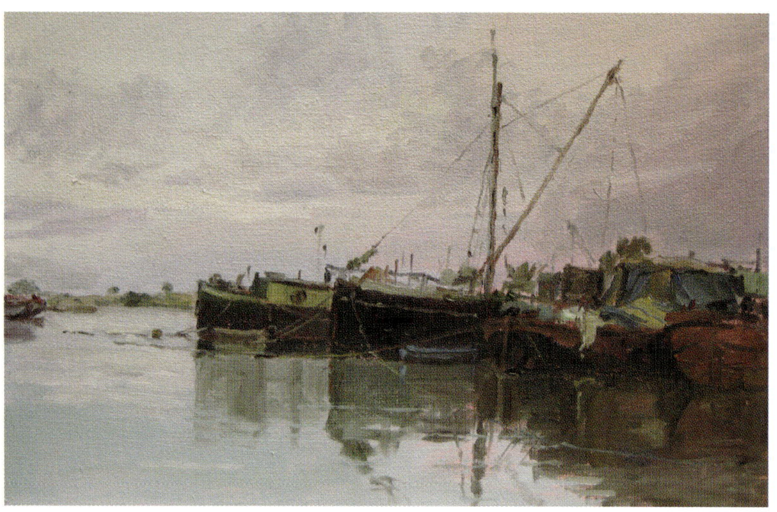

Steven Alexander, Ebbing Tide, St Osyth Creek. Oil.

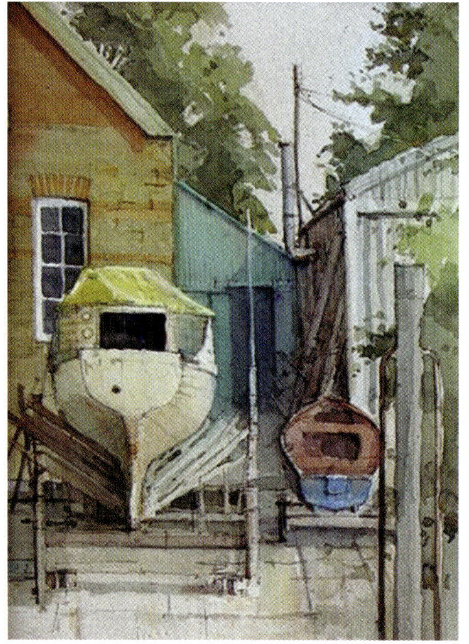

Paul Banning, Boats At Rest. Watercolour.

John Bryce, View to Tower Bridge. Watercolour.

STEVEN ALEXANDER

Steven Alexander was born in Thanet in 1951. He started drawing in the 1960s under the guidance of his father and master draughtsman, Chris Alexander. Steven began to paint during the early 1980s and has been self taught since this time.

An exhibitor at the RA Summer Exhibition, Steven's work was featured during the 1983, 1984 and 1986 shows. Other prestigious exhibitions include Royal Society of British Artists, Royal Society of Marine Artists, New English Art Club and the Royal Watercolour Society.

Steven was elected to The Wapping Group of Artists in 2006 and is currently the Secretary. Painting mainly townscape and landscape, mostly in oils, Steven also enjoys painting in watercolours and has travelled and painted in France, Italy and Spain.

PAUL BANNING

Paul Banning was born in Trinidad in 1934, and educated at Clifton College, Bristol, and the West of England College of Art, gaining NDD Honours in Furniture Design. He served two years National Service obtaining a commission in the Army and subsequently became a furniture designer in industry.

Mainly a *plein air* painter, Paul loves the challenge of painting direct from the subject whenever possible. He travels extensively and has exhibited in France, Holland, Italy, United States of America, Dubai, and in many galleries in the United Kingdom. His work has been regularly accepted in the New English Art Club, and the Royal Institute of Oil Painters, and he has been selected for the Singer and Friedlander/*Sunday Times* watercolour competition in 2003 and 2006, as well as for the Royal Academy Summer Exhibition in 2006.

Paul Banning is a member of the Royal Institute of Painters in Watercolours; the Royal Society of Marine Artists; The Wapping Group of Artists; the Chelsea Art Society and the Armed Forces Art Society. He is an associate member of the Royal Institute of Oil Painters and the Farnham Art Society.

JOHN BRYCE

Before retirement, John Bryce worked as a research scientist at the Royal Aerospace Establishment, Farnborough. He now pursues an active artistic career as a painter and printmaker.

As a member of The Wapping Group of Artists, John enjoys painting river and marine scenes directly from the subject.

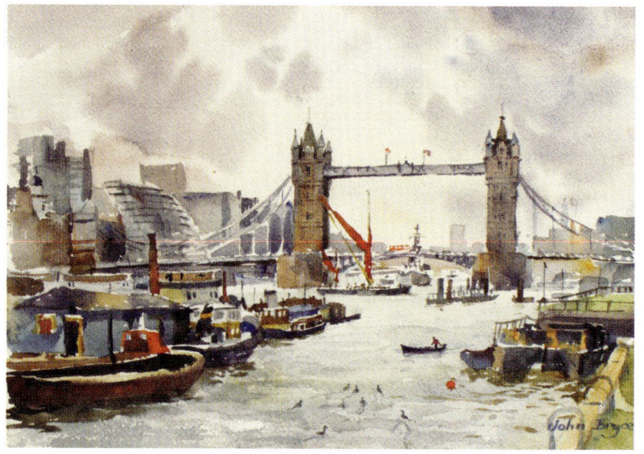

He is also a member of the Society of Wood Engravers and an associate of the Royal Society of Painter-Printmakers. John also creates original print images through the challenging medium of wood engraving. Another interest is painting aircraft and he is a full member of the Guild of Aviation Artists.

In 2007, one of John Bryce's wood engravings was a runner up for the Newcomer's Prize at the Royal Academy Summer Exhibition. In the following year he won the Baker Tilly Prize at the Royal Watercolour Society Open Exhibition.

SIDNEY CARDEW
Sidney Cardew was born in London, worked as a Design Engineer for Ford Motor Company, and started painting in 1970.

He is a member of the Royal Society of Marine Artists, The Wapping Group, The London Sketch Club, Chelsea Art Society and Essex Art Club. Sidney has exhibited his paintings with the Royal Institute; Royal Watercolour Society; and Royal Society of British Artists at the Mall Gallery in London.

Well known for his watercolours of maritime subjects, Sidney Cardew has had several successful one-man exhibitions and his work is to be found in galleries at home and abroad. He has always been fascinated by the changing atmospheres – ideal for watercolour with its colour fusions – but, when a subject dictates, he also enjoys using oil paints.

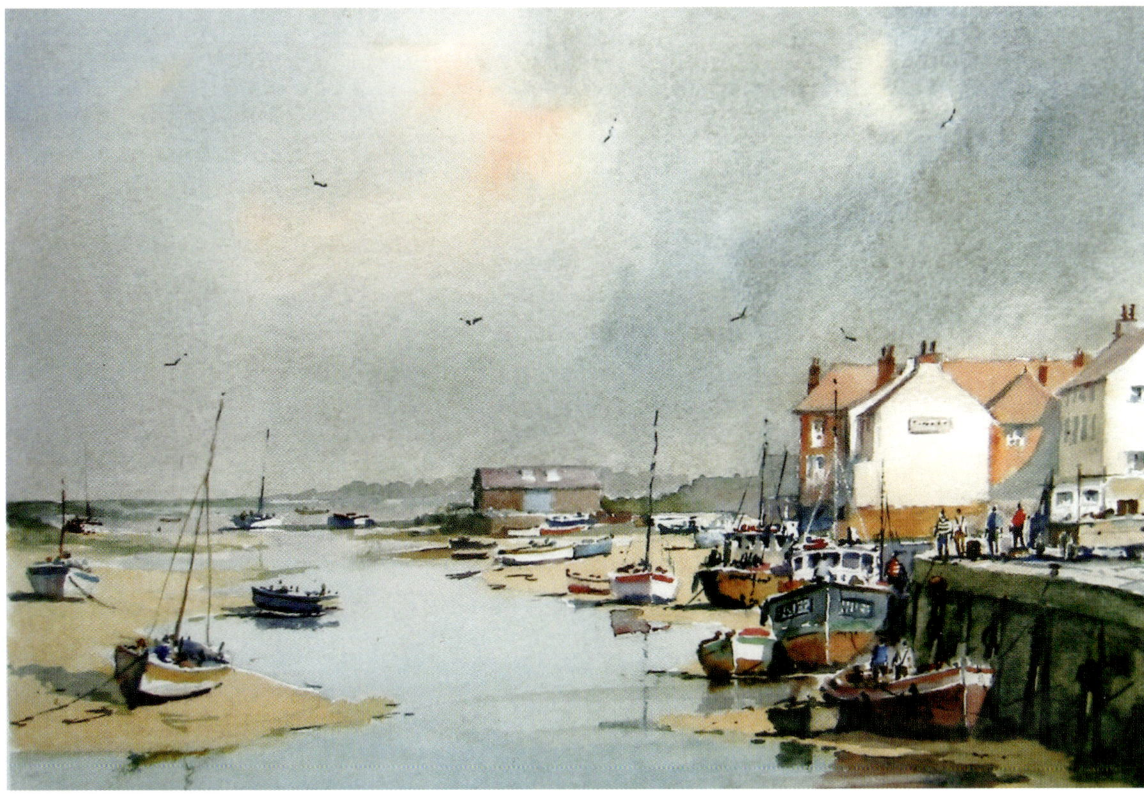

Sidney Cardew, Low Tide, Wells-next-the-Sea. Watercolour.

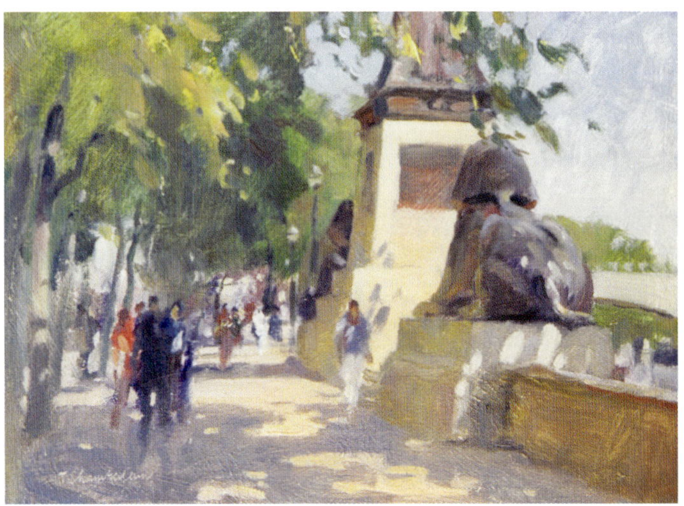

Trevor Chamberlain, Summer Light, Victoria Embankment. Oil.

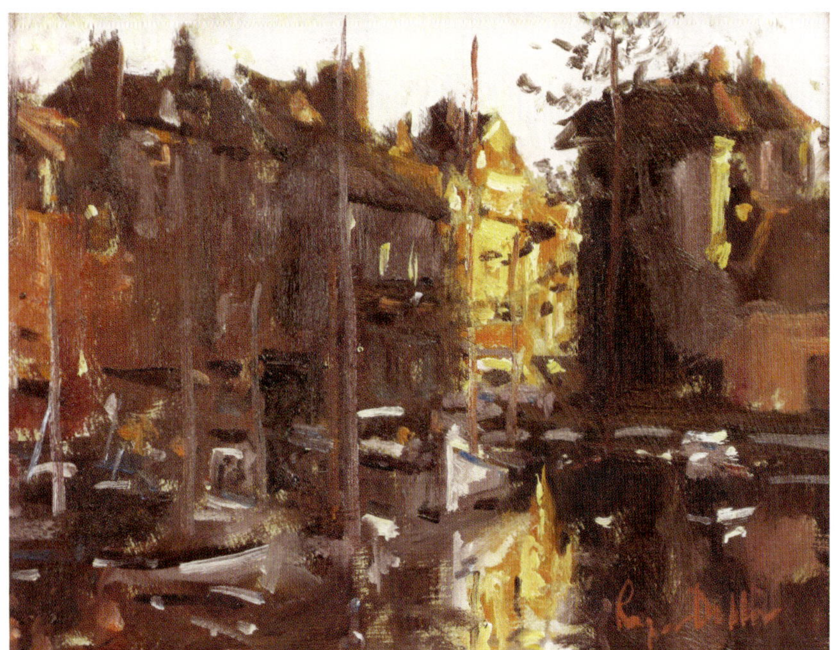

Roger Dellar, Honfleur, Oil.

TREVOR CHAMBERLAIN

Trevor Chamberlain was born in Hertford in 1933 and had no formal art school training. He worked initially as an architectural assistant, but from 1964 he has painted professionally. His main subjects of interest are marine, figure, town and landscape, preferring to paint *alla prima* from life, with a particular emphasis on atmosphere and light.

Regularly exhibiting in London, the provinces and abroad, Trevor has also staged over twenty one-man exhibitions. He has received many awards for his paintings, including the Lord Mayor of London's Award and six different awards at the Royal Institute of Oil Painters exhibitions, where he is a member. Trevor Chamberlain is also a member of the Royal Society of Marine Artists and served as President of The Wapping Group of Artists and The Chelsea Art Society.

Trevor Chamberlain's work has featured on British television and has been included in two programmes for Connecticut television. He has had several books published, the most recent being released in 2006 celebrating sixty years of painting entitled, *England and Beyond*. His work is represented in many highly prestigious museum collections and features in significant private collections.

ROGER DELLAR

Roger Dellar is a self-taught professional artist and his studio is based in Surrey. Roger's keen interest in people reflects in his figurative paintings. Working in most mediums, Roger also has a particular interest in marine subjects and is fascinated as a subject is transformed by the play of light. Working mainly on the spot he is a great enthusiast for the sketch book.

Roger was elected as a member of The Wapping Group in 1996 and is a member of The Chelsea Art Society; The Langham Sketching Club; The Royal Institute of Painters in Watercolour; The Pastel Society; The Royal Institute of Oil Painters.

He has exhibited at the Royal Watercolour Society; Royal Society of Marine Artists; The New English Art Club; The Royal Institute of Painters in Watercolour; The Royal Institute of Oil Painters; The Royal Society of Portrait Painters; The Royal Society of British Artists; The Singer and Friedlander/*Sunday Times* Watercolour Exhibition; The Royal West of England Academy; The Royal Academy.

RICK HOLMES

Rick Holmes has been painting for twenty years with a small group of eminent artists and firmly believes that to mingle with fellow artists is of tremendous benefit. Rick finds the exchange of painting techniques and offers of advice to be generally advantageous and is one of the reasons why he regularly attends workshops and life classes.

He is an exhibiting member at both Farnham and Guildford Art Societies and has shown at the Royal Watercolour Society at

Bankside, as well as The Chelsea Art Society. Rick Holmes has also exhibited his paintings in France and with The Royal Society of Marine Artists at the Mall Gallery. A number of Rick's paintings regularly feature at KD Fine Art Gallery at Compton, near Guildford, and he exhibits on a regular basis with Lincoln Joyce Fine Art at Great Bookham, near Leatherhead.

Rick Holmes has held a number of one-man shows in Surrey and Hampshire and his paintings feature in many private collections in Europe and around the world.

JOHN KILLENS

John Killens left his job to become a full time artist in 2000. Selling from the first time he exhibited, in 2001, he then had two highly successful joint exhibitions in 2004 and 2008.

He has exhibited in the Royal Society of Marine Artists and the Royal Watercolour Society open exhibitions and was elected a member of The Wapping Group in 2008.

John was brought up near the sea in Essex and with the surrounding countryside it is not surprising that marine and landscape now feature as his two favourite subjects. Paintings by John Killens are held in private collections as far away as India and the United States of America.

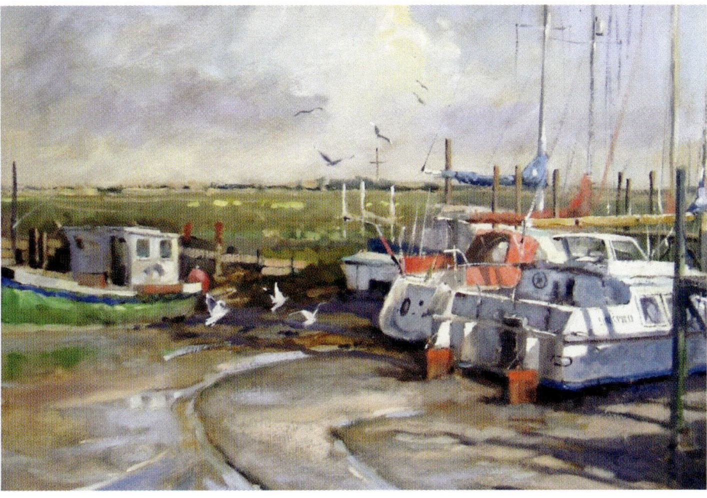

John Killens, Tollesbury, September Morning. Oil.

ROBIN MACKERVOY

Robin Mackervoy generally prefers to work from life. Preparatory sketches are made in pencil, pen or watercolour and the final pieces are usually in oil or acrylics. Robin was elected to membership of The Wapping Group of Artists in 1992. He is President of the Lea Valley Art Society, a member of Chelsea and Hertford Art Societies, and Past President and Trustee of the London Sketch Club. He has demonstrated painting in all mediums to art societies throughout the home-counties and East Anglia for many years.

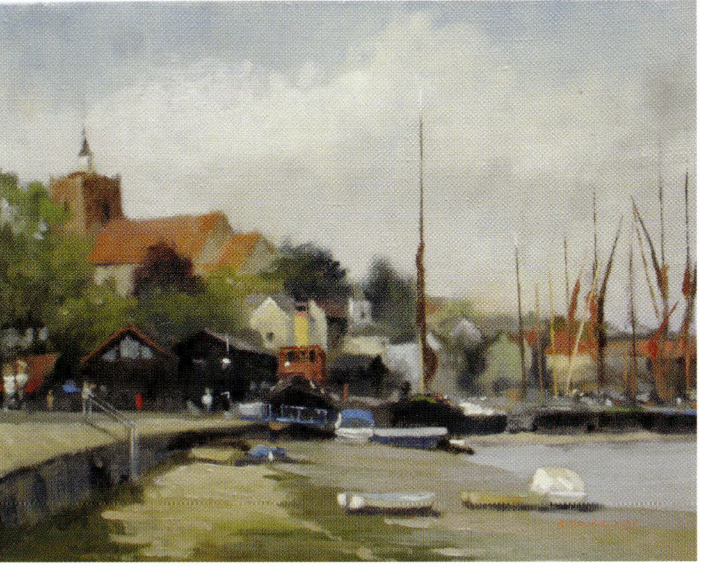

Robin Mackervoy, Low Water Maldon Creek. Oil.

Robin has exhibited at the Royal Society of Marine Artists exhibitions from 1995 and the Royal Institute of Oil Painters annually since 1997. He was awarded the Stanley Grimm prize at the Royal Institute of Oil Painters exhibition of 1999. He was elected to Associate Membership of the Royal Institute of Oil Painters in 2006 and to full membership in November 2008.

DENIS PANNETT

Denis Pannett became a professional artist in 1982. He has exhibited in the Royal Institute, Royal Society of Marine Artists, The RAF Museum at Hendon, The Royal Festival Hall, The National Maritime Museum, Greenwich, and in the United States of America and Hong Kong, where he had two family exhibitions with his mother, Juliet, and sister, Liz.

Denis Pannett is President of The Wapping Group of Artists; a member of the Guild of Aviation Artists; an Honorary Freeman of The Painter Stainers Company; Past President of The Arun Art Society and Chairman of the Chiltern Painters.

DAVID PENNY

David Penny was brought up in Southampton and Guildford, and loved drawing from an early age. He trained and worked in architecture until 1991 when recession led to redundancy, whereupon he started to paint, working with watercolour in particular. Enjoying Farnham Art Society's outdoor painting programme, David has exhibiting regularly with them and occasionally elsewhere.

David Penny was elected to The Wapping Group in 2000, and has found the challenge

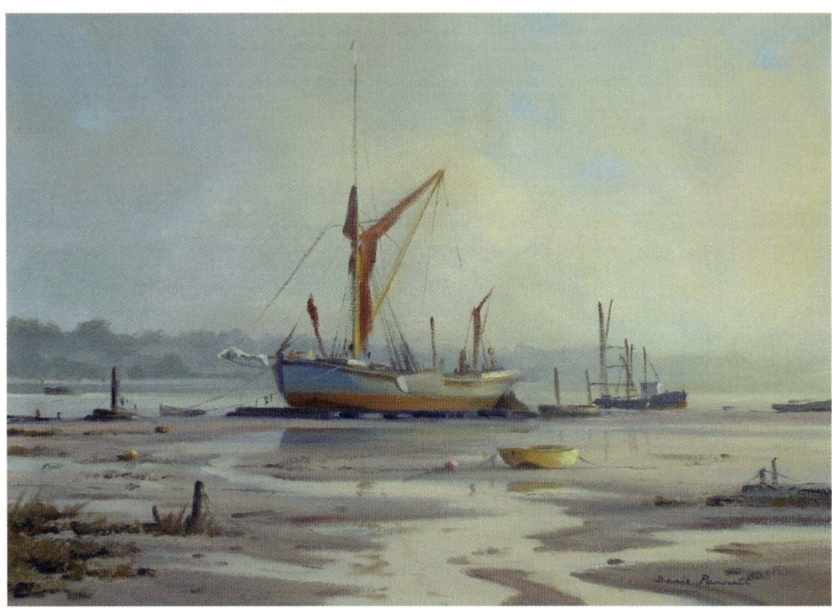

Denis Pannett, Low Water, Pin Mill. *Oil.*

of continuing to develop outdoor painting in stimulating locations a tremendous inspiration. He has also enjoyed the companionship and experience of working alongside his fellow members a great source of motivation and pleasure. Seeking strongly structured compositions, David's architectural background is often evident in his paintings. He enjoy the subtlety of transparent watercolour and the more direct impact of oils, which can also be more practical to use on damp days.

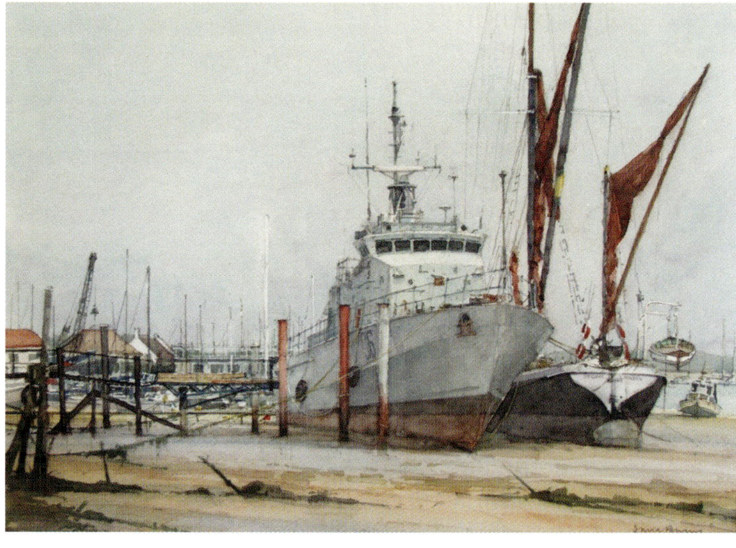

David Penny, Defender *and* Dulcima *at* Heybridge. *Watercolour.*

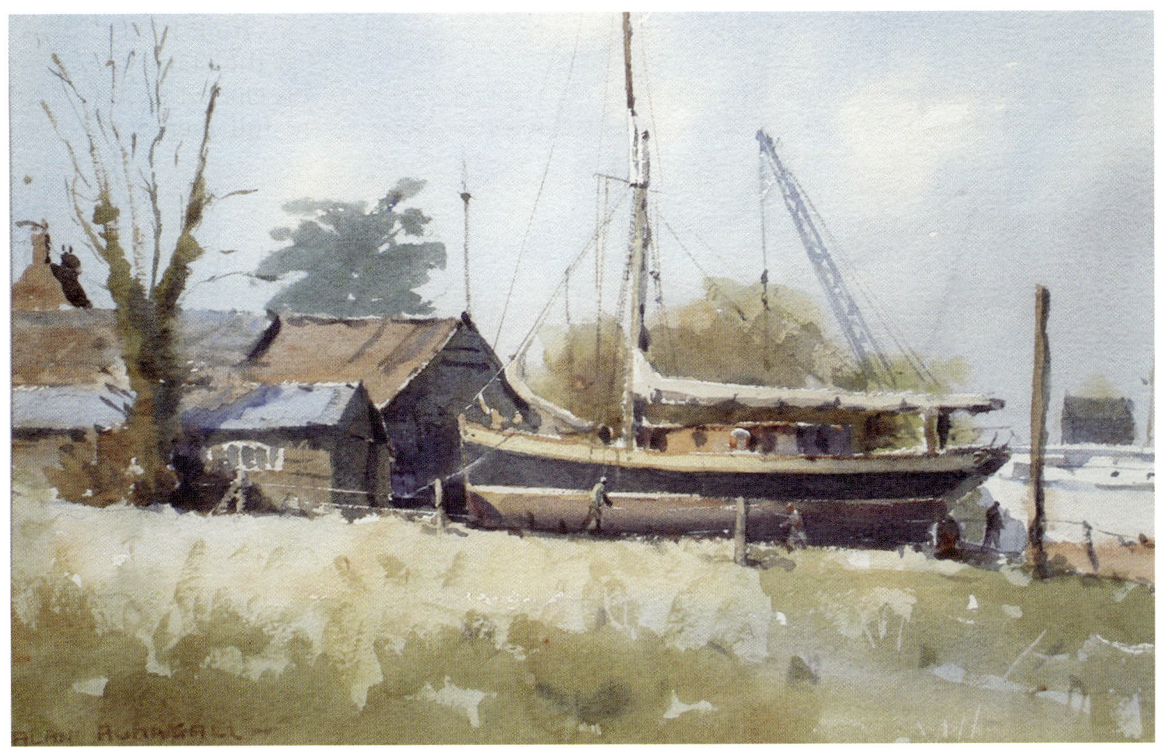

Alan Runagall, Downs Road Boatyard. Watercolour.

ALAN RUNAGALL

Alan Runagall is self taught and has been painting since a young age. He now paints solely in watercolour, specialising in all types of shipping, past and present. He particularly likes East Coast subjects, including the Thames barge, smacks, tugs and dock scenes. He has been involved with the river for a number of years having worked in the India Docks and Tilbury Docks for the Port of London Authority after leaving school in 1957.

Alan Runagall is a founder member of the East Anglian Group of Marine Artists, and also a member of the Royal Society of Marine Artists as well as The Wapping Group of Artists. He is a past winner of the prestigious St Cuthberts Mill Award at the annual exhibition of the Royal Society of Marine Artists for the best watercolour.

JOHN SHAVE

John teaches oil painting privately and at summer schools for several residential centres. He exhibits regularly at regional galleries. In 2008 he exhibited at the Mall Galleries London in The Wapping Group exhibition, the ROI, the RSMA and the East Anglian Marine Artists exhibitions and previously with the Royal Society of Portrait Painters. About forty of John's paintings have been reproduced as greetings cards. Along with his

John Shave, Downs Road Boatyard. Watercolour.

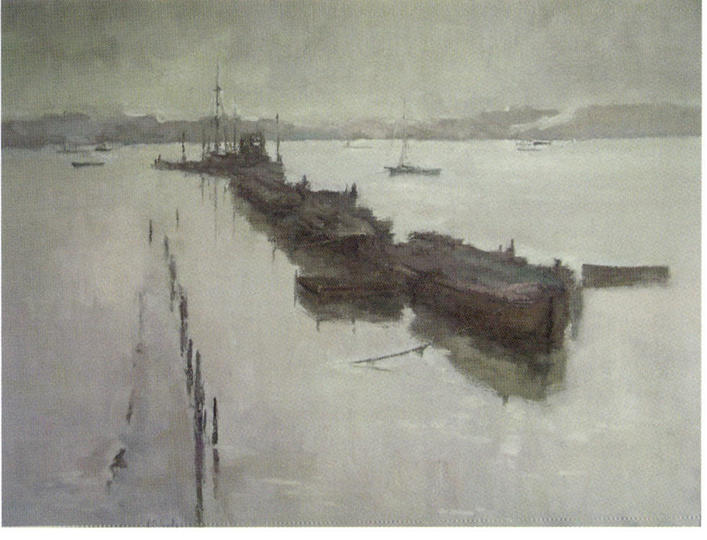

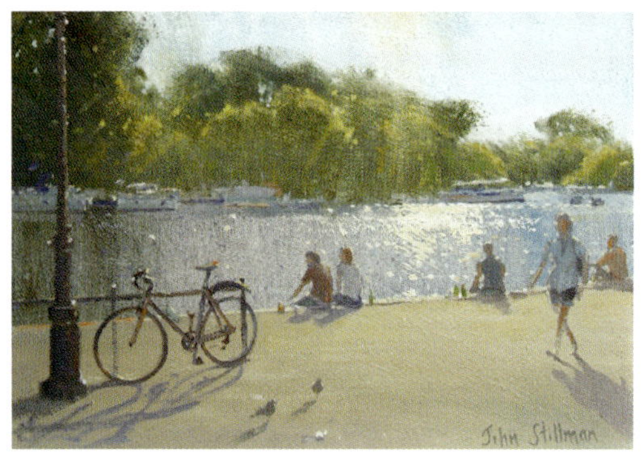

John Stillman, Brilliant Light, Richmond. Oil.

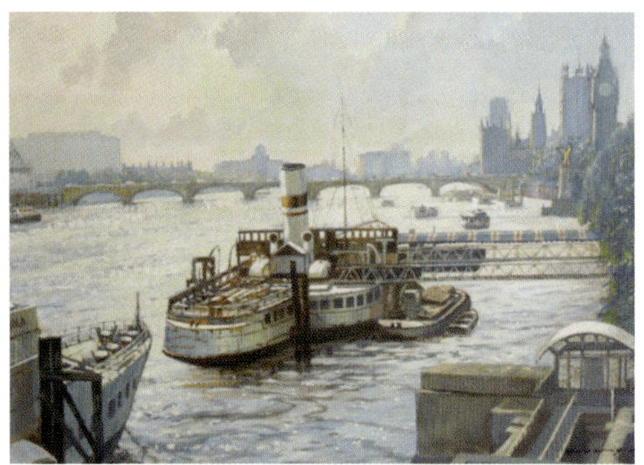

Bert Wright, Evening Light, Westminster. Oil.

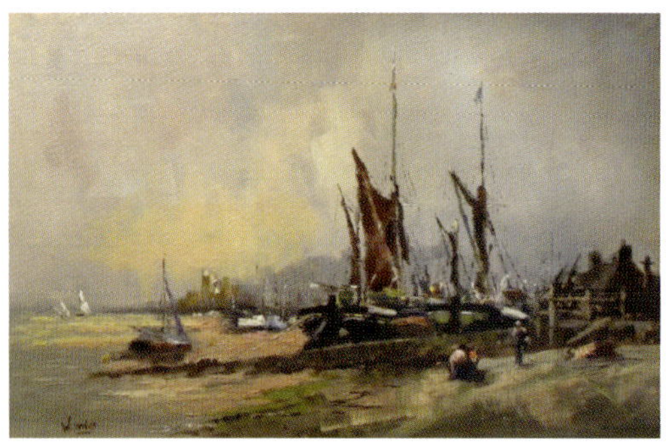

William Davies, Barges on the Medway. Oil.

membership of The Wapping Group of Artists, he is a Fellow of The Royal Society of Arts in South Australia. He paints mainly in oils but also in watercolour, pastel, guoache and all drawing mediums, using a wide variety of subject matter to depict and celebrate his love for light colour and atmosphere

JOHN STILLMAN

John Stillman was born in Carshalton, Surrey, in 1968 and is completely self-taught, drawing and painting ever since he can remember. He is now a professional artist but previously worked as an illustrator for books and as a graphic artist in advertising in London.

In April 2009, John was elected a full member of The Wapping Group of Artists. He is also a member of The Chelsea Arts Society and The Croydon Art Society where his paintings are exhibited annually. Amongst the varied subjects that John likes to paint are the landscapes and scenes of Surrey and marine subjects, where membership of The Wapping Group provides the opportunity to paint at locations along the River Thames.

John Stillman exhibits his paintings regularly at the Royal Society of Marine Artists and Royal Institute of Oil Painters at the Mall Galleries in London, and at The Royal Academy. He has also staged one-man exhibitions and his paintings are held in numerous private collections in the United Kingdom, the United States of America, France and Australia.

BERT WRIGHT

Bert Wright has been a practicing artist for many years. He sold his first painting at the age of 16 years in 1946, and has since had a career in art covering many different aspects of this profession. He initially embarked on a career as an illustrator working on a diverse range of paintings depicting planned architectural subjects for major companies.

Particular interests are marine, landscape and town subjects. He principally works outdoors, in all weathers, and likes to complete a painting in one sitting whenever possible.

Bert Wright served as a President of the Royal Society of Marine Artists and the London Wapping Group. He is currently President of the Ealing Art Group and a member of the Chelsea Art Society. He has been a Governor of the Federation of British Artists and his work is exhibited at a number of National and International Galleries.

WILLIAM DAVIES

Born in 1928, William Davies is a past President of The Wapping Group of Artists. Following service in the Royal Navy he began painting in 1962 and turned professional in 1986. Self taught he works mostly in oil using a very impressionist style and, following in the impressionists' footsteps, prefers to work almost entirely on site.